War on Family Property Rights

As of 2020 South Korea has 14 firms listed on the global Fortune 500, including Samsung, Hyundai, SK, POSCO and LG. The country along with Japan is also one of the only two countries in Asia that are members of the OECD and its Development Assistance Committee (DAC) simultaneously. Furthermore, Korea boasts of its membership in the seven-country 50-30 Club (countries with a population of more than 50 million and a GDP of $30,000 per capita). However, unlike its official status as one of the most developed economies in the world, it still suffers from the backward struggle between the state and the family firms over the issue of property rights and family successions. The corporate governance issue has damaged the reputation of Korean *chaebols* (family conglomerates) for many decades as founders, and their families had been imprisoned and/or fined for violating inheritance tax laws and related laws associated with the issue of protecting their family properties. The democratically elected governments in Korea since 1987 have tried to reform the *chaebol* governance structures to ease asset concentration by family members, although many of those have failed due to corruptive practices between the state and the *chaebol*. This book spells out the current governance problems within the *chaebol*, state reform policies and both success and failures of the reforms. It was originally published as a special issue of the *Asia Pacific Business Review.*

Ingyu Oh is Professor of Business and Cultural Industries at Kansai Gaidai University, Osaka, Japan. His main teaching and research interests include organizational studies, innovation, international business, political economy, political sociology, business history and cultural studies. He has published numerous books, monographs and journal articles over the last 25+ years. He is Associate Editor of *Asia Pacific Business Review.*

Chris Rowley is Visiting Fellow at Kellogg College at the University of Oxford, UK, and Visiting Professor at the Graduate School of Education at Tohoku University, Japan, and at the University of Business and International Studies, Switzerland. He is Professor Emeritus at Bayes Business School at the City, University of London, UK. He has over 30 years' experience in university systems in the UK, Europe, and Asia and has won several international grants. He is the Editor of the important SCI-rated journal *Asia Pacific Business Review* and has published over 700 articles, books, chapters and practitioner pieces. He regularly provides interviews, expert comments and opinion pieces to the international media, including news services, TV, radio and practitioner outlets.

Yong Wook Jun is Invited Professor at Business School at Seoul National University, South Korea. He is Academician, Businessman and Consultant, having worked for universities, business corporations and consulting firms in the past 40 years. He was Dean of Global Learning Institute at Sookmyung Women's University, Seoul, South Korea. Prior to this, he was Vice President of Sejong University, Vice President of Woosong University and Dean of SolBridge International School of Business. Professor Jun has served as Non-Executive Director, Counsellor and Consultant for many major Korean corporations including Hynix, Samsung Electronics, Hyundai Motors and SK Telecom. His capabilities are balanced in both practice and academia. He has also published numerous articles and textbooks in the field of International Business.

War on Family Property Rights

Rethinking Governance Reforms for the South Korean Chaebol

Edited by Ingyu Oh, Chris Rowley and Yong Wook Jun

Routledge
Taylor & Francis Group
LONDON AND NEW YORK

First published 2023
by Routledge
4 Park Square, Milton Park, Abingdon, Oxon, OX14 4RN

and by Routledge
605 Third Avenue, New York, NY 10158

Routledge is an imprint of the Taylor & Francis Group, an informa business

British Library Cataloguing-in-Publication Data
A catalogue record for this book is available from the British Library

ISBN13: 978-1-032-41059-3 (hbk)
ISBN13: 978-1-032-41062-3 (pbk)
ISBN13: 978-1-003-35608-0 (ebk)

DOI: 10.4324/9781003356080

Typeset in Myriad Pro
by codeMantra

Publisher's Note
The publisher accepts responsibility for any inconsistencies that may have arisen during the conversion of this book from journal articles to book chapters, namely the inclusion of journal terminology.

Contents

Citation Information vi
Notes on Contributors vii

1 Inertia: Stalled governance reforms in the Korean chaebols amid economic maturation 1
Ingyu Oh, Chris Rowley and Yong Wook Jun

2 The end of rent sharing: corporate governance reforms in South Korea 16
Ingyu Oh, Soon Suk Yoon and Hyo Jin Kim

3 Successors' discretion and corporate restructuring in family firms in South Korea: from an institutional perspective 38
JungYun Han

4 The shadow of a departing CEO: outsider succession and strategic change in a business group 65
Changsu Kim, Jong-Hun Park, Jiyoon Kim and Youngjoo Lee

5 Remains on the board: outside directors' behaviour and their survival chance in Korean firms 87
Taeyoung Yoo and Yunsung Koh

6 Transforming Korean business? Foreign acquisition, governance and management after the 1997 Asian crisis 111
Robert Fitzgerald and Ji Woong Kang

Index 131

Citation Information

The chapters in this book were originally published in the journal *Asia Pacific Business Review*, volume 28, issue 1 (2022). When citing this material, please use the original page numbering for each article, as follows:

Chapter 1

Corporate governance reforms amidst economic maturation and democratization: the case of the Korean chaebol since the 1990s
YongWook Jun, Chris Rowley and Ingyu Oh
Asia Pacific Business Review, volume 28, issue 1 (2022) pp. 1–15

Chapter 2

The end of rent sharing: corporate governance reforms in South Korea
Ingyu Oh, Soon Suk Yoon and Hyo Jin Kim
Asia Pacific Business Review, volume 28, issue 1 (2022) pp. 16–37

Chapter 3

Successors' discretion and corporate restructuring in family firms in South Korea: from an institutional perspective
JungYun Han
Asia Pacific Business Review, volume 28, issue 1 (2022) pp. 38–64

Chapter 4

The shadow of a departing CEO: outsider succession and strategic change in a business group
Changsu Kim, Jong-Hun Park, Jiyoon Kim and Youngjoo Lee
Asia Pacific Business Review, volume 28, issue 1 (2022) pp. 65–86

Chapter 5

Remains on the board: outside directors' behaviour and their survival chance in Korean firms
Taeyoung Yoo and Yunsung Koh
Asia Pacific Business Review, volume 28, issue 1 (2022) pp. 87–110

Chapter 6

Transforming Korean business? Foreign acquisition, governance and management after the 1997 Asian crisis
Robert Fitzgerald and Ji Woong Kang
Asia Pacific Business Review, volume 28, issue 1 (2022) pp. 111–129

Notes on Contributors

Robert Fitzgerald is Professor of Business History and International Management at Royal Holloway, University of London, UK. He has written on global history and business, including the economies of Japan, Korea and China.

JungYun Han is Assistant Professor at National Taiwan University, Taipei, Taiwan. She works on family business and firm strategy. She has published papers in the *Academy of Management Journal* and *European Journal of Innovation Management*. She received her PhD degree from INSEAD, France.

Yong Wook Jun is Invited Professor at Business School at Seoul National University, South Korea. He is Academician, Businessman and Consultant, having worked for universities, business corporations and consulting firms in the past 40 years. He was Dean of Global Learning Institute at Sookmyung Women's University, Seoul, South Korea. Prior to this, he was Vice President of Sejong University, Vice President of Woosong University and Dean of SolBridge International School of Business. Professor Jun has served as Non-Executive Director, Counsellor and Consultant for many major Korean corporations including Hynix, Samsung Electronics, Hyundai Motors and SK Telecom. His capabilities are balanced in both practice and academia. He has also published numerous articles and textbooks in the field of International Business.

Ji Woong Kang gained his doctorate at Royal Holloway, University of London, UK. He works in the Strategic Planning and Corporate Business Support Teams at Samsung.

Changsu Kim is Professor of International Business at Sogang University, Seoul, South Korea. He earned his PhD at Rutgers University, USA. His research has been published in *Journal of International Marketing, Journal of Business Ethics* and *Journal of Business Research*.

Hyo Jin Kim is Professor of Accounting and Tax at Jeonju University, South Korea. Her teaching and research interests include financial accounting and tax accounting. She has published 3 books and more than 30 journal articles over the last 15 years.

Jiyoon Kim is PhD Candidate of International Business in Business Department at Sogang University, Seoul, South Korea. Her research interests include strategic leadership and international management.

Yunsung Koh is Professor at the College of Business Administration at the Hankuk University of Foreign Studies, Seoul, South Korea. He holds a PhD from the School of Business at Yonsei University, Seoul, South Korea. His research topics include corporate governance, R&D investment, dividends and tax avoidance. His research has appeared in journals such as *Asian Business & Management, Asian Review of Accounting* and *Asia Pacific Business Review.*

Youngjoo Lee is Associate Professor of Finance at Sogang University, Seoul, Korea. She received her PhD from the School of Management at the State University of New York, Buffalo, USA. Her research interests are corporate finance, corporate governance and financial institutions.

Ingyu Oh is Professor of Business and Cultural Industries at Kansai Gaidai University, Osaka, Japan. His main teaching and research interests include organizational studies, innovation, international business, political economy, political sociology, business history and cultural studies. He has published numerous books, monographs and journal articles over the last 25+ years. He is Associate Editor of *Asia Pacific Business Review.*

Jong-Hun Park is Professor of Strategic Management at Sogang University, Seoul, South Korea. He obtained his PhD from the Sauder School of Business at the University of British Columbia, Vancouver, Canada. His research has been published in *Academy of Management Journal, Journal of International Business Studies* and *Journal of Management Studies.*

Chris Rowley is Visiting Fellow at Kellogg College at the University of Oxford, UK, and Visiting Professor at the Graduate School of Education at Tohoku University, Japan, and at the University of Business and International Studies, Switzerland. He is Professor Emeritus at Bayes Business School at the City, University of London, UK. He has over 30 years' experience in university systems in the UK, Europe and Asia and has won several international grants. He is the Editor of the important SCI-rated journal *Asia Pacific Business Review* and has published over 700 articles, books, chapters and practitioner pieces. He regularly provides interviews, expert comments and opinion pieces to the international media, including news services, TV, radio and practitioner outlets.

Taeyoung Yoo is Professor at the College of Business Administration at the Hankuk University of Foreign Studies, Seoul, South Korea. He holds a PhD in Management from Birkbeck College, University of London, UK. His current research interests draw on organizational and institutional changes in light of identity roles and socio-economic arrangements. His research has appeared in journals such as *Asian Business & Management, British Journal of Sociology, Corporate Governance, Organization Studies* and *Target.*

Soon Suk Yoon is Professor of Accounting at the School of Accounting, Finance, Economics, and Decision Sciences at Western Illinois University, Macomb, USA. His teaching and research interests include financial accounting and corporate finance. He has published numerous books and more than 50 journal articles over the last 35 years.

Inertia: Stalled governance reforms in the Korean chaebols amid economic maturation

Ingyu Oh, Chris Rowley and Yong Wook Jun

ABSTRACT

This collection of research deals with a broad issue of business organizations and history that awaits unremitting refinements and improvements by scholars who always find fresh enigmas that might wobble the established theories in the field. A new conundrum about South Korea and its conglomerate businesses – the *chaebol* – is its organizational resilience that seems to protect them from the relentless attention from the government and civic interest groups as to issues such as their so-called 'backward' corporate governance structures. Of course, this is a conundrum as it is this very *chaebol* corporate governance that helped create the 'Miracle on the Han' and unprecedented wealth for the nation during its entire postwar history. Therefore, this special issue features empirical studies of the *chaebol* corporate governance and its evolution with a variety of foci. These are: (a) rent-sharing, (b) succession, (c) outsider board members and (d) the reforms after the 1997 Asian financial crisis.

Introduction

The recent radical announcement by a scion of the Samsung founding family, Jae-Yong Lee of Samsung Electronics, that labour unions would be legalized and the father–son succession of the ownership and control structure of the family conglomerate has ended, seems at first sight to signal the end of the classic *chaebol* governance structure that we used to know of. The *chaebol* of South Korea ('Korea' for shorthand from now on) have tenaciously maintained family ownership, male heir succession and family control, despite harsh criticisms from society and unsympathetic governments of various periods (Jung 1995; Oh 2018; Oh and Jun 2016; Oh and Park 2001; Redding 2004; Rowley and Bae 2004; Rowley and Warner 2014; Warner and Rowley 2014).

This particularistic governance structure of big family conglomerates (i.e. the fusion of family ownership and control, male heir succession, etc.) derived from the new type of state-business relations in East Asia, which was set up in the immediate postwar years.

Then the fundamental purpose of the family firms was survival, first under the US military occupation and later under the civilian or military governments in Japan, Korea and Taiwan. The Japanese family firms were the first that had been liquidated by the US occupation forces in 1945, followed by the Korean family firms, most of which were confiscated by the first military government in 1961 and the Taiwanese family firms that were impounded by the occupying Kuomintang government from the mainland China in 1949 (Hattori 1999; Jung 1995; Kuo and Myers 2012; Oh 2018). Even during the period of rapid economic growth and development (the 1960s–1980s), the protracted threat of government hostility had always been there, at least in the background, in order for the illegitimate governments to curb the property rights of business proprietors. It is by no coincidence, therefore, that several large-scale family firms went bankrupt as soon as the state decided not to bail them out from debt defaults.

What greatly concerns external observers of the Korean *chaebol* is not the inimical state-business relations *per se* but how *the chaebol has managed to remain resilient all those years and posted phenomenal business success despite state hostility*. Most extant studies of the *chaebol* corporate governance have evaded this question by taking either a 'crony capitalism' view of disregarding the hostility altogether (i.e. the state has always sponsored and safeguarded the *chaebol)* or a 'revisionist' view that the Korean state has been super efficient in accomplishing an economic miracle via the *chaebol* (for the former, see Corsetti, Pesenti, and Roubini 1999; Fischer 1998; Goldstein 1998; Hahm and Mishkin 2000; for the latter, see Amsden 1989; Chang 2009; Haggard 1990; Wade 2003). A third view, which to us has some good explanatory traction, is organizational relativism – that the Korean version of corporate governance for the *chaebol*, like the US M-forms, had a strategic fit with the global market as the Korean family firms constantly adjusted their structures to fine tune to the changing global market (Hoskisson, Hill, and Kim 1993; Hoskisson and Hitt 1994; Hoskisson et al. 2000; Kim et al. 2004). This third view, nonetheless, does not deal with state-business relations at all, excluding it from the changing market environments. Therefore, our aim in this collection is to explain all three elements: *how did the chaebol neutralize state hostility and maintain governance structure in order to demonstrate miraculous firm-level performance even though tainted with crony capitalism?*

What we deem pivotal in the study of the *chaebols* is their resilience and success not only in domestic, but also in global, markets through technological and organizational innovations. We also argue that corporate governance is fundamental in disentangling this puzzle because it has been both efficient and of full of corruption. For example, their unique family ownership and control was pivotal in the success of electronics and semiconductor firms like Samsung and their ultimate global victory over Sony, Panasonic, Toshiba and other Japanese electronics giants (Chang 2008; Cherry 2003; Fitzgerald and Kim 2004; Jun 1987; Oh and Jun 2016). Under the rubric specified so far, this special issue features the following five contributions (Table 1).

The up- and downside of governance reforms

As briefly indicated above, restructuring and/or reforming the *chaebol* governance structure has been a buzzword in Korea since 1961. The attractiveness of transaction cost economics (TCE) and new institutional economics (NIE) is their capability in identifying sources of organizational strength in adapting to the changing environment by gradually or

Table 1. Summary of contributions.

Authors	Research question	Theories used	Data and methodology	Findings
Ingyu Oh et al.	How do *chaebols* strategically respond to series of reforms and reinforce corruptive practices to maintain family capitalism?	Rent-sharing view of corporate governance (CG)	*Chaebol* financial data Multiple regression, etc.	Despite top-down CG reforms by government, *chaebol* families continue to share rents with government either illegally or legitimately Minority group of *chaebols*, including Samsung, refuse to adopt holding company system or HCS (resilience) Those that adopted HCS institutionalized male heir succession and continue to illegally accrue family profits by intragroup trading (IGT)
Han	Does Confucianism work as institutional blue print that legitimizes male heir system and motivate *chaebol* restructuring by successors?	New Institutionalism	*Chaebol* financial data Logit regression	In Confucian culture, when a successor in a family firm is the first-born child and male, he is likely to implement a spin-off.
Kim et al.	Do outsider successors in *chaebols* bring in reforms and strategic changes, despite internal resistance?	Social Network Theory	*Chaebol* financial data Generalized least squared (GLS) procedures	Both firm and group-level outsider successions were significant predictors of strategic change. Continuing presence of departing CEO within group suppressed incoming CEO's strategic change initiative. Group-level outsider succession had counterbalancing impact on presence of departing CEOs within group, whereas firm-level outsider succession had no impact.
Yoo and Koh	Do outside directors refrain from taking proactive roles of *chaebol* reforms to safeguard their positions?	Role based Agency Theory	*Chaebol* financial data Exploratory factor analysis	Outside directors have lower survival chance when they proactively perform their roles regardless of whether this involves monitoring or advising When they survive, their proactive behaviour increases Tobin's q. Foreign ownership and EMBA degrees have moderating effect on proactive behaviours.
Fitzgerald and Kang	Has foreign ownership brought in CG reforms in *chaebols*?	Cross-border capitalism	Interview and other qualitative data Semi-structured interviews and case study	Contrary to local perceptions, 'fire-sales' and financial opportunism had not motivated foreign buyers, which sought to transform their acquisitions. Nor does government pressure to reform or poor liquidity fully explain strategies of their Korean counterparts.

drastically reforming organizational and institutional structures. Organizational structures can be changed periodically in order to adapt to idiosyncratic environmental changes, although institutional change that is intended to curb systemic environmental changes is few and far between in many dormant economies (Aoki 2013). From this point view, we can deduce that reforming the overall institution of the economy in Korea would have been difficult, although short-term periodic adjustments to external pressures were common.

Over the decades since 1961 both the government and the *chaebol* have carried out various governance reforms while relentlessly pursuing diversifications and M&As. Although the overall corruptive framework of state-business collusion [*jeonggyeong yuchak*] and family capitalism had persisted resiliently, the *chaebol* have managed to post phenomenal profits nonetheless – not only from the monopolistic domestic market but from the global markets filled with intense competition. In less than six decades, the Korean economy emerged as one of the 10 biggest in the world, while the leading *chaebols* occupied high places in the global 500 firms ranking (e.g. Samsung and Hyundai ranked #15 and #83, respectively in 2021). Periodic recessions and the 1997 Asian financial crisis had forced some delinquent *chaebols* to go bankrupt, although the surviving ones have continued to maintain family capitalism.

Contrary to the rosy picture of the Korean economy and the *chaebol* performance in global markets, the downside of the periodic fine tuning to their idiosyncratic environments without a major overhaul of the system itself are many. As Table 2 shows, political democratization in Korea has resulted in added pressures on the *chaebol* for a tangible and substantial corporate governance reforms that would ultimately signal the end of the *chaebol* or family capitalism. However, as the table also clearly shows, the top-down legal sanctions on *chaebol* governance has only been piecemeal and had been enacted only after irregularities were found despite the previous reform bills. A seemingly endless chain of legislation and amendments due to the *ex post facto* loopholes found in the legislation exists and is unlikely to end in the near future. The core of the legislation is to try to delimit family capitalism. Various administrations in the democratic government in Korea have repeatedly targeted family ownership succession by imposing huge inheritance taxes, while imprisoning chaebol CEOs who had evaded paying such taxes. Simultaneously, the social demand of meritocracy and managerial professionalism in *chaebols* has been accumulated into a social and political force, furthering the pressures of *chaebol* reforms (Cho et al. 2014; Jun, Kim, and Rowley 2019; Kim and Lee 2018; Oh 2018; Redding 2004; Rowley 2003; Rowley and Bae 2004).

Furthermore, despite the *chaebol* reforms in labour relations and corporate governance, Samsung remained adamant about preserving the infamous 'no union' policy and the father–son succession of ownership and control. The final blow against Samsung came after the election of the Moon government that had arrested the previous president for corruption, directly implicating Samsung in the process (Doucette 2017). Lee Jae-Yong, although paroled during his 30-months sentence for the violation of inheritance tax laws, labour relations laws, and anti-corruption laws, finally gave in and openly announced the end of the 'no union' policy in Samsung and the ending of the father-son succession of the top managerial position in the *chaebol*. As he promised, Lee indeed permitted unions in Samsung, although the father–son inheritance via both ownership and managerial control still awaits his decision at the time of his actual retirement.

Table 2. Evolution of corporate governance reforms in Korea (1987–2019).

Key regulations imposed on *chaebols*	Date imposed
Prohibition of cross-shareholding	April 1987
Restriction on the voting rights of affiliated financial and insurance companies	April 1987
Prohibition on the creation of holding companies	April 1987
Ceiling on the total amount of equity investment by firms in business groups	April 1987
Specialization policy to encourage greater focus on core activities	1991
Prohibition of debt guarantees	April 1993
'Big Deals' – swaps of the groups' firms in eight key industries	July 1998
Requirement to disclose large-scale intra-group transactions	April 2000
Requirement to disclose important matters related to non-listed companies	April 2005
Requirement to disclose business group's status	June 2009
Restriction on the pursuit of personal interests	February 2014
Prohibition of new circular shareholding	July 2014
Introduction of Stewardship Codes	February 2016
Requirement to disclose intragroup trade and non-dividend income including consulting fees and rents	December 2019

Source: Korea Fair Trade Commission (KFTC).

The consequences of these cyclical corruptions and legislative responses to them was the clear-cut deterioration of corporate governance among the *chaebol*. As Table 3 shows, the quality of Korean corporate governance was ranked 9th in Asia, lower than Thailand, Malaysia and India and only one notch above China. The downside of the Korean governance reform, therefore, entails the continued collusion between the state and *chaebol* officials leading to the arrest of *chaebol* CEOs and even former presidents of the country. For example, the former President Park Geun-hye is serving a 20-years sentence in jail for allegedly extorting bribes from Samsung.

The ostensible failure of the government-initiated governance reforms in Korea, therefore, calls for the review of the entire reform agenda and its ideas and policies. One reaction to the policy failure was to take sides with the *chaebol* by arguing that their form of corporate governance is similar to that of M-form in the US in bringing about organizational and business efficiencies and profitability (Chang 2003; Kim et al. 2004). The lack of agency problem within the *chaebol* and its organizational resilience braced by diversification and intragroup trading, were three important pillars of the *chaebols'* success during the tumultuous years of development and globalization (Chang and Hong 2000). While the government policies change from one party rule to another based on democratic

Table 3. Corporate governance ranking in the Asia Pacific (2018 and 2020).

Changes in market rankings/Underperforming categories		
2018	2020	Underperforming categories 2020
1. Australia	1. Australia	Government and Public Governance; Regulators
2. Hong Kong	2. Hong Kong	Investors; Listed Companies
3. Singapore	2. Singapore	Investors; Listed Companies
4. Malaysia	4. Taiwan	Investors; CG Rules
5. Taiwan	5. Malaysia	Government and Public Governance; Civil Society
6. Thailand	5. Japan	Listed Companies
7. Japan	7. India	Government and Public Governance; Investors
7. India	8. Thailand	Government and Public Governance; Civil Society
9. Korea	9. Korea	Civil Society; CG Rules
10. China	10. China	Investors; Civil Society
11. Philippines	11. Philippines	Investors; Civil Society
12. Indonesia	12. Indonesia	Investors; Regulators

Source: Asia Corporate Governance Association.

elections, the *chaebol* family would maintain their strong grip on their property rights through direct control and ownership succession by male heirs. The *chaebol* have grown 'too big to thrash'.

However, as long as the democratic government also maintains its democratic ideal of fair competition and the protection of shareholder rights along with labour union rights to participate in management, the *chaebol* will continue to face the cyclic misfortunes of imprisonment for briberies and illicit successions and intragroup trading. In other words, both sides of the table face stalemate, not being able to see any hope of future resolutions of the problems surrounding *chaebol* corporate governance reform. Against the backdrop, the research in this collection intends to answer why the stalemate has occurred, why the state wants to enforce governance reforms repeatedly and why such reform efforts are met by botches and hold-ups.

The rent sharing view (RSV) of corporate governance

Oh et al. present their original theory of RSV in the explanation of the *chaebol* corporate governance reforms. The authors set out with a bold comment that 'RSV of corporate governance may well explain the current logjam in Korea', as the Korean state is persistently interested in maximizing illicit rents from the *chaebol*. To meet the state demands of rent sharing, the firms need to lobby the government for exclusive business opportunities in the domestic and/or export markets and/or find innovative ventures to triple or quadruple their surplus profits. In so doing, the owning families need to violate laws outright sometimes in order to protect their property and succession rights. The logic goes like this: as long as the *chaebol* pay extortion fees to the state for the violation of new corporate governance regulations, the former can conserve family capitalism along with the succession of male progeny. The RSV, therefore, shies away from the popular Rent-Seeking or Rent-Augmenting Theory, given that it proposes an opposite outlook that rent sharing will motivate economic growth more efficiently than the free market, especially when an infant stage of the free-market economy does not fully guarantee private property protection unless such property is safeguarded by the state or parallel institutions that cartelize violence (Gambetta 1996; Oh 2018).

When the free-market economy is mature and democracy is fully developed, as in the case of Korea in the twenty-first century, rent sharing between the state and business is fraught with difficulties as each incumbent government fails to completely eradicate rent sharing due to the acute need of the huge amount of cash needed for election campaigns and the distribution of the rents among the contributors of election victories. The *chaebol* also find it unacceptable to abandon their family capitalism with a built-in mechanism of male heir succession as long as they have continuously donated 'slush funds' to political leaders. Therefore, it is unlikely the state and the *chaebol* will reach an agreement on a reform package that would convert the *chaebol* into an M-form or the holding company system, both of which the state sees as a more transparent form of corporate governance than family capitalism.

Developing from the RSV, the authors then find implications of the theory to test hypotheses. They propose to test five hypotheses within the following areas: 1) property protection and the adoption of new corporate governance; 2) different rent sharing behaviours between those that adopted new corporate governance and those that refused; 3) different patterns of ownership-control disparity between new and old corporate governance; and 4) the mechanism of intragroup trading (IGT) in new corporate governance. Their statistical analyses reveal that chaebols now can refuse to adopt new corporate governance if that threatens their property rights and in so doing, they should increase rents to be shared with the state through IGT. Furthermore, new corporate governance did not end the vicious cycle of corruption and rent sharing, as firms now focus on IGT to strengthen family capitalism.

The cultural and institutional view of succession by male primogenitures

Han's contribution uses new institutionalism (NI) to explore the possibility of corroborating the mechanism of how national culture can legitimate and motivate strategic change, including corporate governance reforms, in major Korean firms. Han's rendition of NI presumes that institutions are complete when they perform regulative, normative and cognitive functions and each function provides a basis for gaining legitimacy in society (Scott 1995). The regulative view of institutions (e.g. Barnett and Carroll 1993) suggests that individual and organizational changes result from coercive means, the legal system and regulations. The normative view of institutions (e.g. Selznick 1948) emphasizes the role of social obligation and norms, and informal structures comprising the environment of organizations (e.g. Powell and DiMaggio 2012). Lastly, the cognitive view of institutions stresses changes in conceptual beliefs and interpretations of shared meanings (DiMaggio 1997). The cognitive phase of institutionalization requires a process called 'internalization' for a full acceptance of firm's strategic changes, a social process where policies, behaviours and decision-making acquire 'taken-for-granted' status (Meyer and Rowan 1977).

One implication of this version of NI is that national culture is a critical source of institutional internalization for strategic change in a firm. In other words, a firm's strategic change is not a decision-maker's individual preference, but a highly contested institutional process where the cognitive internalization of such change among organizational members must be pre-conditioned. Therefore, the legitimacy and acceptance of the change initiated by a new successor in a firm who has gone through the process of successor 'routinization' (i.e. gaining legitimacy through charismatic, traditional or legal-rational norms) become a single most important factor of organizational change (Ingram and Silverman 2002; Johnson, Dowd, and Ridgeway 2006; Suchman 1995).

Based on NI, Han then proposes to test two hypotheses, the first concerning the tendency of the strategic change initiated by the first-son heir and the second regarding the intensity such change by the first-son heir when he has many siblings. The dependent variable is operationalized into firm spinoffs or firm splits [*bunga*]. By this we mean that one firm is split into two or more to give them out to sons and daughters who do not become the successor. Although it may seem odd to consider spinoffs as strategic change in a firm, *bunga* is a culturally critical process during the transition period from the father to the first son. Han's data analysis confirms both hypotheses leading to an interesting finding that Confucianism works not as an overall cultural setting that prevents strategic change from happening but as a cultural legitimizer that motivates new successors to engage in changes that involve spinoff and the consequent CG reforms.

Agencies and networks in understanding outside CEOs and directors

Two contributions to this collection utilize Agency and Social Network Theory in a complementary fashion to advance our understanding of outside successors or outside directors in the Korean *chaebol*. Kim et al. investigate different types of outside successors or 'outsiders' and their impact on strategic change in business groups in Korea. Social Network Theory, they believe, allows them to distinguish different types of outsiders in those firms, while it may also explain why departing CEOs still retain their influence on incoming CEO's policies of strategic change. Therefore, Kim et al.'s study takes up a very similar topic to that of Han's, although the latter takes culture as the most important institutional and cognitive factor, emphasizing the illegitimacy of any successor who is not a male primogeniture in a Confucian institutional and cognitive framework.

Kim et al.'s central theses are anchored in the view of CEOs as entities 'embedded' in the social network of a business group. Embeddedness, according to Granovetter (1992, 33), refers to 'the fact that economic action and outcomes, like all social action and outcomes, are affected by actors' dyadic (pairwise) relations and by the structure of the overall network of relations'. Researchers later found that both relational embeddedness (e.g. the characteristics of relationships) and structural embeddedness (e.g. the characteristics of the relational structure) influence the nature and scope of relationships (Burt 1992; Coleman 1988; Uzzi 1996). Applying this theory to Korean business groups, Kim et al. are interested in identifying the embeddedness discrepancy of incoming and departing CEOs on the basis of their cross-cutting interpersonal ties in a business group boundary (Cao, Maruping, and Takeuchi 2006).

One important implication of this theory is that the impact of CEO succession on strategic change depends on the portfolio of relationships of both the incoming and departing CEOs within a business group network. Based on this implication, the authors find that two types of outsiders exist: outsides who have ties with in-group members of the firm (e.g. directors of affiliated firms) and those who are purely outsiders with no such ties. Kim et al. then test four hypotheses drawn from their theoretical outlook: (1) pure outsiders are more associated with strategic change than are either insiders or in-group outsiders; (2) the retention of the outgoing CEO in the firm has a negative effect on the strategic change by an incoming CEO; (3) the degree of the negative effect of the ex-CEO on new CEO is the weakest for pure outsiders; and (4) the 1997 Asian financial crisis has a moderating effect on the first two hypotheses. All four hypotheses are corroborated by the authors' data analysis. They conclude by urging further study of how to invite more pure outsiders to Korean business groups.

Yoo and Koh's contribution takes an alternative view of outside directors to the one corroborated by Kim et al. The former postulates that most outside directors are not supposed to be proactive decision makers, including strategic change and corporate governance reforms. Yoo and Koh contend that the palpable influence of outside directors on performance is in no way conclusive (Adams, Hermalin, and Weisbach 2010; de Andrés, Arranz-Aperte, and Rodriguez-Sanz 2017). Even in the US outside directors' roles have often labelled 'rubber-stamping' (Herman 1981), while their nomination was anchored in personal connections and ingratiation (Westphal and Stern 2007). The situation is worse in Korea, where outside directors have outright personal or familial connections with CEOs or controlling family members, almost forcing them not to carry out any tangible monitoring roles. Therefore, their contribution to the firm has mostly been negligible, if not unconstructive, measured in terms of ROA, Tobin's q and shareholder returns (Yoo and Jung 2015). Therefore, it is in family capitalism's interest to create agency problems among the outside directors.

Provided that Agency Theory is not readily applicable to outside directors as monitors and advisors, Yoo and Koh elect to introduce Network Theory as an alternative perspective with which to explain the discrepancy between the prescribed roles and actual behaviours of outside directors. Indeed, outside directors' personal and socio-political connections with their proprietors turns out to be another factor in their unsatisfactory performance (Khatri, Tsang, and Begley 2006). Yoo and Koh find that Social Network Theory can further distinguish between proactive and conformist outside directors, just as Kim et al. divided outsiders into two types. Yoo and Koh argue that networked reciprocity between *chaebol* owners and outside directors is pivotal for such a distinction. According to them, reciprocity 'explains why outside directors avoid constraining CEOs when conducting their expected roles, regardless of whether they are monitoring or advisory'. Furthermore, 'such constraints could harm the exchange relationship between the outside directors and the appointers, who tend to be CEOs or controlling family members of the focal firms' (Herman 1981; Ma and Khanna 2016).

Yoo and Koh test three hypotheses, including a moderating variable that basically explores ways to enhance the number of proactive outside directors: (1) all outside directors choose to act out a conformist role to protect their tenure at the firm; (2) nonetheless, proactive outside directors post far better contributions to firm performance than conformists; and (3) foreign ownership and outside directors' expertise enhance proactive behaviours during high growth and low growth periods, respectively. The authors find that all three hypotheses are corroborated against their data, producing intriguing implications for theory and practice. For one thing, the study found that foreign ownership and outside directors' expertise do matter in retaining them on the board even though they play out proactive roles. For another, legal means should be applied in order to delimit the selection and employment of outside directors only to those who have MBA or higher degrees.

Cross-border capital and foreign pressures in corporate governance reforms

In the final contribution to our collection, Fitzgerald and Kang examine whether foreign ownership has in fact cleared up the barriers to corporate governance reforms in Korea since the Asian financial crisis in 1997. Their research questions are threefold:

- Firstly, to what extent did acquisition by a foreign multinational as a result of the 1997 Asian Crisis transform the governance and management of *chaebol* affiliates, and which factors determined the outcomes?
- Secondly, were changes in governance and management within foreign-owned multinational subsidiaries fundamentally different to developments in Korean-controlled *chaebol* affiliates?
- Thirdly, following the change to foreign ownership, did the capabilities and long-term competitiveness of the acquired *chaebol* affiliates increase or diminish?

These questions of comprehensive before-after assessment of corporate governance reforms in the *chaebol* that were possible only because of the external pressures such as the financial crisis and 'fire sales' of *chaebol* subsidiaries to reduce the debt-to-equity ratio. In answering why the crisis occurred to begin with, the authors deliberately shy away from either the crony capitalism thesis (Corsetti, Pesenti, and Roubini 1999; Fischer 1998; Goldstein 1998; Hahm and Mishkin 2000) or the strong state thesis (Amsden 1989; Chang 2009; Haggard 1990; Wade 2003). Instead, Fitzgerald and Kang take a third view: the failure of Korea, Inc. occurred because of the institutional failure to control cross-border capital movements and the banking sector (Feldstein 1998; Kalinowski 2008; Zhang 2010). Key to this failure was the lack of mature corporate governance that would have monitored any irregularities within the globalizing banking sector and the *chaebol's* own financial institutions (Fields 1995).

According to the authors, the answers to these questions are indeed *pis aller*. While some cases do show improvements in terms of financial governance especially for cross-border capital, 'internal debates on the advantages of quick decision-making, risk-taking and long-term versus short-term profitability and financial sustainability continued'. The factors that determined the success of post-reform performance were relevant to 'technological leadership, competitive capabilities, and profitability levels'. Despite the crisis and foreign ownership, the 'old' Korean management style creeped in and sabotaged reform efforts. However, the corporate governance reforms that both indigenous and foreign ownership had carried out resulted in similar consequences due to the urgency of the crisis. Foreign ownership mattered a lot in this regard more than partially owned foreign subsidiaries of multinational companies, as managerial change in wholly owned multinational subsidiaries proved comparatively more extensive, deeper and durable than otherwise. Finally, the authors find that although 'wholly owned subsidiaries in Korea proved better able, when strategically motivated, at transferring resources and capabilities than in identified examples of international joint ventures, the extent the multinationals invested in their subsidiaries or transferred resources and capabilities varied significantly'.

Theoretical and practical implications of corporate governance reform in Korea

Fitzgerald and Kang's final assessment of the corporate governance reform in Korea before and after the financial crisis echoes through our collection. The authors state: '[After the crisis], the established owners of business groups, moreover, increased circulatory share ownership as a means of maintaining control, and prosecutions revealed notorious breaches of transparency and accountability'. This means that foreign ownership alone, even if it is coupled with an external crisis, cannot be a sole theoretical basis of successful corporate governance reform. It also entails that outside directors and CEOs cannot bank on foreign ownership and the crisis as a solid springboard for leapfrogging into radical strategic change within Korean *chaebols*. However, the picture is not as simple as it looks, as many cases within Korea contradict each other: Some are very successful in bringing about radical changes in corporate governance and strategic changes, while others are not. This demands further theoretical investigation.

While the whole picture is still fuzzy in the theoretical arena of foreign ownership and external crises, the NI approach to strategic change within the *chaebol* and other business groups in Korea clearly resonate with us who want a simple and logical answer for the whole debate. Confucianism works as a legitimating force in the institution of the *chaebol* allowing much needed legitimacy and prop for the male primogenitures who may want to pursue strategic change and corporate governance reforms to defend his property rights. However, this clear-cut view awaits further justification in the area of why this cannot be legalized by the government that keeps treating it as unjust and even unacceptable. The disparity between national culture and legal systems leads to a rent-sharing view of corporate governance reforms in Korea, where the legality of succession by male primogenitures must be negotiated with the state, which wants to retain economic interests of maximizing rents. The political need of rent sharing, therefore, presupposes the illegality of Confucian national culture, a very ironic fact about Korean family capitalism, about which the extant theories have failed to address and thus needs to be continued in major scholarly forums like this.

On a practical note, the whole debate about the Korean *chaebols* leaves us with some policy implications. Firstly, the state should not pursue rent sharing to begin with and liberalize succession methods as long as the national culture permits it (e.g. male heir succession). However, the drivers of foreign ownership and global financial capitalism must work as potential threats to Korean family capitalism so that the latter can continue its high performance and complete corporate governance reforms to be paralleled with the global standards.

Future prognosis

The conclusion of our collection is in no way complete, making our project an ongoing one with immediate needs of fine tuning and developing our research. We need, for example, to develop theories and methods of identifying networked characteristics of agents and their roles in the *chaebol* as reform leaders. Another acute necessity is to develop theories and methods to identify the precise impact of foreign ownership and external crises on the *chaebol* corporate governance reforms and strategic change by the agents. Finally, we also need to continue our discussion of the nature of the Korean state in formulating and revising its regulatory regime designed to curtail the property rights of the *chaebol*. The resilience of the *chaebol* has indeed been braced not by foreign pressures *per se* but by the governmental hostility in various historical periods. As long as it continues to exert its force in *chaebol* reforms, the topic needs to be carefully studied from various perspectives and make better use of both cross-disciplinary and inter-disciplinary insights.

Conclusion

This collection on Korean *chaebol* corporate governance and reforms is blessed with five contributions from experts in their own fields. The broad range of its topics, perspectives, and methodologies is something that other collections cannot so easily garner. Nonetheless, all five contributions had one common underlying theme: what are pivotal in transforming *chaebol* corporate governance and other strategic contingencies? Theories and implications used in each contribution range from the rent sharing view to national culture as institutions, to agency and network theories and to external and foreign factors. While four contributions relied on various quantitative analyses, the final contribution utilized qualitative data. As all the contributions have made it convincing, the big question of *chaebol* reform has three crucial dimensions: the state, culture and foreign pressures. This is an important finding that differentiates our collection from previous ones that highlighted crony capitalism, the efficient state or meticulous family capitalism. We nonetheless want to see the debate continue in the future.

Disclosure statement

No potential conflict of interest was reported by the authors.

ORCID

Ingyu Oh http://orcid.org/0000-0002-1645-8767

References

Adams, R., B. Hermalin, and M. Weisbach. 2010. "The Role of Boards of Directors in Corporate Governance: A Conceptual Framework and Survey." *Journal of Economic Literature* 48 (1): 58–107. doi:10.1257/jel.48.1.58.

Amsden, A. 1989. *Asia's Next Giant: South Korea and Late Industrialization*. Oxford: Oxford University Press.

Aoki, M. 2013. *Comparative Institutional Analysis: Theory, Corporations and East Asia*. Cheltenham: Edward Elgar Publishing.

Bae, J., and C. Rowley. 2003. "Changes and Continuities in South Korean HRM." *Asia Pacific Business Review* 9 (4): 76–105. doi:10.1080/1743792X.2003.11878825.

Bae, J., C. Rowley, D.-H. Kim, and J. J. Lawler. 1997. "Korean Industrial Relations at the Crossroads: The Recent Labour Troubles." *Asia Pacific Business Review* 3 (3): 148–160. doi:10.1080/13602389700000009.

Barnett, W. P., and G. R. Carroll. 1993. "How Institutional Constraints Affected the Organization of Early US Telephony." *Journal of Law, Economics and Organization* 9: 98.

Buchanan, J. M. 1983. "Rent Seeking, Non-compensated Transfers, and Laws of Succession." *Journal of Law and Economics* 26 (1): 71–85. doi:10.1086/467026.

Burt, R. S. 1992. *Structural Holes: The Social Structure of Competition*. Cambridge: Harvard University Press.

Cao, Q., Maruping, L. M., and Takeuchi, R. 2006. "Disentangling the Effects of CEO Turnover and Succession on Organizational Capabilities: A Social Network Perspective." *Organization Science* 17 (5): 563–576.

Chang, D. O. 2009. *Capitalist Development in Korea: Labour, Capital, and the Myth of the Developmental State*. New York: Routledge.

Chang, S. J., and J. Hong. 2000. "Economic Performance of Group-affiliated Companies in Korea: Intragroup Resource Sharing and Internal Business Transactions." *Academy of Management Journal* 43 (3): 429–448.

Chang, S. J. 2003. *Financial Crisis and Transformation in Korea: The Rise and Fall of Chaebol Business Groups*. Cambridge University Press.

Chang, S. J. 2008. *Sony Vs. Samsung: The inside Story of the Electronics Giants' Battle for Global Supremacy*. Hoboken: Wiley.

Cherry, J. 2003. "The 'Big Deals' and Hynix Semiconductor: State–business Relations in Post-crisis Korea." *Asia Pacific Business Review* 10 (2): 178–198. doi:10.1080/13602380410001677209.

Cho, Y. H., G. C. Yu, M. K. Joo, and C. Rowley. 2014. "Changing Corporate Culture over Time in South Korea." *Asia Pacific Business Review* 20 (1): 9–17. doi:10.1080/13602381.2012.755321.

Coleman, J. S. 1988. "Social Capital in the Creation of Human Capital." *American Journal of Sociology* 94: 95–120. doi:10.1086/228943.

Corsetti, G., P. Pesenti, and N. Roubini. 1999. "What Caused the Asian Currency and Financial Crisis?" *Japan and the World Economy* 11 (3): 305–373. doi:10.1016/S0922-1425(99)00019-5.

de Andrés, P., L. Arranz-Aperte, and J. Rodriguez-Sanz. 2017. "Independent versus Non-Independent outside Directors in European Companies: Who Has a Say on CEO Compensation?" *Business Research Quarterly* 20 (2): 79–95.

DiMaggio, P. 1997. "Culture and Cognition." *Annual Review of Sociology* 23 (1): 263–287. doi:10.1146/annurev.soc.23.1.263.

Doucette, J. 2017. "The Occult of Personality: Korea's Candlelight Protests and the Impeachment of Park Geun-hye." *Journal of Asian Studies* 76 (4): 851–860. doi:10.1017/S0021911817000821.

Edlin, A. S., and J. E. Stiglitz. 1995. "Discouraging Rivals: Managerial Rent-seeking and Economic Inefficiencies." *The American Economic Review* 85 (5): 1301–1312.

Feldstein, M. 1998. "Refocusing the IMF." *Foreign Affairs* 77 (2): 20–33. doi:10.2307/20048786.

Fields, K. 1995. *Enterprise and the State in Korea and Taiwan*. Ithaca, NY: Cornell University Press.

Fischer, S. 1998. "In Defense of the IMF: Specialized Tools for a Specialized Task." *Foreign Affairs* 77 (4): 103–106. doi:10.2307/20048970.

Fitzgerald, R., and Y. C. Kim. 2004. "Business Strategy, Government and Globalization: Policy and Miscalculation in the Korean Electronics Industry." *Asia Pacific Business Review* 10 (3–4): 441–462. doi:10.1080/1360238042000264423.

Goldstein, M. 1998. *The Asian Financial Crisis: Causes, Cures, and Systematic Implications*. Washington, DC: Institute for International Economics.

Granovetter, M. 1992. "Problems of Explanation in Economic Sociology." In *Networks and Organizations: Structure, Form and Action*, edited by N. Nohria and R. G. Eccles, 25–56. Boston: Harvard Business School Press.

Haggard, S. 1990. *Pathways from the Periphery: The Politics of Growth in the Newly Industrializing Countries*. Ithaca, NY: Cornell University Press.

Hahm, J.-H., and F. Mishkin. 2000. "The Korean Financial Crisis: An Asymmetric Information Perspective." *Emerging Markets Review* 1 (1): 21–52. doi:10.1016/S1566-0141(00)00003-0.

Hattori, T. 1999. "Zaibatsukaitai to keiei no keizoku: Nihon ni okeru zaibatsukaitai no keiken [The Continuity of Zaibatsu Dissolution: The Experience of Zaibatsu Dissolution in Japan]." *Hyôron Shakaikagaku* 59: 1–33.

Herman, E. 1981. *Corporate Control, Corporate Power*. New York: Cambridge University Press.

Hoskisson, R., C. Hill, and H. Kim. 1993. "The Multidivisional Structure: Organizational Fossil or Source of Value?" *Journal of Management* 19 (2): 269–298. doi:10.1177/014920639301900205.

Hoskisson, R., L. Eden, C. Lau, and M. Wright. 2000. "Strategy in Emerging Economies." *Academy of Management Journal* 43 (3): 249–267.

Hoskisson, R., and M. Hitt. 1994. *Downscoping: How to Tame the Diversified Firm*. Oxford University Press: New York.

Ingram, P., and B. Silverman. 2002. *The New Institutionalism in Strategic Management*. Oxford, UK: Elsevier.

Johnson, C., T. Dowd, and C. Ridgeway. 2006. "Legitimacy as a Social Process." *Annual Review of Sociology* 32 (1): 53–78. doi:10.1146/annurev.soc.32.061604.123101.

Jun, I.-W., K.-I. Kim, and C. Rowley. 2019. "Organizational Culture and the Tolerance of Corruption: The Case of South Korea." *Asia Pacific Business Review* 25 (4): 534–553. doi:10.1080/13602381.2019.1589728.

Jun, Y. 1987. "The Reverse Direct Investment: The Case of the Korean Consumer Electronics Industry." *International Economic Journal* 1 (3): 91–104. doi:10.1080/10168738700080023.

Jung, K.-H. 1995. "Changing Business-government Relations in Korea." *Asia Pacific Business Review* 1 (3): 98–112. doi:10.1080/13602389500000005.

Kalinowski, T. 2008. "Korea's Recovery since the 1997/98 Financial Crisis: The Last Stage of the Developmental State." *New Political Economy* 13 (4): 447–462. doi:10.1080/13563460802436616.

Khatri, N., E. Tsang, and T. Begley. 2006. "Cronyism: A Cross-cultural Analysis." *Journal of International Business Studies* 37 (1): 61–75. doi:10.1057/palgrave.jibs.8400171.

Kim, A., and Y. Lee. 2018. "Family Firms and Corporate Social Performance: Evidence from Korean Firms." *Asia Pacific Business Review* 24 (5): 693–713. doi:10.1080/13602381.2018.1473323.

Kim, H., R. E. Hoskisson, L. Tihanyi, and J. Hong. 2004. "The Evolution and Restructuring of Diversified Business Groups in Emerging Markets: The Lessons from Chaebols in Korea." *Asia Pacific Journal of Management* 21 (1/2): 25–48. doi:10.1023/B:APJM.0000024076.86696.d5.

Kuo, T. C., and R. H. Myers. 2012. *Taiwan's Economic Transformation: Leadership, Property Rights and Institutional Change 1949–1965*. London: Routledge.

Ma, J., and T. Khanna. 2016. "Independent Directors' Dissent on Boards: Evidence from Listed Companies in China." *Strategic Management Journal* 37 (8): 1547–1557. doi:10.1002/smj.2421.

Meyer, J. W., and B. Rowan. 1977. "Institutionalized Organizations: Formal Structure as Myth and Ceremony." *American Journal of Sociology* 83 (2): 340–363. doi:10.1086/226550.

Oh, I., and H. Jun. 2016. "Economic Miracle." In *Handbook of Modern Korean History*, edited by M. Seth, 295–313. London: Routledge.

Oh, I., and H.-J. Park. 2001. "Shooting at a Moving Target: Four Theoretical Problems in Explaining the Dynamics of the Chaebol." *Asia Pacific Business Review* 7 (4): 44–69. doi:10.1080/713999115.

Oh, I. 2018. *Mafioso, Big Business and the Financial Crisis: The State-Business Relations in South Korea and Japan*. London: Routledge.

Powell, W. W., and P. J. DiMaggio. 2012. *The New Institutionalism in Organizational Analysis*. Chicago: University of Chicago press.

Redding, G. 2004. "The Conditional Relevance of Corporate Governance Advice in the Context of Asian Business Systems." *Asia Pacific Business Review* 10 (3–4): 272–291. doi:10.1080/1360238042000264360.

Rowley, C., and J. Bae. 2004. "Big Business in South Korea: The Reconfiguration Process." *Asia Pacific Business Review* 10 (3–4): 302–323. doi:10.1080/1360238042000264388.

Rowley, C., and M. Warner. 2014. "The Changing Contours of Korean Management and Business." *Asia Pacific Business Review* 20 (1): 1–8. doi:10.1080/13602381.2013.859424.
Rowley, C. 2003. "The Korean Economy, Business and Labour: Miracle or Mirage?" *Asia Pacific Business Review* 9 (3): 116–122. doi:10.1080/13602380312331288660.
Scott, P. 1995. *The Meanings of Mass Higher Education*. Buckingham: McGraw-Hill Education.
Selznick, P. 1948. "Foundations of the Theory of Organization." *American Sociological Review* 13 (1): 25–35. doi:10.2307/2086752.
Tullock, G. 2013. *The Economics of Special Privilege and Rent Seeking*. Berlin: Springer Science & Business Media.
Uzzi, B. 1996. "The Sources and Consequences of Embeddedness for the Economic Performance of Organizations: The Network Effects." *American Sociological Review* 61 (4): 674–698. doi:10.2307/2096399.
Wade, R. 2003. *Governing the Market: Economic Theory and the Role of Government in East Asian Industrialization*. Princeton, NJ: Princeton University Press.
Warner, M., and C. Rowley. 2014. "Context and Implications for Korean Management and Business." *Asia Pacific Business Review* 20 (1): 197–207. doi:10.1080/13602381.2013.859428.
Westphal, J., and I. Stern. 2007. "Flattery Will Get You Everywhere (Especially if You are A Male Caucasian): How Ingratiation, Boardroom Behavior, and Demographic Minority Status Affect Additional Board Appointments at U.S. Companies." *Academy of Management Journal* 50 (2): 267–288. doi:10.5465/amj.2007.24634434.
Yoo, T., and D. Jung. 2015. "Corporate Governance Change and Performance: The Roles of Traditional Mechanisms in France and South Korea." *Scandinavian Journal of Management* 31 (1): 40–53. doi:10.1016/j.scaman.2014.08.005.
Zhang, X. 2010. "Global Forces and Corporate Reforms in South Korea." *International Political Science Review* 31 (1): 59–76. doi:10.1177/0192512109354472.

The end of rent sharing: corporate governance reforms in South Korea

Ingyu Oh, Soon Suk Yoon and Hyo Jin Kim

ABSTRACT

As the imprisonment of Samsung's heir, JY Lee, clearly indicates, South Korean conglomerate groups (*chaebol*) face enormous difficulties in protecting their private property via father-son inheritance of the entire group. High party polarization (i.e. intense competition between ideologically divided political parties) within Korean democracy has continuously threatened the chaebols' private property and family succession system, criticizing the unusually high economic concentration enjoyed by the top ten chaebols. Using the rent sharing view (RSV) of corporate governance, this contribution to the special issue examines key variables in the evolution of Korean corporate governance: the impact of the traditional corporate governance (TCG) and the new holding company system (HCS) on intragroup trading (IGT), non-dividend incomes hoarded by owning families, ownership-control disparity (OCD) and family succession. We find that private property protection through rent sharing continues to overshadow chaebols' choices about their future corporate governance structure, while the new HCS fails to curb IGT, non-dividend incomes, OCD and family succession.

Introduction

The South Korean (hereafter, Korean or Korea) chaebol, roughly defined as family-owned and controlled conglomerates with high levels of intermarket corporate diversifications, has been understood by many as having the following five salient characteristics (Choi, Han, and Lee 2014; OECD 2018; Choi and Cho 2021):

(1) Regardless of corporate governance reforms and strict legal enforcements to curb ownership and control concentration by minority shareholders, including direct family members, chaebols continue to increase their number of affiliated firms.

(2) Regardless of corporate governance reforms and strict legal enforcements to curb ownership and control concentration by minority shareholders, including direct family members, the top four chaebols' share of the total assets and profit owned and generated by the top 30 chaebols continues to grow; it was as high as 70% in 2017.

(3) Regardless of corporate governance reforms and strict legal enforcements to curb ownership and control concentration by minority shareholders, including direct family members, the inside ownership of the chaebol has continuously risen to 60% of total shares by 2016 through circular shareholding, even though family shareholding has decreased to less than 4%.
(4) Regardless of corporate governance reforms and strict legal enforcements to curb ownership and control concentration by minority shareholders, including direct family members, chaebols' profitability has been continuously influenced by intragroup trading.
(5) Regardless of corporate governance reforms and strict legal enforcements to curb ownership and control concentration by minority shareholders, including direct family members, chaebols' profitability is continuously linked to inside (particularly, family) ownership.

As Table 1 shows, the Korean government and civil society have enacted a series of corporate governance reforms to ameliorate the above five problems, not to mention other related ones, such as the family succession of chaebol ownership and control by male progenies. However, chaebols' structural resilience has outwitted these reform efforts by the government, as vindicated by the above five characteristics, all of which are still fecund today. Despite repeated reprisal against the chaebols, the overall reputation of Korean corporate governance therefore remains tarnished, although the overall firm level performance has been more than prodigious in terms of any macro and microeconomic indicators (Table 2). The weakest area of Korean corporate governance reform has turned out to be its inability to bolster the corporate governance rules within each chaebol, as Table 2 confirms.

What sharply demarcates Korean corporate governance before and after 1987 is the end of the 'rent-sharing' regime that had been dominant from the birth of the first military government in 1961. Rent-sharing refers to corruptive collusion between the state and the chaebol family in order to achieve economic development and simultaneously to share the rent, accrued from the collusion, with the managers of the military state. It was an effective means of governing the system, awarding both legitimate and illegitimate rents to chaebol owners in exchange for either legitimate or illegitimate extortions to be collected later by the state (Oh and Varcin 2010; Oh and Jun 2016; Oh 2018 [1999]).

Under the first civilian democratic leadership from 1992, and especially after the Asian financial crisis of 1997, policymakers enacted many measures intended to curb chaebols' monopoly and thus a pathological propensity in the Korean economy by prohibiting intragroup debt guarantees and encouraging business specialization. Immediately after political democratization in 1987, the government reconfirmed an old rule by banning the holding company system (HCS). However, during the Asian financial crisis in 1997, the state officials had to capitulate to the demand of foreign investors and the IMF, both of whom demanded that the ban on holding companies be lifted. Furthermore, as this ban on HCS inspired a new precarious practice of circular holding that allowed chaebol families to own and control their conglomerates without majority shares and enabled the succession of the chaebol to male offspring, the government in turn encouraged HCS to ban any new circular holdings in 2014. As of May 2021, consequently, 22 chaebols have

Table 1. Evolution of corporate governance reforms in Korea (1987–2019).

Key Regulations Imposed on Chaebols	Date Imposed
Prohibition of cross-shareholding	April 1987
Restriction on the voting rights of affiliated financial and insurance companies	April 1987
Prohibition on the creation of holding companies	April 1987
Ceiling on the total amount of equity investment by firms in business groups	April 1987
Specialization policy to encourage greater focus on core activities	1991
Prohibition of debt guarantees	April 1993
'Big Deals' – swaps of the groups' firms in eight key industries	July 1998
Requirement to disclose large-scale intra-group transactions	April 2000
Requirement to disclose important matters related to non-listed companies	April 2005
Requirement to disclose business group's status	June 2009
Restriction on the pursuit of personal interests	February 2014
Prohibition of new circular shareholding	July 2014
Introduction of Stewardship Codes	February 2016
Requirement to disclose intragroup trade and non-dividend income including consulting fees and rents	December 2019

Source: Korea Fair Trade Commission (KFTC)

Table 2. Corporate governance ranking in the Asia Pacific (2018 & 2020).

Changes in market rankings/Underperforming categories		
2018	2020	Underperforming categories 2020
1. Australia	1. Australia	Government & Public Governance; Regulators
2. Hong Kong	2. Hong Kong	Investors; Listed Companies
3. Singapore	2. Singapore	Investors; Listed Companies
4. Malaysia	4. Taiwan	Investors; CG Rules
5. Taiwan	5. Malaysia	Government & Public Governance; Civil Society
6. Thailand	5. Japan	Listed Companies
7. Japan	7. India	Government & Public Governance; Investors
7. India	8. Thailand	Government & Public Governance; Civil Society
9. Korea	9. Korea	Civil Society; CG Rules
10. China	10. China	Investors; Civil Society
11. Philippines	11. Philippines	Investors; Civil Society
12. Indonesia	12. Indonesia	Investors; Regulators

Source: Asia Corporate Governance Association

completely adopted the HCS, while 32 others still tenaciously retain traditional chaebol governance (TCG) with the proscribed circular holding system (Korea Fair Trade Commission 2020a).

As of May 2020, Korean corporate governance is fraught with difficulties. The HCS is not fully embraced by all leading chaebols, while the chief of Samsung Chaebol is behind bars for bribery extended to the ex-President, who is also in jail. Furthermore, what is striking is the fact that HCS is now demonstrating higher degrees of ownership-control disparity (OCD), intragroup trading (IGT) and tunnelling than TCG groups (KTFC 2020). The new disclosure requirement for non-dividend income under the new regulatory restrictions also makes it clear that HCS chaebols garner more consulting, brand royalties and rent incomes for chaebol families than TCG groups (KTFC 2020). Although these new sets of data and scholarly analyses make abysmal revelations about chaebol corporate governance, none of the previous studies on the HCS among Korean chaebols has provided adequate theoretical explanations for the failure of the governmental regulation of chaebol corporate governance.

Therefore, the research question of our contribution to this special issue is twofold: (1) what is the theoretical background relevant to the Korean evolution of corporate governance and the importunately pernicious effect of chaebols' resistance to governance reforms imposed on them by the government? and (2) why is HCS producing more disparaging effects relating to OCD, IGT and other means of tunnelling than TCG? To answer these questions, we employ various statistical analyses, including trend scanning and a regression analysis, to compare HCS and TCG in terms of their OCD, IGT and tunnelling practices and to test hypotheses regarding the theoretical basis that explains the differences between two groups of Korean chaebols. We would also like to suggest policy implications for future corporate governance reforms for chaebols based on our findings, in addition to the theoretical and managerial implications of the Korean experience of corporate governance reforms.

Literature review and hypotheses

Transaction cost economics (TCE) and new institutional economics (NIE)

The Korean experience of corporate governance evolution casts a strong doubt on the TCE or NIE views of corporate governance, which predict a steady and smooth evolution of corporate governance into credible commitments from credible threats (see *inter alia* Williamson 1983, 1984; North and Weingast 1989; North 1993, 1995). Unlike the implications of TCE and other branches of NIE, the Korean experience represents a ferocious, irregular and capricious outcome from the stalemate between the firms that resist governance reforms and the state, which insists on imposing new regulations on the former.

The failure to explain the irregularity of Korean corporate governance despite its phenomenal level of economic growth also fails to explain why the perception of Korean corporate governance is shoddier than that of Malaysia, Thailand and India (Table 2). This theoretical loophole in TCE and NIE arises from their inattention to the importance of the state in the evolutionary process of corporate governance, an important agent in the rent-seeking, rent-augmenting and rent-sharing theory of economics (Buchanan 1983; Tullock 2013). As we will explain in detail below, when private property rights are not fully institutionalized in an economy that is experiencing rapid economic growth due to an unexpected demand explosion in the global export market, it is historically manifest that the state assumes a mercantilist role in promoting and regulating international trade. The interventionist state therefore becomes highly interested in selling protection to the exporting firms for 'fees', which are equal to the sharing of the rent amassed by the monopolist or oligopolist firms that are allowed to participate in international trade.

Rent sharing view (RSV) of corporate governance

The RSV of corporate governance may well explain the current logjam in Korea, as it predicts that the state will be intrinsically interested in imposing new regulations on chaebols in order to maximize illicit rents from the latter, which are left with no option other than to violate the regulation in order to protect its private property. As long as the chaebol pays extortion fees to the state for the violation of new corporate governance regulations, the former can conserve TCG along with the succession of male progeny (see Tables 3 and Tables 4).

RSV therefore veers away from the mainstream rent-seeking or rent-augmenting theory, which prophesies that the economies run by rent-seeking and rent-augmenting mechanisms will be less efficient in the long run than perfect competition in the free market system (e.g. Buchanan 1983; Edlin and Stiglitz 1995; Tullock 2013). On the contrary, RSV advances a contrasting argument that rent sharing will motivate economic growth more efficiently than the free market, especially given that the free-market economy does not fully guarantee private property protection unless such property is safeguarded by the state or parallel institutions that cartelize violence (Gambetta 1996; Oh 2018 [1999]). Furthermore, if it is the case that the transition to credible commitment with a multidivisional form of corporate governance or HCS, which is popular in the US, will only exacerbate their family ownership and control over assured male-heir succession or TCG, chaebol families will opt out of HCS. They will choose the option of co-opting the state; the latter in fact cannot destroy a globally successful family conglomerate like Samsung or Hyundai by risking the confirmed rent, which is only being augmented and can be shared with the state anytime. This observation is congruous with Li and Ouyang (2007), who verified a theorem that predicts firms' continuous use of bribery, even if they are caught and punished routinely, as long as the state in a widely corrupt society (i.e. where all the chaebols provide bribes to the state for rent) finds the game-like cycles of bribery-punishment beneficial to it, as each cycle escalates the total sum of the bribery.

In the typical prisoner's dilemma game (Table 3), with the dominant payoffs for the chaebol and the state deployed by (5,0) and (0,5), the Nash equilibrium results in a concomitant choice of a suboptimal payoff of (1,1). However, if rent sharing can benefit both the state and the chaebol in the form of monopoly rents harnessed by a chaebol that will faithfully pay the state's extortion fees, which are far greater than the fines collected by the state after punishment, the payoff structure changes to the extent that the new Nash equilibrium allows both parties to choose the second best outcome despite playing the same prisoner's dilemma game, as Table 4 below explicates.

In this modified prisoner's dilemma game, the payoff structure of (3,3) has moved to the top left cell to reflect a new compromise between the state and the chaebol over the sharing of the monopoly rent. As long as this new game is played out continuously from one cycle to another, the chaebol is informally allowed to hand down their private property illegally from the father to the first son in each succession cycle. Any new government policy that threatens this

Table 3. State-Chaebol prisoner's dilemma game.

		Chaebol	
		Break laws	Don't break
State	Punish	1,1	5,0
	Don't	0,5	3,3

Table 4. Modified prisoner's dilemma game.

		Chaebol	
		Break laws	Don't break
State	Punish	3,3	5,0
	Don't	0,5	1,1

conventional rule of the game will be vehemently resisted by the chaebol. Therefore, in chaebol corporate governance, private property protection and family succession loom large as key factors of opting out of transition to HCS or any other US-style corporate governance that has been advocated by state officials since the Asian financial crisis of 1997.

H_1: If HCS threatens the protection of private property and family succession, chaebols will opt out of it.

HCS and firm-level rent seeking

As part of a tumultuous (rather than seamless) transition to credible commitments from credible threats, we postulate that the transition to HCS from TCG in Korea occurred due to pressures from foreign investors, who demanded a transparent disclosure of corporate information and the option for hostile takeovers of Korean firms by foreign hedge funds (Lee and Rhyu 2019). Even though the chaebols had no fear of the agency problem, they had to capitulate to the demands of the government, who decided to lift the ban on HCS in the course of negotiations with foreign investors and the IMF during the 1997 Asian financial crisis (Lee and Rhyu 2019). In other words, corporate governance in Korea has evolved into the Anglo-American form of HCS or multidivisional form not because the chaebols wanted it but because foreign financial interests did, as it meant the government could no longer protect the chaebols from foreign pressures. Nevertheless, as we mentioned above and will reiterate below, a sizable number of leading chaebols are still resisting the transition to HCS from TCG.

The benefit of HCS was not very clear to the chaebols initially, as the Korean version did not allow the fusion of financial and industrial subsidiaries under one holding company. As such, many chaebol groups eschewed espousing it as much as possible unless the chaebol in question did not own or control financial firms (Hypothesis 1). However, as Daems (2012 [1978], 113) substantiated a long time ago, HCS provides the owners of holding companies with a great advantage in 'control over corporate assets', which enables them to implement corporate policies that can maximize their profitability. This further implies that a holding company will want to merge other companies, either related or unrelated, as vertical subsidiaries (son, grandson and great-grandson companies, etc.) in order to maximize profitability through directorate interlocking (Daems 2012 [1978], 122).

However, previous studies of HCS have unfortunately neglected the fact that HCS can be unstable when both domestic and foreign political and economic pressures on domestic firms are extraordinarily threatening or hostile. In Korea, where political risk remains high (Dalton 2008), HCS therefore cannot be a stable governance form, unlike in Europe or in pre-war Japan. Table 5 is a party polarization index, which was accumulated between 1996 and 2016 from various nation-states throughout the world. The purpose of this index is to ascertain (a) how unstable each country is in terms of its economic policies, especially in terms of its monopolistic firms, such as chaebols; and (b) how this instability has been intensified by the rapid change in party polarization (e.g. right vs. left wing parties). The table shows that Korea is the most politically unstable country in terms of polarization changes (Change = 3.22), while the most recent polarization score was the second highest (PPI = 3.92), second only to the Czech Republic (PPI = 4.77).

As we explained above, this stability issue will augur an elongating vicious cycle where the chaebol and the state will continue to play the game of the former paying bribes and

Table 5. Party polarization index (1996–2016).

Nation	Time 1	Time 2	Time 3	Time 4	Change
Australia	2.04	1.96	2.50	2.71	0.67
Canada	1.83	2.06	2.87	3.27	1.44
Czech Rep.	5.44	5.43	5.15	4.77	−0.67
Germany	2.51	2.70	3.63	3.34	0.83
Israel	3.99	3.87	2.14	2.33	−1.66
Japan	3.30	3.30	2.13	2.53	−0.77
Korea	0.70	3.55	3.08	3.92	3.22
Mexico	1.29	2.10	2.95	3.00	1.71
New Zealand	3.81	3.35	3.33	3.88	0.07
Philippines	1.33	0.46	0.88	0.26	−1.07

Source: Comparative Study of Electoral Systems; available from www.cses.org.

other forms of extortion to the latter, which importunately revises laws curbing first-son succession within the chaebol (i.e. changing laws to increase extortion). Under these conditions, family owners of holding companies will prioritize their private wealth accumulation by exploiting the assets of son, grandson and great-grandson companies in their holding companies. This is done to stack up personal wealth for use as bribes later in the succession season, especially when the plausibility of garnering dividends and other forms of legitimate incomes is dismal. Therefore, firm-level rent-seeking by family owners (i.e. living off the firm, instead of stewarding it) looms large in Korean HCS.

H_{2a}: Chaebols that have adopted HCS will maximize their family rents through IGT, including tunnelling, more than those that rejected HCS by maximizing the number of vertical subsidiaries.

Non-dividend incomes as new rents hoarded by the HCS chaebols

Related to H_{2a} is the task of specifying the new types of rents that these freshly established HCS chaebols are hoarding in order to maximize their family rents through IGT. The holding companies are essentially passive investment companies, since they do not have operating business segments other than holding equity interests in their subsidiaries (Daems 2012 [1978]). By nature, holding companies are supposed to have dividend income only. However, the resourcefulness of HCS chaebols, acquired through long-term interactions with volatile state leaders in the past, has allowed them to find a crevice in the system, which can be used to award the owning families enormous wealth in the form of non-dividend incomes. The advantage of their excessive control over ownership rights of subsidiary firms has enabled this crack to open up wide for the families. Non-dividend incomes typically include brand royalty payments, consulting fees and rental charges, which these families amass primarily from their subsidiaries and affiliates.

According to the KFTC (KFTC Press Release 2018), we can discern that the lower the family ownership in their subsidiaries, the higher the non-dividend incomes projected. Unlike dividend incomes, which are determined proportionally to shareholders' cash flow rights, non-dividend incomes do not rely on shareholders' proportionate interests in their affiliates (Penman and Sougiannis 1998). Therefore, the non-dividend income is a convenient way for HCS chaebol owners to collect rents from their subsidiaries. HCS chaebols use pyramidal structures to secure OCD through indirect second- and third-tier subsidiaries (e.g. grandson or great-grandson subsidiaries). Therefore, the pyramidal structure helps chaebol owners to save investment outlays while also assuring them of collecting rents from indirect subsidiaries in the lower tiers of the pyramid. Furthermore, a considerable portion of the IGT, along with their subsidiaries and affiliates, results in non-dividend income transactions and takes the form of non-market transactions. According to the Korea Fair Trade Act (KFTA), big IGTs exceeding 500 million won (or roughly £300,000) are subject to approval by the board of directors and internal monitoring. However, individual IGT contracts are not substantial in monetary terms; hence they do not need approval from the board of directors, nor are they subject to internal monitoring.[1]

Typically, dividend income is a primary source of revenue for holding companies in many countries. It is therefore normal for these firms not to expect non-dividend incomes, and even if it does arise, it accounts for an infinitesimal portion of the operating income of holding companies (Penman and Sougiannis 1998). However, in Korea, non-dividend income accounts for a significant proportion of the operating income for some HCS chaebols (KFTC White Paper, 2018). What is bewildering is the fact that the source of the non-dividend income is none other than HCS's subsidiaries and affiliates. HCS chaebols hoard the non-dividend income from the forced discretionary contracts imposed on their subsidiaries and affiliates, tapping their owners' powerful position. The resulting unfair prices and quantities allow chaebol owners to amass tremendous wealth for personal use and storage. Their successors, equipped with increasing ownership trends, will inherit the control of the chaebols under the disguise of formal contract-based transactions. It is the *new normal* for HCS chaebols to follow suit in order to benefit from the imposition of easy, unfair and unilateral non-dividend income transactions on their affiliates. Chaebols' unscrupulous use of non-dividend incomes to tunnel business resources to chaebol owners is more pronounced when their affiliates are controlled by a holding company. The HCS might have enhanced chaebols' transparency by prohibiting their circular ownership practices, which are the main cause of the blame placed on the OCD. However, at the same time, the holding company system leads chaebols to resort to the unethical and opportunistic practices of maximizing the non-dividend income of chaebol owners.

When did this new normal start among the HCS chaebols? Records show that GS Group initiated the stockpiling of brand royalties in Korea from their affiliates in 2004, when GS Group was separated from LG Group and adopted the HCS for the first time. LG Group followed suit by hoarding brand royalties in 2005 after turning itself into an HCS. Many other HCS chaebols similarly require subsidiaries to pay brand royalties, because as pure holding companies they have a limited source of family income. The practice is reported to have spread even to non-chaebol HCS business groups (Lee 2008).

Based on the above discussion, we state H_{2b} as follows, to test the new normal of collecting non-dividend income from subsidiaries and affiliates:

H_{2b}: Chaebols that have adopted HCS will maximize their family rents through non-dividend income more than those that rejected HCS.

HCS and ownership and control structure

Intragroup rent seeking by family owners of chaebol holding companies lucidly shows how HCS allows their rent seeking activities by enlarging the number of vertical subsidiaries in the firm (H_{2a}). Related to this theoretical perspective is the overall nature of ownership and control structure within HCS among Korean chaebols. Provided that family level rent seeking emerges as a dominant payoff strategy for chaebol family owners, it is undeniable that they will pursue the related operational tactic of widening the gap between ownership and control, as long as vertical diversification is key to maximizing non-dividend incomes from IGT, tunnelling and other profit sources. In other words, it is apparent that non-dividend incomes awarded to chaebol families become bigger than ever, as the indirect control of subsidiary firms in the vertical hierarchy within HCS (i.e. OCD) becomes ever more intensified (KFTC White Paper 2018).

However, it has been documented by previous studies that foreign investors will shy away from firms that have high levels of OCD in Korea. As this foreign pressure on Korean corporate governance reform was crucial during the post-Asian financial crisis in Korea, the HCS in fact served, albeit temporarily, to impede the enlarging tendency of OCD among HCS chaebols (Choi, Cho, and Sul 2014; Lee and Cho 2016). Simultaneously, holding on to the old TCG despite the government threats and foreign pressures gave an additional measure of protection to TCG chaebols from possible hostile takeovers by foreign hedge funds. Indeed, the government restricted cross holding (and even circular holding in some cases) among HCS chaebol affiliates, though it is still prevalent among TCG chaebol affiliates, which do not have such legal constraints (Jun, Sheldon, and Rhee 2010). Therefore,

H_3: OCD in TCG chaebols is more predominant than in HCS chaebols even though we expect OCD will grow substantially among the latter in the near future as well.

Indirect ownership leverage within HCS chaebols

What is interesting about the HCS chaebols is their ability to control subsidiaries with only a small portion of subsidiary shares (e.g. 25–35%), unlike the usual 100% ownership requirement imposed on holding companies in other countries (Choi 2011). As we have suggested in H_3, OCD will be unusually high for Korean HCS chaebols, and it is also noteworthy that this OCD could be a new means of indirectly controlling subsidiaries in order to maximize IGT.

As is widely known, in the pyramidal ownership structure of HCS chaebols, the founding family directly holds equity shares only in the holding company. The holding company then controls its son subsidiaries, which own their lower-tier subsidiaries (KFTC White Paper 2020: 268–271). Chaebol owners can therefore exercise control over the subsidiaries indirectly. This neatly allows us to use the concept of *indirect ownership leverage* to investigate the relationship between IGT and ownership structure (i.e. a mixture of H_2 and H_3). The idea is that the lower the indirect ownership interest in the subsidiaries of the pyramid, the higher the probability of opportunistic IGT that will benefit chaebol owners. Therefore, the following hypothesis is possible:

H_4: There will be a negative relationship between IGT and the indirect ownership interest in the subsidiaries.

HCS and succession

The main organizational functions of the HCS are: (1) sustaining corporate governance; (2) transferring corporate ownership and control to a successor; (3) controlling and restructuring an entire corporate group under the direction of a holding company; (4) neutralizing environmental threats; and (5) amassing profits inside a corporate group (Koike 1991, 25; Quigley and Hambrick 2012; Yu 2014; Park, Kim, and Shin 2020). The evolution of the HCS has always taken (1), (2) and (5) seriously, although its advance in major capitalist economies in the 19th and 20th centuries in the form of monopolies and/or concentration of assets forced governments in various countries to curb its spread (Koike 1991). In fact, both Japan and South Korea banned the HCS after the Second World War due to the notoriety of Japanese-style family holding companies, or *zaibatsu*, which dominated the prewar economy through concentration based on the holding company system.

The usual method of intergenerational succession in HCS chaebols takes the option of succession through spinoffs [*bunhal seunggye*], as utilized by the LG and SK groups (Choi 2011; Yi 2012). In order to secure first-son ownership of the entire HCS, the chaebol will divide up its entire affiliates into those that will remain key enterprises for the group and those that will be abolished or given away to other siblings and family members. This practice is similar to *fenjia*, which is popular among Taiwanese *guanxi* firms (Wakefield 1998). All in all, we notice that the HCS has clearly provided the chaebols that adopted the new system with an easy means of increasing and transferring shares of the holding company to potential successors and other family members, especially with the Korean government's provision of tax incentives for HCS chaebols to convert their corporate governance to the HCS. Therefore, our final hypothesis is:

H_5: HCS, more so than TCG, allows chaebol family owners to make substantial increases to the shares of potential family successors, if HCS can save sufficient funds from the reduced corporate taxes imposed on holding companies.

Theoretical model

Our theoretical discussion so far, which takes the rent sharing view seriously in the explanation of the corporate governance evolution within Korean chaebols, can be recapitulated using the following theoretical model adopted in this paper (Figure 1).

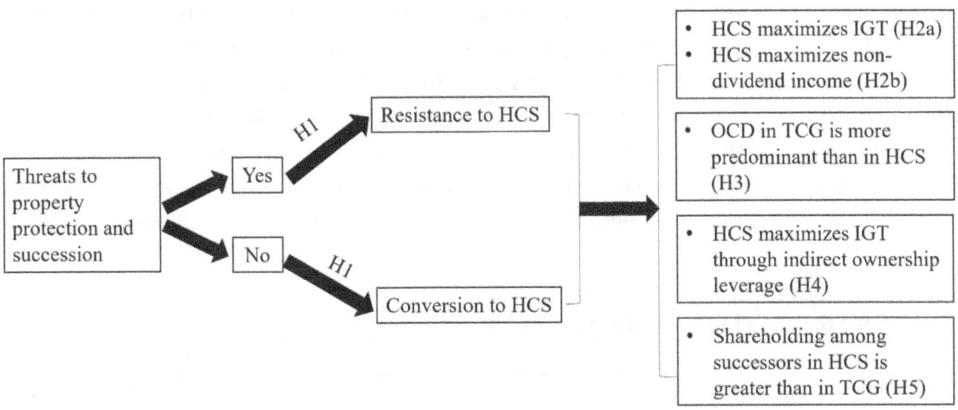

Figure 1. Evolution of chaebol corporate governance.

Data

In order to corroborate the above hypotheses, we rely on two data sources. First, we use the press releases and white papers issued by the KFTC. The KFTC periodically discloses these germane sources in order to publicize its policy updates in tandem with other relevant analyses of its new policies and implications. We piled up most of the time series data from the KFTC press releases for the period from 2015 to 2020, during which a major shift in government policy occurred regarding chaebol corporate governance: the new holding company system and its impact on our key dependent variables. We use the data included in the KFTC press releases for the trend analyses and the regression analysis.

Secondly, we utilize the 2021 chaebol data from the DART system (Data Analysis, Retrieval and Transfer System) operated by the Financial Supervisory Services of Korea. We limited our sample to chaebols with natural persons as controlling shareholders of their holding companies or representative companies. Hence, we excluded the chaebols with business entities as controlling shareholders. We also eliminated from our sample those chaebols with only financial affiliates. Our 2021 DART sample consists of 22 HCS chaebols and 24 TCG chaebols.

Analyses

Financial revenues (test of H_1)

To test H_1, that chaebols will opt out of the government-led transition to HCS if doing so threatens their private property rights and family succession, we test the mean difference in the ratio of financial revenues over total revenues between the HCS and TCG chaebols. Table 6 shows that the TCG chaebols have significantly higher financial revenues than the HCS chaebols. Financial revenues for the TCG chaebols, on average, accounts for 13.3% of total group revenues, whereas the ratio for the HCS chaebols is virtually zero at 0.2%. Of course, the statistical significance should be noted due to the design of the regulatory policy that the HCS chaebols are not allowed to have financial affiliates. To do so, we need to show the actual ratio of the financial revenues over total group revenues for the TCG chaebols.

We examine some individual TCG chaebols in order to ascertain the ratio of the financial revenues over total group revenues. Kiwum Daum Group has the highest ratio of financial revenues over total revenues with 85.2%, followed by Taegwang Group with 80.2%, Hanwha Group with 49.4%, Yujin Group with 48.7%, Kakao Group with 21.0%, Samsung Group with 20.6%, Naver Group with 10.7% and Hyundai Motor Group with 3.7%. It is well known in Korea that the top five chaebols, including Samsung, Hyundai and Hanwha, are reluctant to convert themselves to HCS since they do not want to give up

Table 6. Ratio of financial revenue over total revenue.

	HCS chaebols	TCG chaebols	t Stat	$P(T \le t)$ one-tail
Mean	0.002	0.133	−2.495	0.010
S.D.	0.006	0.257		
Obs.	22	24		

their lucrative financial business segments, which would mean forsaking their private properties and family successions.

Total IGT difference between the HCS and TCG chaebols (test of H_{2a})

To test H_{2a}, we first examine whether there is a statistically significant IGT difference between the HCS and TCG chaebols. Panel A in Table 7 shows that the HCS chaebols have significantly higher IGT than the TCG chaebols in 2020 when the KFTC Press Release data is used. The 22 HCS chaebols have an average of 11.5% of IGT, whereas the 24 TCG chaebols have an average of 8.1% IGT. The difference is statistically significant at a 5% significance level. To corroborate the Panel A findings, we also use the 2021 data available from the DART and replicate the test.

We use two measures of IGT: (1) domestic IGT divided by total group revenue, as in 2020 KFTC Press Release data; and (2) total IGT (domestic plus international) divided by total group revenue. Panel B in Table 7, reporting the between-group difference test based on the first definition of IGT, shows that IGT is not statistically different between the HCS and TCG chaebols. Panel C in Table 7, reporting the between-group difference test based on the second definition of IGT, also shows that IGT is statistically insignificant. The results are mixed in terms of statistical significance. However, the results show that the HCS chaebols engage in IGT more actively than the TCG chaebols, even though the between-group differences are more attenuated in 2021 than in 2020. As such, we document that even though the statistical significance is not strong, the HCS chaebols are more actively engaged in IGT than their TCG counterparts.

Chaebols often use IGTs opportunistically in order to benefit their owners. Chaebol owners can enjoy personal benefits when they have more IGTs with non-listed affiliates they own or control than IGTs that do business with their publicly listed affiliates, over which they only have weak control. As per the 2018 KFTC White Paper, chaebols rely more on non-listed firms than listed firms for IGT. More specifically, the ratio of domestic IGT over total group revenues for the population of 51 chaebols, including both HCS and TCG chaebols, with natural persons as controlling shareholders averages 8.2% for listed firms

Table 7. IGT difference between the HCS and TCG chaebols.

Panel A. KFTC Press Release (November 2020) data and IGT defined as domestic IGT over total group revenue

	HCS chaebols	TCG chaebols	t Stat	P(T< = t) one-tail
Mean	0.115	0.081	1.767	0.043
S.D.	0.079	0.046		
Obs.	22	24		

Panel B. DART data (May 2021) and IGT defined as domestic IGT over total group revenue

	HCS chaebols	TCG chaebols	t Stat	P(T< = t) one-tail
Mean	0.112	0.089	1.179	0.123
S.D.	0.077	0.050		
Obs.	22	24		

Panel C. DART data (May 2021) and IGT defined as total IGT over total group revenue

	HCS chaebols	TCG chaebols	t Stat	P(T< = t) one-tail
Mean	0.207	0.151	1.257	0.108
S.D.	0.166	0.134		
Obs.	22	24		

Non-listed firms owned by chaebol owners as primary vehicles in IGT (an additional test of H_{2a})

and 22.1% for non-listed firms. Hence, we examine the analysis focusing on IGT with non-listed affiliates, using three different metrics.

First, we examine how non-listed firms owned internally by the chaebol families affect IGT. To this end, we identify *one* non-listed firm with the largest IGT for each chaebol and ascertain whether there is any difference between the HCS and TCG chaebols. Secondly, it is well known that chaebol owners provide their successors with favourable IGT privileges in order to help them to succeed smoothly. We also noticed that the non-listed firms with the largest IGT are either wholly or almost wholly owned internally. Therefore, we test whether there is a difference in inside ownership – defined as family plus affiliates' ownership – between the HCS and TCG chaebols. Thirdly, we examine the extent to which IGT is accounted for by all the non-listed firms in each chaebol.

Panel A in Table 8 shows that the ratio of the IGT provided by one non-listed firm with the highest IGT to total non-listed firms' IGTs is higher, but statistically insignificant, for the TCG chaebols than for the HCS chaebols. As an in-depth related analysis, we identified the types of non-listed firms with the highest IGT in each group. We found that chaebols typically use privately-owned IT and construction firms to provide a considerable portion of their IGT demands. Six non-listed IT firms – four in the HCS chaebols and two in the TCG chaebols – are the largest IGT firms, providing between 16.4% and 76.4% of the non-listed firms' IGT. Five non-listed construction firms provide between 27.2% and 85.9% of the non-listed firms' IGT. For the remaining chaebols, the largest IGT suppliers provide goods or management services closely related to their main business needs.

Panel B in Table 8 shows that the inside ownership is significantly higher for the TCG chaebols than for the HCS chaebols. The inside ownership of non-listed firms with the highest IGT ranges from 50% to 100%. Panel C in Table 8 shows that the IGT accounted for by all the non-listed firms within each chaebol is lower for the HCS chaebols than the TCG chaebols. However, the between-group differences are insignificant. These results imply that the HCS chaebols engage less in IGT than the TCG chaebols, but the difference is not statistically significant.

Table 8. Using non-listed firms owned by chaebol owners in IGT: HCS and TCG chaebols.

Panel A. Ratio of the IGT provided by the non-listed firm with the largest IGT to total non-listed firms' IGT				
	HCS chaebols	TCG chaebols	t Stat	P(T ≤ t) one-tail
Mean	0.419	0.482	−1.169	0.124
S.D.	0.185	0.176		
Obs.	22	24		
Panel B. Inside ownership of the non-listed firms with the largest IGT				
	HCS chaebols	TCG chaebols	t Stat	P(T ≤ t) one-tail
Mean (%)	83.747	95.316	−2.183	0.019
S.D.	22.672	10.653		
Obs.	22	24		
Panel C. Ratio of the IGT accounted for by all the non-listed firms in each chaebol				
	HCS chaebols	TCG chaebols	t Stat	P(T ≤ t) one-tail
Mean	0.383	0.408	−0.315	0.377
S.D.	0.234	0.400		
Obs.	22	24		

Non-dividend income as a primary income source for HCS holding companies (test of H_{2b})

To test H_{2b}, we examine differences in non-dividend income between the HCS and TCG chaebols. As mentioned earlier, the holding companies of the HCS chaebols do not have operating business segments other than investments in their subsidiaries. In contrast, the 'representative' companies of the TCG chaebols are typically the largest in their respective chaebols. We define non-dividend income as the sum of the consulting fees, rental incomes and brand royalties divided by the holding company's or representative company's revenue. Typically, non-dividend incomes, probably except rental incomes, originate from IGT contracts imposed on the subsidiaries by the holding companies. Those IGT transactions are typically not based on market terms; hence, they are used as the primary vehicles for tunnelling corporate resources to chaebol owners.

Table 9 reveals that non-dividend income is significantly larger for the HCS chaebols than for the TCG chaebols. Income from brand royalties, which account for about two-thirds of non-dividend income, are also significantly larger for the HCS chaebols than for the TCG chaebols. Table 9 therefore supports H_{2b}.

Table 9. Comparison of non-dividend income between the HCS and TCG chaebols.

	Total non-dividend income		Brand royalties	
	HCS chaebols	TCG chaebols	HCS chaebols	TCG chaebols
Mean (%)	0.277	0.006	0.176	0.005
S.D.	0.198	0.013	0.163	0.013
Obs.	22	24	22	24
t Stat	6.415		4.892	
$P(T \le t)$ one-tail	0.000		0.000	

Ownership-control disparity (test of H_3)

To test H_3, we ascertain whether there is a difference in OCD between the HCS and TCG chaebols. We measure OCD as the ratio of inside ownership minus family ownership divided by inside ownership. Here, the inside ownership includes both family and affiliates' ownership in the holding company for the HCS chaebols, and the 'representative' company for the TCG chaebols. The result in Table 10 shows that the TCG chaebols have significantly higher OCD than the HCS chaebols. The reason for this is that the TCG chaebols rely on crossholding between affiliated firms, while the HCS chaebols are not allowed to do so.

Table 10. OCD differences: HCS vs. TCG chaebols (2021 DART data).

	HCS chaebols	TCG chaebols	t Stat	$P(T \le t)$ one-tail
Mean (OCD)	0.295	0.441	−1.725	0.046
S.D.	0.277	0.299		
Obs.	22	24		

Impact of the indirect ownership leverage by HCS chaebols on IGT (test of H_4)

To test H4, we propose the following regression model:

$$IGT = \beta_0 + \beta_1 FOHC + \beta_2 HCOSS + \beta_3 IOLLS + \varepsilon_r$$

where IGT denotes intragroup trading as a percentage of the total group revenue. FOHC and HCOSS respectively denote the family ownership interest in the holding company by chaebol owners and the average ownership interest in the son subsidiaries (first-tier indirect ownership in the pyramid) under each holding company. IOLLS represents the indirect ownership leverage in the lower-tier subsidiaries of the pyramid. Specifically, we define the IOLLS as the ratio of the average ownership interest of the son (grandson) subsidiaries in the grandson (great-grandson) subsidiaries over the average ownership interest of the holding company in the son subsidiaries.

The regression result reported in Table 11 reveals that: (1) the lower the holding company's ownership interest in the son subsidiaries (HCOSS), the higher the IGT; and (2) the lower the indirect ownership leverage in the grandson and great-grandson subsidiaries (IOLLS), the higher the IGT. The higher the indirect ownership leverage in the lower tiers of the pyramid, the higher the dividend income to the chaebol owners from the lower-tier subsidiaries of the pyramid, and *vice versa*. The indirect ownership leverage implies that subsidiaries from which chaebol owners have high dividend income will have lower IGT and *vice versa*. The results are consistent with the expectations. Overall, the HCS chaebols structure their holding companies to engage in IGT in order to tunnel profits from IGT with their subsidiaries and affiliates and thus benefit the chaebol owners.

Table 11. Indirect ownership leverage and the 2020 IGT (n = 22 HCS chaebols).

	Coeff.	t Stat.	P-val.	Adj. R^2
Intercept	74.386	3.989	0.001	0.299
FOHC	0.009	0.151	0.882	
HCOSS	−0.491	−3.390	0.003	
IOLLS	−24.612	−3.006	0.008	

Data source: Fair Trade Commission Press Release (November 2020)

Ownership succession (test of H_5)

H_5 postulates that chaebols use the holding company system to ensure smooth succession of chaebols to their family members. To test H_5, we use a trend analysis examining the successor ownership interest relative to the controlling shareholder's ownership interest from 2015 to 2020. We also compare the trends with all the HCS firms and the TCG chaebols. Panel A in Figure 2 shows that the family ownership interest in the 22 chaebol holding companies ranged from 45% to 50% during the 2015–2020 period. It is noteworthy that successors' ownership interest increases as controlling shareholders' ownership interest decreases, indicating that chaebol owners prepare for the succession

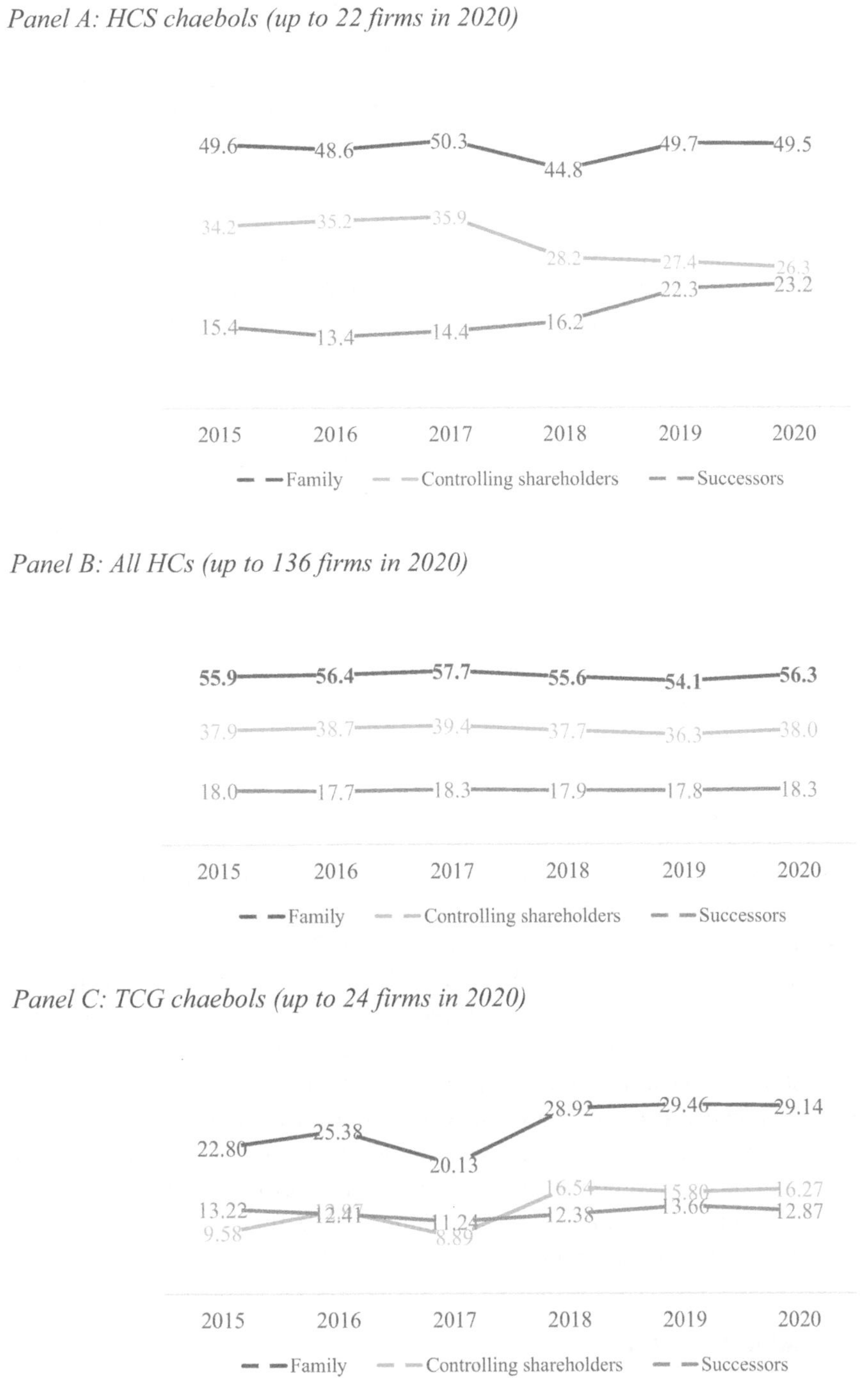

Figure 2. Trends of family ownership breakdown of the holding companies over the 2015–2020 period (unit: %). Sources: Fair Trade Commission Press Release (November 2020) and 2021 DART data

of their businesses to their successors. Compared to the lowest ownership interest of 13.4% in 2016, the successors' average ownership interest increased by 9.8 percentage points to 23.2% in 2020. The successors' ownership interest in the HCS chaebols was lower than that of all the holding companies until 2017. The successors' ownership interest increased a little in 2018. It then picked up in 2019 and further increased to an all-time high level of 23.2%.

The trends contrast with those of the entire set of holding companies (Panel B) and the TCG chaebols' representative companies (Panel C). Panel B shows that the controlling shareholders' and their successors' average ownership interests hovered around 38% and 18%, respectively, for the entire set of HCS business groups. On the other hand, Panel C shows that the family ownership interests of the TCG chaebols were all much lower than those of the HCS chaebols. Furthermore, the successors' ownership interest stayed stable, ranging from 11.24% to 13.66%, while the controlling shareholders' ownership interest increased rapidly in the 2018–2020 period compared to the 2015–2017 period.

The trend analyses show that HCS chaebol owners use the HCS as a vehicle for facilitating succession to their successors. In contrast, the TCG chaebol owners do not have the incentives or abilities to do the same. A sudden increase in the HCS chaebol successors' ownership interests in the 2018–2020 period ensued from the 2017 chaebol policy changes by the KFTC to promote the holding company system. The change in the chaebol ownership composition shows that chaebols are quick to take advantage of any favourable government policy changes in order to transfer their wealth to their successors.

Summary of findings

All five hypotheses displayed statistical significance from our various tests and analyses. H_1 confirmed the political threat to chaebols' private property, which forced chaebols to shy away from the government advice to adopt the HCS. Furthermore, our statistical tests and analyses all confirmed H_{2a}, H_{2b}, H_3 and H_4. These results bolstered our suspicion that the rent sharing norm has in fact encouraged the HCS chaebols to exploit and maximize IGT, tunnelling and non-dividend incomes through OCD and indirect ownership leverage since the HCS reform was introduced. Finally, H_5 was corroborated by our analysis, which correctly identified the tax incentive as a main reason for buttressing the successor's shareholding in an HCS chaebol. Therefore, the HCS reform has not produced any positive result that can be considered better than the TCG. This further implies that the chaebols that resolutely hold on to the TCG will continue their battle against the government to protect their private property rights and father-son succession.

Theoretical implications

Corporate governance can be approached from various perspectives, including financial (Fama 1980; Jesen 1994), economic (Buchanan 1983; Williamson 1984; North and Weingast 1989; Tullock 2013) and sociological (Aguilera and Jackson 2003). This paper contributes yet another perspective to the long debate – an economic sociological approach through the rent sharing view (Gambetta 1996; Oh 2018 [1999]). The RSV of corporate governance intends to resolve the conundrum surrounding corporate governance in non-Anglo-American cultures: why do some forms of rent sharing and outright collusion between the state and business monopolies lead to sustainable economic growth through phenomenal innovation? Furthermore, why does this economic success through rent sharing continue to be subject to acrimonious criticism from voters and party polarization, leading to the imprisonment of key business and political leaders who have conspired in the grand design of rent sharing? While most theories of corporate governance have neglected the importance of the state in the picture, the RSV of corporate governance puts it centre-stage in order to facilitate comprehension of this complicated matter. Our pragmatic cases for this perspective are South Korea, Japan, China, Thailand, Turkey and Russia, among others.

The unique factor in the RSV of corporate governance is its reliance on the game theoretic perception of the entire evolution of corporate governance, a theoretical stance widely shared by most economic and financial views of corporate governance, although RSV buttresses the evolving nature of the game under the tenet of augmenting and sharing the monopoly rents created by the alliance between the state and conglomerates. The prognosis of this kind of theorization of the concept of corporate governance includes the resilient nature of the way business and political leaders are keen to cling to rent sharing as a *new normal* in the political economy of developing countries. Therefore, the whole gamut of RSV satisfies our burning desire to know why the chaebols have not been easily dissolved by the irate state and its supportive voters in a similar fashion to that of the prewar zaibatsu in Japan. The benefit of rent sharing appears greater than the benefit of dismantling it to both chaebols and political leaders, both of whom want to continue the game with only minor changes in the form of corporate governance that still enables the partners in the deal to share rents. The holding company system, therefore, is another utter disaster of policy failure that could never have stopped rent sharing in the first place. In this regard, the RSV of corporate governance theoretically contributes to corporate governance literature.

Practical implications

Policy implications drawn on in this study for business leaders in Korea include the importance of their capacity as generators of rents, mostly by actively participating in the global economy through innovations in technologies, production process and business models (e.g. agility). Agility, indeed, has been a core competence of Korean business organizations (Mun 2016). This agility will serve as a formidable bulwark against state hostility towards chaebols in the form of threats and extortions. On the other hand, implications for state policymakers include the need to strengthen their power over chaebols by reducing their financial reliance on the gargantuan economic families of the country. To do this, the state policymakers must nurture and guide alternatives to chaebols by diversifying market niches for startups, new ventures and small and medium firms. The success of Kakao, Coupang and Naver in the Korean economy is a good example. Given their enormous success in a relatively short time, these firms have been shown to be more flexible than chaebols in adopting the new corporate governance structures, including family succession conditions, recommended by voters and parties.

Furthermore, our study provides wisdom regarding the formulation of corporate governance reform packages for chaebols. A lopsided reliance on the Anglo-American style of corporate governance as an ideal terminal structure is an extremely dangerous diagnosis for Korea. The division between ownership and control on the one hand, and the tenet of credible commitments on the other, can hardly be realized in a non-Anglo-American cultural context. The point is to reduce the state's reliance on chaebols politically, economically and financially. To resolve this convoluted problem, the Scandinavian model of social democracy and corporate governance could be an alternative way out (for this see Yi 2006; Hansen 2007).

Limitations and future research

The major hurdle in the study of Korean chaebols is the inability to find concrete data on rent sharing, as there are virtually no tangible and reliable data for the rents shared between chaebols and the government in the form of extortions, illegal hoarding, bribes and/or slush funds. Anecdotal news reports following the indictment and imprisonment of chaebol owners and their political partners, usually in the presidential palace (the Blue House), have revealed some figures pertaining to rent sharing, although they are meagre tips of a huge iceberg. This paucity of data is not an issue that can be easily resolved in the near future. Therefore, we need to develop other indirect measures of rent sharing that can predict a stronger correlation with chaebols' decision to opt out of the HCS in order to avoid endangering the benefit of rent sharing than is currently shown by this study. A comparative study of rent sharing can then be designed in order to substantiate its relationship with corporate governance evolution in non-Anglo-American cultures where family ownership and succession are prevalent.

Conclusion

Our contribution to this special issue started with one question in mind: what is the goal of Korean corporate governance and where have the recent governance reforms been in terms of leading the whole of the economy? Our analysis reveals that the deeply rooted norm of rent sharing within the Korean governance structure is hard to dismantle or replace with a new tenet as long as both the government and the chaebols find rent sharing to be much more beneficial to both parties than other competing options. The attempt to assail chaebols' private property by severely taxing conglomerates for legitimate property inheritance has only perversely turned the clock backwards for reforms. Unless the government can completely end its reliance on the chaebols for extortion, taxes and employment of its labour force, it is unlikely that jailing the sons of the chaebol will by itself resolve any legal issues surrounding circular ownership, ownership-control disparity and illegitimate successions. The Korean case therefore serves as an important lesson for any developing countries struggling with corporate governance reforms. Instead of the Anglo-American ideal of M-forms based on credible commitments, a more socially acceptable norm of social democracy, like that found in Scandinavian countries, may well be the true solution to the Korean problem.

Note

1. It is probable that they structure or split the IGTs to be small enough that they can avoid the regulation threshold of 500 million won.

Disclosure statement

No potential conflict of interest was reported by the author(s).

ORCID

Ingyu Oh http://orcid.org/0000-0002-1645-8767

References

Aguilera, R. V., and G. Jackson. 2003. "The Cross-national Diversity of Corporate Governance: Dimensions and Determinants." *Academy of Management Review* 28 (3): 447–465. doi:10.5465/amr.2003.10196772.

Buchanan, J. M. 1983. "Rent Seeking, Noncompensated Transfers, and Laws of Succession." *The Journal of Law and Economics* 26 (1): 71–85. doi:10.1086/467026.

Choi, H., and J. Cho. 2021. "Related-party Transactions, Chaebol Affiliations, and the Value of Cash Holdings." *Sustainability* 13 (2): 699–712. doi:10.3390/su13020699.

Choi, H. M., Y. G. Cho, and W. Sul. 2014. "Ownership-control Disparity and Foreign Investors' Ownership: Evidence from the Korean Stock Market." *Emerging Markets Finance and Trade* 50 (Sup1): 178–193. doi:10.2753/REE1540-496X5001S112.

Choi, J. 2011. "Jaebeoleui Bunhalseunggyewa Gyeongjeryeokjibjungeui Byeonhwa [Chaebol's Succession by Division and the Change of Economic Concentration]." *Gyeongyeongsayeongu* 26 (2): 181–199.

Choi, Y. K., S. H. Han, and S. Lee. 2014. "Audit Committees, Corporate Governance, and Shareholder Wealth: Evidence from Korea." *Journal of Accounting and Public Policy* 33 (5): 470–489. doi:10.1016/j.jaccpubpol.2014.06.001.

Daems, H. P. 2012 [1978]. *The Holding Company and Corporate Control*. Vol. 3. Springer Science & Business Media.

Dalton, R. J. 2008. "The Quantity and the Quality of Party Systems: Party System Polarization, Its Measurement, and Its Consequences." *Comparative Political Studies* 41 (7): 899–920. doi:10.1177/0010414008315860.

Edlin, A. S., and J. E. Stiglitz. 1995. "Discouraging Rivals: Managerial Rent-seeking and Economic Inefficiencies." *The American Economic Review* 85 (5): 1301–1312.

Fama, E. F. 1980. "Agency Problems and the Theory of the Firm." *Journal of Political Economy* 88 (2): 288–307. doi:10.1086/260866.

Gambetta, D. 1996. *The Sicilian Mafia: The Business of Private Protection*. Cambridge: Harvard University Press.

Hansen, J. L. 2007. "A Scandinavian Approach to Corporate Governance." *Scandinavian Studies in Law* 50: 125–142.

Jensen, M. C. 1994. "Self-interest, Altruism, Incentives, and Agency Theory." *Journal of Applied Corporate Finance* 7 (2): 40–45. doi:10.1111/j.1745-6622.1994.tb00404.x.

Jun, I., P. Sheldon, and J. Rhee. 2010. "Business Groups and Regulatory Institutions: Korea's Chaebols, Cross-company Shareholding and the East Asian Crisis." *Asian Business and Management* 9 (4): 499–523. doi:10.1057/abm.2010.26.

Koike, Y. 1991. *Burajiru No Kigyō: Kōzō to Kōdō [Brazilian Corporations: Structure and Behaviour]*. Tokyo: Ajia Keizai Kenkyūsho.

Korea Fair Trade Commission (KFTC). 2018. *White Paper*. Sejong: KFTC.

Korea Fair Trade Commission (KFTC). 2020a. *Press Release*. Sejong: KFTC.

Korea Fair Trade Commission (KFTC). 2020b. *White Paper*. Sejong: KFTC.

Lee, H. 2 June 2008. "Holding Firms Reap Royalties from Subsidiaries." *The Korea Times*.

Lee, S., and S. Y. Rhyu. 2019. *The Political Economy of Change and Continuity in Korea*. Cham, Switzerland: Springer International.

Lee, Y., and M. Cho. 2016. "Does Control-ownership Disparity Matter to Foreign Investors in Korea?" *International Review of Economics and Finance* 44: 219–231. doi:10.1016/j.iref.2016.04.007.

Li, S., and M. Ouyang. 2007. "A Dynamic Model to Explain the Bribery Behavior of Firms." *International Journal of Management* 24 (3): 605–620.

Mun, H. C. 2016. *The Strategy for Korea's Economic Success*. Oxford: Oxford University Press.

North, D. C. March 1993. "Institutions and Credible Commitment." *Journal of Institutional and Theoretical Economics (Jite)/zeitschrift Für Die Gesamte Staatswissenschaft* 1: 11–23.

North, D. C. 1995. "Five Propositions about Institutional Change." Economics Working Paper Archive, WUSTL.

North, D. C., and B. R. Weingast. 1989. "Constitutions and Commitment: The Evolution of Institutions Governing Public Choice in Seventeenth-century England." *Journal of Economic History* 49 (4): 803–832. doi:10.1017/S0022050700009451.

OECD. 2018. "OECD Economic Survey of Korea: Achieving a New Paradigm for Inclusive Growth." shorturl.at/gtyGT

Oh, I., and H. Jun. 2016. "Economic Miracle." In *Routledge Handbook of Modern Korean History*, edited by M. Seth, 295–313. New York: Routledge.

Oh, I. 2018 [1999]. *Mafioso, Big Business and the Financial Crisis: The State-Business Relations in South Korea and Japan*. London: Routledge.

Oh, I., and R. Varcin. 2010. "Rent-sharing: Organizational and Technological Innovations under Military Regimes in South Korea and Turkey." *International Journal of Technology Management & Sustainable Development* 9 (2): 77–94. doi:10.1386/tmsd.9.2.77_1.

Park, J., Y. Kim, and H. Shin. 2020. "Injeokbunhaleul Tonghan Jijuhoisa Jeonhwani Gieopgachiwa Soyugujoe Michineun Yeonghyang [The Effect of Transforming into Holding Companies through Spin-offs on Firm Value and Ownership Structure]." *Jeonmungyeongyeonginyeongu* 23 (3): 1–20.

Penman, S. H., and T. Sougiannis. 1998. "A Comparison of Dividend, Cash Flow, and Earnings Approaches to Equity Valuation." *Contemporary Accounting Research* 15 (3): 343–383. doi:10.1111/j.1911-3846.1998.tb00564.x.

Quigley, T. J., and D. C. Hambrick. 2012. "When the Former CEO Stays on as Board Chair: Effects on Successor Discretion, Strategic Change, and Performance." *Strategic Management Journal* 33 (7): 834–859. doi:10.1002/smj.1945.

Tullock, G. 2013. *The Economics of Special Privilege and Rent Seeking*. Berlin: Springer Science & Business Media.

Wakefield, D. 1998. *Fenjia: Household Division and Inheritance in Qing and Republican China*. Honolulu: University of Hawaii Press.

Williamson, O. E. 1983. "Credible Commitments: Using Hostages to Support Exchange." *The American Economic Review* 73 (4): 519–540.

Williamson, O. E. 1984. "Credible Commitments: Further Remarks." *The American Economic Review* 74 (3): 488–490.

Yi, E. 2012. "Jaebeol Seunggye Eotteoke Irueojina: SK Geurub [How Does the Chaebol Completes Succession: SK Group]." *Gieopjibaegujoyeongu* 44: 119–131.

Yi, W. 2006. "Gieopjibaegujoeui jeongchi gyeongjehak: Jujumodele daehan ironnjeok bipan [Political Economy of Corporate Governance: A Theoretical Critique of the Shareholder Model]." *Hangukjeonchihakhoibo* 40 (3): 263–290.

Yu, J. 2014. "Injeokbunhaleul tonghan jijuhoisa jeonhwani gieopgachiwa soyugujoe michineun yeonghyang [A Study on the Conversion into Holding Companies through Spin-offs]." *Saneopjojikyeongu* 22 (2): 73–95.

Successors' discretion and corporate restructuring in family firms in South Korea: from an institutional perspective

JungYun Han

ABSTRACT
Although a successor's discretion is a key factor in facilitating corporate restructuring, little is known about the source of discretion, particularly about national culture. From an institutional perspective, we argue that when a successor is legitimized by the norms and expectations embedded in national culture, the successor is likely to implement corporate restructuring. Using data of family-run business groups in South Korea, where Confucianism is a dominant value system, we find that when a successor is the first-born child and male in the family, the business group is likely to spin-off, and this effect becomes stronger with the number of siblings.

Introduction

Succession is an important topic in family business research because it enables a founder family to maintain control of the firm over generations (Brockhaus 2004; Lee, Lim, and Lim 2003; Molly, Laveren, and Deloof 2010) as well as determines the competitiveness of family firms (Boyd, Botero, and Fediuk 2014; Boyd et al. 2015; Carney 2005). Succession provides an important opportunity for firms to alter current power structure (Pfeffer and Salancik 1978) and realign their structure and strategic stances to the changing environment (Katz and Kahn 1978; Miller and Friesen 1980; Thompson 1967). Also, it brings profound changes in the dynamics of the strategic decision-making process (Wiersema 1995) and long-held organizational inertia (Tushman and Romanelli 1985), which enables firms to generate new value and knowledge (Wiersema and Bantel 1993).

One of the most dramatic changes caused by succession is corporate restructuring because the change of leadership accompanies the perception that firms need strategic redirection by breaking strategic inertia and routines (Gabarro 1987; Miller 1993; Pfeffer and Salancik 1978; Smart and Hitt 1994; Wiersema 1995). Indeed, incumbent executives have little motivation to reverse their earlier decisions or change a corporate structure because their experiences and repertoires are aligned with current strategies and organizational structure. Also, for incumbent executives, reversing actions can be risky because organization members often take it as leadership failure and miscalculation of organizational adaptation (Brockhaus 2004; Dibrell and Memili 2019; Hambrick and Fukutomi 1991). On the contrary, the newly appointed successor is typically under pressure to demonstrate his or her efficiency and worthiness as a new leader. This cannot be done by maintaining the predecessor's current strategies and routines (Ocasio and Kim 1999; Pfeffer 1981; Wiersema 1995). Therefore, many successors attempt to restructure and shift the organization's attention towards the new strategic direction.

For a successful corporate restructuring, a key is a successor's managerial discretion, which refers to the relative absence of constraint on the executive's actions (Quigley and Hambrick 2012). Depending on the degree of managerial discretion, a successor's latitude on corporate restructuring will be varying, which affects the likelihood of successful structural changes as they are planned. Prior studies suggest that managerial discretion can be determined by several factors such as national system and industry characteristics (Crossland and Hambrick 2007; Hambrick and Abrahamson 1995), firm size, prior performance, resource slack (Finkelstein and Boyd 1998) and a successor's personality (Carpenter and Golden 1997).

In this study, we investigate an unexplored source of managerial discretion, *national culture*, and ask whether and how national culture, as one key component of a cognitive institution, becomes a source of a successor's discretion and affects corporate restructuring in family firms. Institutionalism suggests that norms, expectations and values embedded in national culture create social processes and obligations that take on rule-like status in a society and shape the shared definition of reality that people accept and follow (Hatch 2018; Meyer and Rowan 1977). Such rules define what is appropriate in family, organization and society. Specifically, in an organization, cultural norms and values inform how organization members respond to the decisions made by the executive in charge. From the institutional perspective, we argue that when a family firm successor is culturally legitimized, the successor has great discretion and the firm is likely to implement corporate restructuring. Furthermore, we test whether a successor's discretion in corporate restructuring is moderated by rivalry in a family (i.e. siblings).

Our research context is Korean business groups, a representative form of family business in the country, between 1981 and 2010. Like many other East Asian countries, Korea adopted Confucianism as a fundamental value system over 600 years ago, and its values still have a profound effect on family, firms and society. Our context has an advantage in studying Confucianism and family business because Korea has relatively well-maintained traditional Confucianism, as compared to China or Vietnam that experienced the dramatic period of blending Confucianism with socialism and capitalism (Yang 2012). Here, we examine a successor's position in a founder family in terms of birth-order and gender, both of which – first born and males – are valued in Confucianism. In addition, we examine corporate restructuring among the firms in our sample as an important strategic change. Specifically, we examine a business group's spin-off events for two reasons: first, a spin-off is a definitive form of strategic change that requires an executive's willingness and leadership (Bigley and Wiersema 2002). Second, in family business, a spin-off is an important way for a founder family to increase its influence over the firm by taking another leadership role in a newly spun organization (Miller et al. 2015). Our results show that, among our sample of 67 business groups, when a successor is a first-born child and male, this business group is likely to spin-off, and its main effect is stronger when the successor has more siblings. We interpret the results by explaining how Confucian culture shapes the successor's appropriateness and ability to exercise discretion in spin-offs.

Our unique research setting allows us to observe family firms' succession and spin-offs in South Korea, where Confucianism has shaped the fundamental value system, enabling us to build context-specific hypotheses in this study. Yet, our findings and implications go beyond a specific context and make important contributions to the literatures on succession and managerial discretion, and family business. First, although prior studies identify the sources of a successor's managerial discretion at industrial, organizational and personal levels, little attention has been paid to the institutional factors that shape the appropriateness of a successor, ultimately affecting the successor's managerial discretion. By investigating the role of dominant national culture in determining a successor's appropriateness in the context of Confucianism, our study enhances scholarly understanding of how a cognitive institution (i.e. national culture) can be a source of a successor's discretion. Second, while the literature on family business has extensively discussed how an executive's position in the family such as birth-order and gender affects the succession process and performance (Birley 1986; Brockhaus 2004; Villalonga and Amit 2006), less is explored about how the executive's position in the family and his or her relationship with siblings in terms of birth order affect strategic changes. To address this gap, this study suggests a novel mechanism that explains how family firms' succession and business group spin-offs are embedded in the national culture system. Furthermore, our findings in the context of Koran business groups help scholars to understand the idiosyncratic corporate governance in family conglomerates.

Theory

Succession and corporate restructuring

Succession is an important change in the firm as an adaption mechanism to environmental shifts (Katz and Kahn 1978; Perrow 1986; Thompson 1967). The change of leadership not only brings a new distribution of power among key decision-makers (Pfeffer and Salancik 1978) but also allows the firm to break with routines and inertia (Tushman and Romanelli 1985). This happens because a successor is relatively free from past decisions and strategies that incumbents made. A successor brings a new cognitive framework to the firm and creates new value and knowledge by attempting several strategic changes (Dibrell and Memili 2019; Wiersema 1995; Wiersema and Bantel 1993).

One of the most typical and dramatic strategic changes after succession is corporate restructuring (Quigley and Hambrick 2012; Wiersema 1995). Incumbent executives avoid corporate restructuring because they have difficulty reversing their early decisions and ongoing organizational practices (Hambrick and Fukutomi 1991). They are also psychologically locked into their original plans, and their expertise and skills, which results in the reinforcement of the status quo in the firm (Stevens, Beyer, and Trice 1978). In addition, incumbent executives have little motivation for strategic changes, because their attempt for corporate restructuring may send a signal to stakeholders that the current corporate structure is wrong (Brockhaus 2004). On the contrary, a successor has a high chance of making changes in the firm's strategic decisions without such concerns about his/her early decisions. In addition, as the change of leadership conveys a perception that the firm also needs redirection, a newly appointed successor has great pressure to engage in new strategic initiatives in order to demonstrate his or her own worthiness and efficiency

(Ocasio 1994; Ocasio and Kim 1999; Pfeffer 1981). In the early years of one's tenure, an executive successor needs to prove that he or she can see some problems that the former executive did not acknowledge or address and make changes to solve them. A successor's attempt for strategic changes enables him or her to solidify leadership and exercise influence in the firm more effectively.

Literature on succession views corporate restructuring as a typical and definite form of strategic change after succession. Researchers suggest that the success of corporate restructuring depends on a successor's level of *managerial discretion* (Quigley and Hambrick 2012), which refers to the degree of a successor's freedom without constraint (Hambrick and Finkelstein 1987). The origins of managerial discretion are diverse. At the environmental level, different national culture and industry characteristics determine the overall influence of executives within a specific country/industry (Crossland and Hambrick 2007; Hambrick and Abrahamson 1995). At the organizational level, firm characteristics such as slack, performance, organization culture and size affect the latitude of an executive's discretion (Finkelstein and Boyd 1998; Fiordelisi and Ricci 2014). At the micro-level, an executive's attributes such as personality and background are determinant factors (Carpenter and Golden 1997). In current literature, however, little attention has been paid to how national culture as an institutional-level factor may determine varying degrees of managerial discretion within a country. Exceptionally, Crossland and Hambrick (2007) studied this topic by focusing on how different national cultures lead to different levels of managerial discretion across different countries (e.g. comparing executives' discretion between the United States and Germany). However, our interest – specifically, how national culture affects varying degrees of managerial discretion across firms in one country – is unknown.

Thus, we ask: How does national culture affect a successor's discretion in a family firm and, ultimately, the firm's likelihood of corporate restructuring? To answer this question, we draw insights from the institutionalism literature (North 1990). This research stream suggests that institutions have three key elements including regulative, normative and cognitive institutions and each element provides a basis for gaining legitimacy in the society (Scott 1995). The regulative view of institutions (e.g. Barnett and Carroll 1993) suggests that individual and organizational changes result from coercive means, the legal system and regulations. The normative view of institutions (e.g. Selznick 1948) emphasizes the role of social obligation and norms, and informal structures comprising the environment of organizations (e.g. Powell and DiMaggio 2012). Lastly, the cognitive view of institutions stresses changes in conceptual beliefs and interpretations of shared meanings (DiMaggio 1997).

From the *cognitive* perspective, a firm's strategic change requires internalization, a social process where policies, behaviours and decision-making acquire "taken-for-granted' status (Meyer and Rowan 1977). This means that a firm's strategic change is not a decision-maker's individual determination. A strategic change should experience the cognitive process of internalization among organizational members and by a society, and after this process, the change is finally accepted and legitimized (Ingram and Silverman 2002; Johnson, Dowd, and Ridgeway 2006; Meyer and Scott 1983; Suchman 1995). Organizational members accept the value of strategic change and support it based on their shared beliefs, cultural norms, expectations and values. According to this logic, only when a firm's succession is well institutionalized and legitimized, and a successor obtains broad acceptance from employees and society, he/she is able to exercise sufficient discrepancy in making strategic changes (Chung and Luo 2013). On the contrary, when a successor is not accepted as an appropriate new leader, he or she suffers the legitimacy discount and his or her latitude of actions will be much constrained.

To verify this institutional explanation, this study focuses on national culture as a representative form of an informal cognitive institution. Cultural values exert significant influence on individual actions and perspectives and shape a common belief in a society (Huang and Van de Vliert 2003). When a nation's culture is represented in a specific institution and enacts certain collective beliefs, a particular business system, property rights, and specific management practices are legitimized by the national culture (Hofstede 1993; Meyer and Rowan 1977; Sakano and Lewin 1999). Succession is not an exception. If succession occurs in the context of a specific national culture and a successor's qualification is legitimized by the cultural value, the newly appointed executive (i.e. successor) has fewer constraints on exercising influence in the firm.

In the following section, we will investigate how national culture – specifically, Confucianism in South Korea – affects a successor's managerial discretion and corporate restructuring in a family firm. Here, family firms in Confucianism are ideal to study the relationship between national culture and family firms' succession because Confucianism puts an emphasis on family relationships as the core of its value system and offers key rules and norms that govern the family (Dou et al. 2020; Goel et al. 2012; Gupta and Levenburg 2010; Hamilton and Cheng-Shu 1990). Such a setting allows us to investigate the profound influence of national culture on business practices (i.e. succession) and family firms' strategic changes directly.

Successors' position in a founder family and Confucian culture

In the East Asian countries, Confucianism has been a main construct of the national cultural system for more than 2,000 years. Originated in the Chinese ancient thought system, Confucianism established a broad set of guidelines for proper behaviours and mindsets in the family, organizations, society and country (Hamilton and Biggart 1988; Hofstede 1993; Tu and Du 1996) and offered a grand theory of interpersonal relationships (Dou et al. 2020; Sundaramurthy and Kreiner 2008; Yan and Sorenson 2006). Later, Confucianism spread into other Asian countries in the 10th century and became the foundation of a fundamental value system, moral standard and economic and business system in the Asian countries including China, Taiwan, Korea and Japan, and even countries in South East Asia such as Vietnam. The coverage of Confucianism is huge. If we count the population, its influence covers more than 20% of the world population.

This cultural value system puts family as a focus and defines various relationships around a family (Tu and Du 1996) such as father and son, husband and wife, and elder brother and younger brother. Confucianism's profound influence over family relationship also affects family business because cultural norms and expectations in the family relationship transmits to a family firm and affects people's work-related behaviours and a firm's decision-making (Lu, Rose, and Blodgett 1999; Tan and Akhtar 1998; Yan and Sorenson 2006).

A key concept in Confucianism, patriarchal ideology provides key principles to succession in family firms (Greenhalgh 1985; Han, Shipilov, and Greve 2017). First, male heirs have precedence over females (Greenhalgh 1994), which confers privilege to sons in family business succession. Such gender differences have a historical root in different socioeconomic resources and personal autonomy between a son and a daughter in a family. A son is entitled to be a successor of the family who keeps the family membership, plays a leading role in the family decision-making and has the ultimate obligation of supporting his parents. On the contrary, a daughter does not have such an obligation. As marriage shifts her identity from her maiden family to her husband's family, a daughter is no longer obligated to support her parents (Greenhalgh 1985). Second, in the relationship of siblings, the rule of privilege among children is given to the older ones because the elders have ultimate responsibility for caring for the family (Greenhalgh 1985).

The above two principles in Confucianism apply to succession in family firms. If an executive successor in a family firm is the first-born child and male, then he is accepted as the most legitimate and privileged one to take over the family business because he qualifies for what Confucianism describes as 'taken-for-grantedness' in terms of his gender and birth-order. With regard to this, prior studies in Chinese family business provide empirical support that elder brothers have a high chance of being a successor and taking an executive role, while younger brothers are expected to defer their authority (e.g. Weidenbaum and Hughes 1996). We also find several similar examples that support the legitimacy of the first son in Korean family firms. For example, from major newspapers' interviews with founder families in Korean business groups such as LG, Hanwha, and Kolong groups, we learned that even if the first son lacks educational credentials and working experience as compared to his younger brothers, he is still preferred and the most acceptable chairman because Korean people believe that the first son is the most appropriate as a leader and such succession will lead to a smooth transition of leadership (KyungHyang News 1999).

With this as a backdrop, the next question to ask is: how does a culturally legitimized successor exercise his discretion and implement corporate restructuring in a family firm? To answer this question, in our context of Korean business groups, we examine business group spin-offs for two reasons: first, a spin-off is an important form of corporate restructuring that a successor exercises at own discretion in the organization and controls for rivals' challenges. Second, a spin-off in a family firm is closely related to rivalry among family members. As a successor's major rivals, siblings still remain in the firm and continue to influence the organization. This peculiar structure in a family firm pressures a successor to consider a spin-off as a way to curb rivals' interventions early on and, at the same time, exercise his or her discretion effectively. In particular, given that Confucianism stresses that all sons have equal right to inherit family wealth (Jacobs, Goupei, and Herbig 1995), a successor has some pressure to share his gains with other siblings in running a family business. As such, splitting a family firm and appointing siblings to the executive positions in the newly spun-off firm becomes an effective way to prevent rivals' (i.e. siblings) from intervening and challenging his leadership. At the same time, such action helps the successor to solidify his power because appointing siblings to the newly spun-off business units is well aligned with the 'equal right' rule that Confucianism emphasizes in the society.

Therefore, when a first-born child and male becomes a successor and takes a leadership role in a family firm, he is likely to spin-off some non-core businesses and appoint other siblings to take leadership positions in the new organizations. In doing so, this successor can effectively prevent other family members from complaining equal rights to inherit the family business and, at the same time, demonstrate his discretion in the organization. On the contrary, when a successor is a younger brother or a female, the successor suffers legitimacy discount and, as a consequence, his or her discretion in the firm is not sufficient to make major changes smoothly.

Taken together, we hypothesize that in Confucian culture, a successor's discrepancy is determined by cultural norms and values, which in turn affects corporate restructuring via a spin-off.

Hypothesis 1: In Confucian culture, when a successor is the first child and male in a family firm, the firm is more likely to implement a spin-off.

Successors' siblings in a family firm

Succession is a complex procedure that reflects a successor's relationship with rivals. Prior research suggests that even after rivals lose in succession, they still remain as powerful parties and exercise sufficient power in the organization. Rivals may restrict executives from taking bold strategic actions in order to restrict the executive successor's latitude in the organization (Cannella et al. 2009; Quigley and Hambrick 2012). In doing so, rivals attempt to maintain their power in the organization and look for any chances to take power from current leadership. Of course, such restriction against the current successor may not serve the best interest of rivals and even do harm to their reputation in the organization. However, in reality, rivals still want to impose a constraint on a successor's discretion and challenge the successor's strategic decisions (Shen and Cho 2005). For this reason, prior studies suggest that a successor's rivals put pressure on the successor's latitude and hamper his/her attempt for corporate restructuring.

In this study, as opposed to the prior research that examined rivalry in Western countries, we argue that rivalry in Confucian culture works in a different way. The main rationale of our prediction is that norms and rules in Confucianism not only define the appropriateness of a successor in a family business but also guide the ways that rivals pressure the successor. As mentioned earlier, Confucianism stresses both older and younger brothers have equal right to inherit family property (Jacobs, Goupei, and Herbig 1995). Thus, although parental favouritism towards the first child and male as a successor is legitimized, his siblings also ask the successor to give equal rights in the family business in order to inherit family wealth (Friedman 1991). For this reason, the more siblings he has, the first-born and male successor has great pressure from siblings. In turn, he is more likely to spin-off using his discrepancy, which helps to address siblings' challenges early on and solidify his power in the organization.

Of course, one may raise a question about whether the first-born and male successor can disregard the request from his siblings using his power. However, such possibility is low in Confucian culture for two reasons: first, since his legitimacy and managerial discrepancy are conferred by Confucianism, it is difficult for him to disregard the pressure from siblings who also claim their rights based on the Confucian norms. Given that family-centric goals have a priority in family decision-making in the Confucian culture (Dou et al. 2020), a successor cannot be free from siblings' pressure. If a successor is unwilling to spin-off in spite of siblings' pressure, his legitimacy will be severely tarnished in this culture. Other family members and organization members who endorsed the successor based on Confucian ideology will view his behaviour as inappropriate and push him to comply with cultural norms. Second, in a family firm, siblings remain as major rivals and stakeholders even after the succession. If the successor does not address his siblings' claims early on, then he will face more severe challenges from them during his remaining tenure, because they will keep claiming their appropriate portion of family property.

Therefore, from the institutional perspective, we hypothesize that the culturally legitimized successor's likelihood of corporate restructuring will be much higher when he has more siblings.

Hypothesis 2: In Confucian culture, the positive effect of the successor who is a first-born child and male on the likelihood of a spin-off will be stronger when he has many siblings.

Data and methodology

Sample

We examine 67 Korean business groups' succession and business group spin-offs as a form of corporate restructuring between 1981 and 2010. We start our observation in 1981, the earliest year that data are available from KIS (Korea Information System, the largest credit rating agency that provides company information and financial performance). We also stopped our observations in 2010 due to data access issue and contextual reason. First, as we could not get access to the same data sources for collecting recent data, we had to merge information from multiple other sources including newspapers, business group websites and government website that complies company financial reports. Although these sources are all reliable and contain accurate information, we still want to be careful for merging different data sourses across two periods. Second, our independent (succession) and dependent (business group divestiture) variables are related to lifecycle of a business group chairman. In our context, most successions and group divestitures happened in the 1980s-1990s when most founders resigned, and the late 2000s when the second-generation chairmen left. This means, in the 2010s, the third generation of business group chairmen are still young to consider succession or business group divestitures. Recently, some Korean media reported that several business groups (e.g. Hyosung group) are now preparing for succession and major group restructuring. For these reasons, we do not use the recent data for our main analysis. Instead, in a supplementary test, we run regressions with the updated dataset until 2020.

The list of business groups, so-called chaebols in South Korea, comes from the government's annual report, in which the Korean government announces the top 30 business groups based on their total asset size (Chang and Hong 2000). We include all names appearing in the government reports during our observation period. Using the business group names, we searched business group information, founder family profile, chairman succession and group divestiture events on a yearly basis (see Appendix). Here, as our interest is a founder family's succession and business group restructuring, we examine the succession of business group chairmanship from a founder to his descendants. We find that most business group families experienced succession one time during our observation period. This happens because the succession of family business is related to a corporate leader's lifecycle. In our sample, when succession happens, the average age of the predecessor chairmen is 70.8 and the average age of successors is 50.7. We find 48 successions and 31 business group spin-offs.

We collect data on business groups' spin-offs from the Korean corporate filing system (DART: Data Analysis, Retrieval and Transfer System), which is equivalent to the U.S. Securities and Exchange Commission. The DART publicizes corporate data starting from 1990 up to now; therefore, we track the data before 1990, using five major news archival, business history books (Lee 2004; Seoul News Corporation 2005) and the KIS. Furthermore, to enhance understanding about the history and background of Korean business groups' spin-offs, we extensively search for major newspapers and magazines that include interviews with business group families during the observation period.

Independent and dependent variables

The dependent variable is a business group's spin-off event. If a business group divests its affiliates and sets up a new business group in a given year, the variable, *business group spin-off*, has a value 1, otherwise 0. Here, we do not count the case where a business group simply sells business units or assets. Also, we do not consider a divested business group's spin-offs.

To capture a successor's cultural legitimacy (independent variable), we create a binary variable, *First son*, which has a value 1 if a successor is the first-born child and, at the same time, male in the family. Next, following the tradition of family business literature, we use the two-year window as succession period since the new executive takes the position (Molly, Laveren, and Deloof 2010) and create a binary variable, *Successor* (succession year, year +1). Finally, we create interaction terms, *Successor x First son*, as our main independent variable, which indicates whether a successor is the first child and male in the family firm.

Next, to test the moderating effect of rivalry in family business (Hypothesis 2), we count the number of a successor's male siblings due to the patriarchal principle in Confucian culture (Yan and Sorenson 2006). We name the variable, *Number of brothers*. Next, we create three-way interaction terms, *Successor x First son x Number of brothers*, as well as *Successor x Number of brothers*, and *First son x Number of brothers*.

Control variables

We include several control variables that may affect corporate restructuring and a successor's ability to exercise managerial discretion. First, although we do not consider female siblings as the main moderator, we control for structural rivalry within an organization (e.g. Selznick 1957) by adding a variable, *Number of sisters*. Also, we control for the possibility that potential rivalry among heirs apparent may affect the decision of corporate restructuring. Literature suggests that incumbent executives are reluctant to relinquish their power and prestige after stepping down (Zajac and Westphal 1996). Thus, they prefer selecting familiar heirs apparent (followers) in advance during their terms (Zajac and Westphal 1996). Thus, competition among potential heirs apparent becomes intensive, which in turn affects a successor's corporate restructuring. So, we count the number of sons and daughters of a current chairman and create variables, *Number of sons* and *Number of daughters*, to control for rivalry among heirs apparent. We also add a variable, *Successor's tenure*, by counting the number of years a successor worked in this business group. We do so because his or her tendency of risk-taking and strategic changes will be affected by experiences in this organization. The more years of experience a successor has in a business group before taking the position of chairman, the more likely he or she is to be familiar with current strategic decisions and stick to the current business group structure.

Literature on corporate restructuring argues that firms intend to enhance performance and restore efficiency by divesting unnecessary business (Hoskisson, Johnson, and Moesel 1994; Markides 1992, 1995). Here, we estimate business group performance and size using *ROA (Return on Asset), Sales growth* $((Revenue_{current\ year} - Revenue_{last\ year})/Revenue_{last\ year})$ and *Diversification*. For the variable, *Diversification*, we count the number of markets in which a business group operates, using two-digit SIC codes. Also, given that board members take charge of monitoring and addressing an agency problem, board size is related to an executive's ability to make strategic changes at will (Chaganti, Mahajan, and Sharma 1985; Hambrick, Werder, and Zajac 2008). For this reason, we count the number of outside board members and total board members, and create a variable, *Ratio of outside board directors*. Also, as firm age is related to the probability of firm survival and resilience to organizational changes (Hannan 1998; Stinchcombe 1965), we control for firm age effect, by adding *Business group age* and *Business group age, squared.*

Lastly, we control for several institutional factors and government policies that affect business group restructuring. The Asian Crisis, 1997–2000, brought massive changes in government regulations and economic policies. The Korean government mandated the introduction of outside board directorship, liberalized takeover markets, and imposed stricter regulations on chaebols' diversification (Park and Kim 2008). In particular, to induce chaebols' corporate restructuring, the government gave various incentives such as tax incentives and favourable policies for M&As, and easing labour regulations on layoffs (Pomerleano and Shaw 2005). Also, during the crisis, the Korean government enacted a new law to separate banking and commerce to prevent business groups from diversifying into the banking industry. Furthermore, in 1998, the government assessed the financial solvency of 59 chaebols and pushed them to go into either a voluntary restructuring programme or a workout programme that requires debt forgiveness and/or different repayment plan due to the debtor's inability of original repayment (Pomerleano and Shaw 2005). To control for the effect of the Korean government's intensive restructuring programmes, we create a binary variable, *Asian Crisis*, indicating the period of 1997–2000.

Next, we consider the government's special restructuring plans for top five chaebols-Hyundai, Samsung, Daewoo, SK, and LG, between 1998 and 1999. For these large business groups, the government required them to submit capital structure improvement plans (CSIP), which aims at lowering the ratio of debt to equity, raising capital in the markets and focusing on core businesses. Eventually, this programme pushed the top business groups to shed many of their affiliate firms and work on restructuring their over-diversified portfolios. Thus, we create a binary variable, *Capital restructure improvement plans*, for these top five business groups between 1998 and 1999. Lastly, changes in economic institutions affect firm strategy. The development of market system and economic institutions towards a liberal market may trigger corporate restructuring as a response to the new economic environment. Hence, we include a variable, *Market development*, which indicates the development of economic institution towards a liberal market. Using the three most common indicators in the literature (Čihák et al. 2013; Zheng, Singh, and Chung 2017), we collect information on the ratio of stock market capitalization to total gross domestic product (GDP), the ratio of total domestic credit to GDP, and the number of listed firms. Next, we create a composite measure by averaging three indices with equal weights.

Data analysis

Given that our dependent variable, *Business group spin-off*, is binary, we use Logit regression with clustering business groups in predicting the probability of corporate restructuring via spin-off in a given year. As most business groups experienced group succession and spin-off once during our observation period, we do not employ a longitudinal analysis that is appropriate to measure the repeated observations over time in an individual unit. Also, estimating fixed effects can be challenged when we observe rare events. Instead, we employ *Xtlogit* in a supplementary test.

Furthermore, we also test our hypotheses with an Event history analysis because this technique is appropriate when the dependent variable is a binary variable and the timing of the event's occurrence matters. Following Therneau and Hamilton (1997) approach, we employ the Cox proportional hazard model. The hazard rate at time t is defined as

$$h(t) = \lim_{\Delta t -> 0} = \frac{P(t, t + \Delta t)}{\Delta t}$$

$P(t, t+ \Delta t)$ indicates the probability of a business group's spin-off during Δt. In this study, the time spell is calculated based on the fiscal year of each business group. In the main analysis, we report the results of both Logit and Cox proportional hazard models.

Results

Table 1 reports descriptive statistics. Table 2 shows our results of likelihood of a spin-off with a dependent variable, *Business group spin-off*. In Models 1–4, we report the results using a logistic regression. Model 1 is a baseline. Model 2 includes main variables, *Successor* and *First son*. Model 3 is a full model with the interaction terms, *Successor x First son*. The positive coefficient of interaction terms supports our Hypothesis 1 around the positive effect of legitimized successors' discretion on corporate restructuring. In Model 4, we add the three-way interaction terms, *Successor x First son x Number of brothers*. The positive coefficient supports our Hypothesis 2, the reinforcing effect of rivals on the successor's corporate restructuring in Confucian culture. In Models 5–8, we report the results with a Cox hazard model. Model 7 shows the results of our test of Hypothesis 1, and Model 8 shows our test of Hypothesis 2.

Table 1. Descriptive statistics.

		Mean	S.D.	1	2	3	4	5	6	7	8	9	10	11	12	13	14	15	16	17	18
1	Business group spin-off	0.02	0.15	1																	
2	Successor	0.07	0.25	0.09	1																
3	First son	0.36	0.48	0.06	0.11	1															
4	Number of brothers	2.46	1.78	0.06	0.10	0.01	1														
5	Number of sisters	1.69	1.79	0.02	0.06	0.02	0.22	1													
6	Number of sons	2.33	1.47	−0.04	−0.13	−0.10	0.13	−0.17	1												
7	Number of daughters	1.48	1.30	0.01	−0.07	−0.31	−0.24	−0.01	0.02	1											
8	Successor's tenure	3.22	0.47	0.02	−0.19	−0.09	0.08	0.02	0.19	0.08	1										
9	ROA	0.04	0.19	−0.01	0.00	−0.01	−0.02	0.03	0.02	0.03	−0.06	1									
10	Sales growth	0.00	0.03	0.00	−0.03	−0.03	−0.02	0.00	0.00	0.04	0.01	−0.01	1								
11	Diversification	2.13	0.66	0.15	0.04	0.14	0.26	0.26	0.02	−0.03	0.27	−0.03	0.00	1							
12	Ratio of outside board directors	0.23	0.40	0.08	0.08	0.23	0.05	0.15	−0.20	−0.09	0.20	−0.02	−0.03	0.36	1						
13	Business group age	3.54	0.39	0.08	0.11	0.33	0.15	0.17	−0.04	−0.04	0.53	−0.07	0.00	0.43	0.52	1					
14	Business group age, squared	12.69	2.49	0.08	0.12	0.35	0.14	0.17	−0.07	−0.05	0.50	−0.08	−0.01	0.44	0.57	0.99	1				
15	Asian crisis	0.12	0.33	0.05	0.05	−0.01	0.03	0.06	−0.05	−0.01	0.13	−0.11	−0.07	0.14	0.14	0.17	0.18	1			
16	Capital restructure improvement plans	0.01	0.10	0.23	0.09	0.01	0.09	0.09	−0.07	0.03	−0.03	−0.01	−0.02	0.13	0.12	0.06	0.06	0.27	1		
17	Market development	3.37	2.10	0.04	0.07	0.22	0.06	0.15	−0.19	−0.09	0.21	−0.06	−0.03	0.36	0.76	0.58	0.63	−0.06	0.02	1	
18	Confucianism/Buddhism	0.45	0.49	0.08	0.05	−0.07	0.24	0.16	0.06	0.05	0.08	−0.03	0.01	0.25	0.14	0.01	0.00	0.03	0.07	0.08	1

Variables, 4–9, 11–14, are logged due to skewness.

Table 2. Succession and business group spin-offs.

	Logit model				Cox model				Panel logit	Linear logit	Logit model (extended data)	
	Model 1	Model 2	Model 3	Model 4	Model 5	Model 6	Model 7	Model 8	Model 9	Model 10	Model 11	Model 12
Successor		1.001	−0.921*	−75.273**		0.942+	−0.574	−93.015**	−1.985	−0.040	−1.022*	−87.880**
		(0.611)	(0.445)	(10.368)		(0.516)	(0.493)	(1.111)	(1.452)	(0.025)	(0.450)	(11.389)
First son		0.434	0.079	1.128		0.617	0.330	0.743	13.814	−0.016	−0.035	0.885
		(0.407)	(0.420)	(0.881)		(0.593)	(0.609)	(0.871)	(9.215)	(0.017)	(0.412)	(0.827)
Successor x First son			2.671**	75.520**			2.205**	93.249	3.019+	0.100**	2.933**	88.553**
			(0.663)	(10.579)			(0.583)	(0.000)	(1.654)	(0.031)	(0.687)	(11.675)
Number of brothers	−0.004	−0.002	0.052	0.096	−0.080	−0.047	0.008	−0.013	−2.517*	−0.022**	0.108	0.146
	(0.079)	(0.088)	(0.090)	(0.117)	(0.081)	(0.074)	(0.075)	(0.116)	(1.183)	(0.005)	(0.092)	(0.122)
Successor x Number of brothers				9.332**				11.636**				10.901**
				(1.317)				(0.132)				(1.474)
First son x Number of brothers				−0.381				−0.169				−0.341
				(0.255)				(0.311)				(0.262)
Successor x First son x Number of brothers				−8.752**				−11.100**				−10.421**
				(1.425)				(0.252)				(1.397)
Number of sisters	−0.124	−0.105	−0.106	−0.097	−0.143	−0.127	−0.118	−0.102	5.214	0.009	−0.119	−0.110
	(0.109)	(0.114)	(0.119)	(0.132)	(0.126)	(0.133)	(0.138)	(0.150)	(3.572)	(0.007)	(0.130)	(0.140)
Number of sons	−0.188	−0.140	−0.166	−0.153	−0.133	−0.091	−0.109	−0.084	−0.173	−0.025**	−0.219	−0.203
	(0.156)	(0.146)	(0.140)	(0.131)	(0.161)	(0.162)	(0.156)	(0.149)	(0.982)	(0.006)	(0.148)	(0.137)
Number of daughters	0.009	0.058	0.064	0.080	0.008	0.097	0.111	0.117	6.581	−0.004	0.051	0.065
	(0.124)	(0.137)	(0.133)	(0.141)	(0.132)	(0.137)	(0.134)	(0.139)	(5.221)	(0.007)	(0.118)	(0.124)
Successor's tenure	0.005	0.413	0.519	0.591	0.057	0.514	0.739	0.769	6.761	0.001	0.795	0.833
	(0.449)	(0.549)	(0.645)	(0.726)	(0.441)	(0.628)	(0.732)	(0.792)	(4.548)	(0.014)	(0.629)	(0.686)
ROA	−0.204	−0.307	−0.259	0.065	−1.191+	−1.094	−1.216+	−0.936	−0.121	−0.009	−0.250	0.063
	(1.214)	(1.065)	(1.240)	(1.156)	(0.714)	(0.694)	(0.687)	(0.764)	(1.904)	(0.020)	(1.206)	(1.129)
Sales growth	−0.083	0.481	1.416	1.692	−0.908	−0.620	1.172	1.086	−4.026	0.001	−0.459**	−0.476**
	(3.646)	(3.019)	(2.256)	(2.275)	(7.176)	(6.606)	(4.180)	(4.325)	(14.084)	(0.144)	(0.151)	(0.152)
Diversification	1.790**	1.685**	1.683**	1.789**	1.796**	1.679**	1.624**	1.697**	0.249	0.010	1.243**	1.321**
	(0.524)	(0.463)	(0.417)	(0.449)	(0.623)	(0.511)	(0.451)	(0.485)	(0.780)	(0.013)	(0.298)	(0.313)
Ratio of outside board directors	1.115*	1.090+	1.066+	1.082*	−1.365+	−1.432+	−1.408*	−1.317+	1.045	0.010	1.495**	1.516**
	(0.563)	(0.577)	(0.572)	(0.545)	(0.774)	(0.781)	(0.702)	(0.678)	(1.044)	(0.017)	(0.528)	(0.530)
Business group age	17.583	13.052	13.921	16.026	42.656+	34.773	35.582	38.782	81.355*	0.044	31.556	33.403
	(20.080)	(20.610)	(22.546)	(23.615)	(23.282)	(22.420)	(23.973)	(25.380)	(40.262)	(0.099)	(26.123)	(26.780)
Business group age, squared	−2.270	−1.707	−1.801	−2.125	−5.991+	−5.019	−5.111	−5.569	−13.174*	−0.009	−4.288	−4.562
	(2.799)	(2.861)	(3.121)	(3.265)	(3.224)	(3.079)	(3.285)	(3.478)	(6.162)	(0.017)	(3.528)	(3.613)
Asian crisis	−1.189	−1.102	−1.063	−1.043	−2.105**	−1.995**	−1.931*	−1.862*	−0.131	−0.008	−1.092	−1.089

(*Continued*)

Table 2. (Continued).

	Logit model				Cox model				Panel logit	Linear logit	Logit model (extended data)	
	Model 1	Model 2	Model 3	Model 4	Model 5	Model 6	Model 7	Model 8	Model 9	Model 10	Model 11	Model 12
	(0.821)	(0.798)	(0.806)	(0.810)	(0.759)	(0.773)	(0.767)	(0.764)	(0.919)	(0.014)	(0.793)	(0.802)
Capital restructure	2.559**	2.521**	2.639**	2.540**	3.351**	3.315**	3.353**	3.197**	1.573	0.236**	2.765**	2.671**
improvement plans	(0.748)	(0.847)	(0.749)	(0.741)	(0.944)	(1.013)	(1.005)	(1.035)	(1.255)	(0.042)	(0.785)	(0.783)
Market development	−0.358**	−0.337*	−0.335*	−0.348*	−1.129**	−1.146**	−1.126**	−1.154**	0.070	−0.002	−0.363*	−0.378*
	(0.130)	(0.136)	(0.140)	(0.135)	(0.199)	(0.211)	(0.198)	(0.198)	(0.257)	(0.004)	(0.177)	(0.179)
Constant	−40.392	−33.098	−35.321	−39.403						0.069	−66.254	−69.829
	(36.500)	(37.098)	(40.754)	(42.735)						(0.150)	(48.342)	(49.584)
Observations	1,422	1,422	1,422	1,422	1,366	1,366	1,366	1,366	499	1,422	1,687	1,687
R-squared										0.063		
Log likelihood	−121.2	−119.3	−116.8	−115.2	−141	−138.6	−136.5	−135.2	−67.18	842.9	−131.2	−129.9

Robust standard errors in parentheses, ** $p < 0.01$, * $p < 0.05$, + $p < 0.10$.
In a Cox Model, the number of our observation is reduced to 1,366 because this technique drops the case when the time span between succession and a spin-off is zero.

In Table 2, results show that in Model 3, the coefficient of the interaction terms, *Successor x First son*, is statistically positive and significant ($p < 0.01$). Also, when we calculate the probability of a spin-off, we find that the probability of first-son's succession is 0.84 which is higher than the probability of a non-first son's succession, 0.28. Furthermore, marginal effect of *Successor* is higher when he is the first child and male (*First son = 1)*(0.04), as compared to non-first son (*First son = 0)*(−0.01). Our Hypothesis 1 is supported. Next, in Model 4, the coefficient of interaction terms, *Successor x First son x Number of brothers*, is negative ($p < 0.01$). However, the coefficient of three-way interaction terms is hard to interpret in a nonlinear model. Following Hoetker (2007) suggestion, we calculate the marginal effect of *Successor x First son*, depending on the numbers of brothers. We find that as the number of brothers increases (ranging from Mean-1 S.D. to Mean + 1 S.D), the marginal effect of the *First son* successor's spin-off increases from 0.054 to 0.124. This result supports our prediction in Hypothesis 2, confirming that in Confucian culture, a legitimized successor with many siblings is more likely to spin-off using his discretion. Also, in a Cox hazard model analysis (Model 7), we find that a hazard ratio of a successor who is the first child and male (*First son = 1)* is equal to 12.2. This result shows that the rate of a business group spin-off exponentially increases when a new chairman is the first child and male (*First son = 1)* in the family. In Model 8, as the number of brothers increases from Mean-1S.D. to Mean+ 1 S.D, a hazard ratio of a successor who is the first child and son (*First son = 1)* increases from 1.56 to 2.97. This result is consistent with our prediction, reinforcing effect of siblings in *First son* successor's spin-off.

Tests for institutional variation

An institution is not static or uniform. We take into account two possibilities: whether institutional transition towards a liberal market affects the relationship between business groups' succession and spin-offs, and whether individual families are equally affected by Confucian culture. First, we investigate a possible effect of a country's institutional transition towards a liberal market. Studies in Confucianism suggest that the cultural value has experienced substantial modification with Westernization (Lam 2006). Market transition brought the introduction of meritocracy and professionalism in top management (Rowley and Bae 2004; Rowley and Warner 2014). This means, the dissolution of family-centred structure, and the development of a modern society has diluted family value and principle in the family (Bennett and Meredith 1995; Davis-Friedmann 1991), which in turn may weaken the role of Confucianism in shaping a successor's discretion. To test this possibility, using the variable, *Market development*, we create the interactions terms, *Successor x First son x Market development*. Our result in Model 1 in Table 3 shows that the coefficient of interaction terms is not statistically significant. Also, we test this possibility using the alternative measure of institutional development, *Economic freedom*, by *Index of Economic Freedom* (www.heritage.org) (Blumentritt and Nigh 2002; Kane, Holmes, and O'Grady 2007). The Heritage Foundation Index of Economic Freedom provides a measure of nine characteristics that reflect a country's adherence to free-market principles and flexibility, including business freedom, trade, fiscal, government spending, monetary, investment, financial, property rights, freedom from corruption, and labour deregulation (Kane, Holmes, and O'Grady 2007; Shinkle, Kriauciunas, and Hundley 2013).

Table 3. Institutional variation, succession and business group spin-offs.

	Model 1	Model 2	Model 3
Successor	−1.855	−11.874**	−0.603
	(1.735)	(1.100)	(0.610)
First son	0.675	0.007	0.466
	(1.090)	(0.657)	(0.484)
Successor x First son	3.889+	13.556**	2.303**
	(2.353)	(1.442)	(0.839)
Market development	−0.246		
	(0.166)		
Successor x Market development	0.209		
	(0.313)		
First son x Market development	−0.155		
	(0.256)		
Successor x First son x Market development	−0.277		
	(0.460)		
Confucianism/Buddhism		0.462	
		(0.593)	
Succession x Confucianism/Buddhism		10.924**	
		(1.109)	
First son x Confucianism/Buddhism		0.429	
		(0.828)	
Succession x First son x Confucianism/Buddhism		−10.986**	
		(1.606)	
Foreign university			1.218+
			(0.683)
Successor x Foreign university			−11.630**
			(1.103)
First son x Foreign university			−1.625*
			(0.790)
Successor x First son x Foreign university			11.960**
			(1.601)
Number of brothers	0.019	0.058	0.092
	(0.097)	(0.094)	(0.109)
Number of sisters	−0.116	−0.143	−0.163+
	(0.117)	(0.134)	(0.096)
Number of sons	−0.141	−0.114	−0.148
	(0.152)	(0.124)	(0.142)
Number of daughters	0.071	0.101	0.024
	(0.136)	(0.129)	(0.158)
Successor's tenure	0.563	0.252	0.435
	(0.644)	(0.595)	(0.678)
ROA	−0.233	−0.025	−0.090
	(1.197)	(1.041)	(0.896)
Sales growth	1.802	2.324	1.308
	(2.226)	(1.949)	(1.876)
Diversification	1.721**	1.437**	1.490**
	(0.435)	(0.393)	(0.439)
Ratio of outside board directors	1.064+	0.119	0.305
	(0.576)	(0.516)	(0.488)
Business group age	10.866	24.053	23.879
	(22.404)	(23.706)	(25.591)
Business group age, squared	−1.382	−3.285	−3.312
	(3.084)	(3.211)	(3.488)
Asian crisis	−1.066	−0.650	−0.533
	(0.814)	(0.820)	(0.803)
Capital restructure improvement plans	2.732**	2.735**	2.503**
	(0.707)	(0.805)	(0.766)
Constant	−30.331	−52.361	−51.967
	(40.475)	(43.738)	(46.713)
Observations	1,422	1,422	1,422
Log likelihood	−116.4	−117.1	−117.1

Robust standard errors in parentheses, ** $p < 0.01$, * $p < 0.05$, + $p < 0.10$.

Using this index, we still find that the coefficient of interaction terms is not statistically significant. This implies that as opposed to our prediction, the institutional development does not affect the role of Confucianism in determining a business group spin-off.

Second, we test whether business group families are equally affected by the Confucian value in two ways. First, we collect information on business group families' religious affiliations using newspapers, magazines and their autobiographies. In South Korea, more than half of the population are affiliated with one of three major religions: Protestantism, Catholicism, and Buddhism. Among the major religions, Buddhism has actively adopted the Confucian value system and has incorporated many of its values and norms (Kim 2002). Also, although Confucianism is not a religion itself, Korean people often equate this cultural belief and religion and present their religion as Confucianism. For this reason, we create a binary variable, *Confucianism/Buddhism*, as a proxy of family preference for Confucianism and add three-way interaction terms, *Successor x First son x Confucianism/Buddhism* in the model. Our result in Model 2 in Table 3 shows that a coefficient of the three-way interaction terms is negative. However, when we calculate a marginal effect, we find that the first-son (*First son = 1)* successor's marginal effect for Confucianism/Buddhism is higher (0.12) than the marginal effect for other religions (0.06). This means, when a founder family takes Confucianism as a core belief system in the family and presents strong familiarity with this culture, then the effect of Confucian values is more salient. Second, we investigate whether a business group chairman received an educational degree from a foreign university. If a chairman has educational credentials abroad, he or she may be less inclined to take the Confucian value system as granted and, therefore, this business group family is less influenced by Confucianism. In addition, in our data, most chairmen who received degrees from foreign universities studied in the United States. Hence, we create a variable, *Foreign experience*, indicating whether a chairman received a degree from a foreign university (binary variable) and add an interaction term, *Succession x First son x Foreign experience*. Our result in Model 3 shows that the coefficient of the interaction term is positive ($p < 0.01$). But, marginal effect of the first-son (*First son = 1)* successor having foreign experience (0.08) is smaller than a chairman without foreign experience (0.09). Also, as a stringent form of test, when we run the regression with foreign university degrees in the United States only, the result is even stronger. Taken together, the above two tests show that when a founder family has religious affiliation with the Confucianism or no foreign experience, the effect of cultural value on a business group spin-off is salient.

Supplementary tests

We conduct several robustness checks. First, although we use a logistics regression and a Cox hazard model in the main analyses, we also test our main hypothesis (H1) by employing Xtlogit with fixed effects. As fixed effects remove time-invariant characteristics, our observations are reduced to 499. In Table 2, we find that our result is the same (ß = 3.019, $p < 0.1$, Model 9), supporting our hypothesis. Second, we run regressions with the extended dataset till 2020. Albeit less frequent than previous years, a few business groups (e.g. LG group) implemented succession to a young chairman. Our results in Table 2 show that in Model 11, the coefficient of main interaction terms, *Successor x First son*, is positive and significant ($p < 0.01$). The marginal effect of first son during the succession is

0.04. Also, in Model 12, although the coefficient of three-way interaction terms, *Successor x First son x Number of brothers*, is negative, we find that the marginal effect of first son's succession increases from 0.054 to 0.125 as the number of brothers increases (from −1S.D + mean to 1S.D.+mean). These results from the extended dataset (1981–2020) are consistent with our main regressions in Models 3–4 (1981–2010). Our arguments are supported. Third, in South Korea, daughters' power and position in a family has increased over time. For example, the Korean government amended the law of succession in 1991 and allowed daughters to claim equal rights to inherit family wealth. To test the possibility of the changing status of females in a family firm, we run a regression with female siblings by adding the term, *Number of sisters x First son x successor*, however, we find that the coefficient is not statistically significant. Fourth, as the Korean government has imposed heavy inheritance taxes on business group families to induce corporate governance reforms (see Call for Papers 2020), a business group paying high inheritance taxes may promote corporate restructuring in order to secure funds. Using the national tax bureau's reports, we create a variable, *High inheritance tax*, which indicates business groups that paid more than 10 million (USD) as inheritance tax in a given year. When we include this variable in the main analysis, our result does not change. Fifth, the Korean government made major revisions to the inheritance tax law in 1993 and 2000 by adopting extra charges for business group families (Shim and Park 2018). We create a variable, *New inheritance tax law*, add it into our analysis and find consistent results. Sixth, although the outbreak of the global financial crisis, 2007–2008, did not directly affect the Korean economy (Hong 2010), in a supplementary test, we add the variable, *Global financial crisis*, to the model and find that our result does not change.

Discussion

Although prior research on executive succession and corporate restructuring suggests that a successor's managerial discrepancy is a key factor that determines the success of corporate changes, relatively little attention is paid to the source of managerial discretion, particularly a macro-level factor. From the institutional perspective, this study explores how national culture as an informal institution affects a successor's discretion in a family firm, and ultimately the likelihood of corporate restructuring. In the context of Korean business groups' spin-offs, we find that in Confucian culture, when a successor in a family firm is the first-born child and male, he is likely to implement a spin-off. This happens because in the context of Confucian norms and value system, he becomes the most appropriate person for succession and, therefore, is able to exercise influence in the firm via a spin-off. We also find that the positive effect of a successor's legitimacy on a spin-off is stronger when he has more siblings. Taken together, our findings in the context of Confucian culture suggest that in a family firm, a successor's discretion and rivalry are deeply embedded in cultural norms and expectations.

Theoretical implications

Here, we develop and test our hypotheses in a specific country context. However, our findings contribute to the literatures on succession and managerial discretion, and family business. First, while prior literature focuses on executives' managerial discretion as a key factor that determines the relationship between executive succession and corporate restructuring (Quigley and Hambrick 2012; Wiersema 1995), relatively little attention has been paid to where successors obtain managerial discretion. For this, prior research suggests some sources of managerial discretion such as national culture (Crossland and Hambrick 2007), industry characteristics (Hambrick and Abrahamson 1995), firm characteristics (Finkelstein and Boyd 1998) and personal attributes (Carpenter and Golden 1997); however, none of them explored the role of national culture, which produces heterogeneity of discretion across successors within a country. Our study uncovers the role of national culture in shaping a successor's discrepancy and suggests a novel mechanism of cultural legitimacy in a family firm that allows certain successors to exercise greater influence in a corporate restructuring than others.

Second, family business research has extensively discussed the idiosyncratic characteristics of succession in a family firm, focusing on how a successor's position in the family and family relationship affect firm performance (Birley 1986; Brockhaus 2004; Villalonga and Amit 2006). However, little attention has been paid to its effects on a family firm's strategic changes. To fill this gap, from the institutional perspective, which views national culture as a cognitive institution, we investigate whether and how a successor's position in the family and relationship with siblings affect corporate restructuring as an important form of strategic decisions. This helps scholars to better understand the unique nature of family firms' succession and strategic changes embedded in national culture.

Furthermore, our study contributes to the literature on family conglomerates, particularly studies focusing on the Asia Pacific region. Governance reforms in family conglomerates have been an important topic in the literature (Oh and Park 2001; Redding 2004); however, we know little about how the cultural value system shapes top executives' perception about appropriate models for corporate governance. Our study helps scholars to advance their understanding about why family conglomerates maintain an idiosyncratic corporate governance.

Practical implications

This research helps policy makers to identify the patterns of the succession and corporate governance of family firms in Confucian countries and introduce regulations accordingly. For example, historically, the Korean government has pushed hard for chaebol reforms, specifically corporate governance, by imposing heavy inheritance taxes and restricting their entry into banking industries. However, until recently, the government's efforts have fallen short of expectations. Our findings about the role of national culture in determining family firms' successions and strategic decision-making can give policy makers a new angle to understand corporate governance in family firms in the Confucian countries and help their policy-making.

Limitations and future research

Of course, our study is not limit-free. First, one may wonder whether the influence of Confucianism in the society may vary depending on each country context. As our empirical setting is Korean family firms only, we acknowledge our limitation. For example, business practices and behaviours of family firms in China have been largely influenced by the blended belief systems among Confucianism, socialism and capitalism (Yang 2012). Japan is an another interesting case. Unlike traditional Confucianism's emphasis on blood heirs' succession, Japan has widely accepted the practice of adult child adoption as a way to maintain the unity of family business (Dinh and Calabrò 2019). Such idiosyncratic development of Confucianism, in turn, may affect family firms' corporate structure in a different way. On the contrary, Taiwan has much similarity with Korea. It has a long-history of family division (*fenjia*) that allows sons' claim on family wealth and economic independence from parents (Tsu 2020). For such differences across countries, we welcome more research that compares family business strategy in other Asian countries with ours from the perspective of institutional development. Second, in a supplementary test, we find that market development towards a liberal market does not affect the role of Confucian values in family business succession and strategic changes. For this result, we do not think this is counter-intuitive because market transition and the introduction of Western business practices do not simply replace the role of Confucian culture in family business. Instead, we observe that in modern businesses in South Korea, these two different value systems and business practices coexist. LG group is a representative case. From the founder, Koo InHiu, LG group has maintained the rule of chairman succession to the eldest son, while filling CEO positions in affiliate firms with professional managers (HanKook Ilbo 2019). Such peculiar dual structure enables the founder family to keep control in the group based on Confucian culture, while adopting professional business practices from Western countries. Third, in a supplementary test, we find that our results are consistent with the extended data set (1981–2020). This implies that Confucian culture is still deeply embedded in South Korea and plays a major role in business group succession and group divestiture. However, at the same time, very recently, we observe a new pattern of corporate restructuring due to stricter government regulations. As the current government, under President Moon (2017-present), takes an unprecedentedly hard-line stance against chaebols, Korean business groups face severe challenges, particularly in their corporate governance (see Call for Papers 2020). The recent arrestment of Samsung chairman, Lee Jae-yong, for example, shows that the father-son succession of chairmanship may come to end, which will also affect corporate structure. We find this very interesting and anticipate that such changes will affect business group succession and corporate restructuring in the near future. For this, we encourage future research on these recent changes.

Conclusion

In sum, this study answers whether and how a cognitive institution (i.e. national culture) affects a successor's discretion and corporate restructuring in a family firm. By combing the literatures on succession, institutionalism, and family business, we suggest the ways national culture shapes a successor's discretion and his or her likelihood of corporate restructuring in a family firm. Furthermore, we present a contingency of a successor's rivals in the relationship between the successor's legitimacy and corporate restructuring. Taken together, this study advances our understanding of an unexplored sources of a successor's discretion and strategic changes in a family firm from the institutional perspective.

Disclosure statement

No potential conflict of interest was reported by the author(s).

References

Barnett, W. P., and G. R. Carroll. 1993. "How Institutional Constraints Affected the Organization of Early US Telephony". *Journal of Law, Econmics and Organization* 9: 98.

Bennett, P., and W. H. Meredith. 1995. "The Modern Role of the Grandmother in China: A Departure from the Confucian Ideal." *International Journal of Sociology of the Family* 25: 1–12.

Bigley, G. A., and M. F. Wiersema. 2002. "New CEOs and Corporate Strategic Refocusing: How Experience as Heir Apparent Influences the Use of Power." *Administrative Science Quarterly* 47 (4): 707–727. doi:10.2307/3094914.

Birley, S. 1986. "Succession in the Family Firm: The Inheritor's View." *Journal of Small Business Management* 24: 36.

Blumentritt, T. P., and D. Nigh. 2002. "The Integration of Subsidiary Political Activities in Multinational Corporations." *Journal of International Business Studies* 33 (1): 57–77. doi:10.1057/palgrave.jibs.8491005.

Boyd, B., I. C. Botero, and T. A. Fediuk. 2014. "Incumbent Decisions about Succession Transitions in Family Firms: A Conceptual Model." *International Journal of Financial Studies* 2 (4): 335–358. doi:10.3390/ijfs2040335.

Boyd, B., S. Royer, R. Pei, and X. Zhang. 2015. "Knowledge Transfer in Family Business Successions." *Journal of Family Business Management* 5: 17–37. doi:10.1108/JFBM-05-2014-0009.

Brockhaus, R. H. 2004. "Family Business Succession: Suggestions for Future Research." *Family Business Review* 17 (2): 165–177. doi:10.1111/j.1741-6248.2004.00011.x.

Call for Papers. 2020. "Governance Reforms in the South Korean Chaebol: Implications for Family Conglomerates in the Asia-Pacific and Beyond." *Asia Pacific Business Review*. doi:10.1080/13602381.2020.1793486.

Cannella, S. F. B., D. C. Hambrick, S. Finkelstein, and A. A. Cannella. 2009. *Strategic Leadership: Theory and Research on Executives, Top Management Teams, and Boards: Strategic Management*. New York, USA: Oxford U.

Carney, M. 2005. "Corporate Governance and Competitive Advantage in Family-Controlled Firms." *Entrepreneurship Theory and Practice* 29 (3): 249–265. doi:10.1111/j.1540-6520.2005.00081.x.

Carpenter, M. A., and B. R. Golden. 1997. "Perceived Managerial Discretion: A Study of Cause and Effect." *Strategic Management Journal* 18 (3): 187–206. doi:10.1002/(SICI)1097-0266(199703)18:3<187::AID-SMJ861>3.0.CO;2-U.

Chaganti, R. S., V. Mahajan, and S. Sharma. 1985. "Corporate Board Size, Composition and Corporate Failures in Retailing Industry [1]." *Journal of Management Studies* 22 (4): 400–417.

Chang, S. J., and J. Hong. 2000. "Economic Performance of Group-Affiliated Companies in Korea: Intragroup Resource Sharing and Internal Business Transactions." *Academy of Management Journal* 43 (3): 429–448.

Chung, C. N., and X. R. Luo. 2013. "Leadership Succession and Firm Performance in an Emerging Economy: Successor Origin, Relational Embeddedness, and Legitimacy." *Strategic Management Journal* 34 (3): 338–357. doi:10.1002/smj.2011.

Čihák, M., A. Demirgüč-Kunt, E. Feyen, and R. Levine. 2013. "Financial Development in 205 Economies, 1960 to 2010."

Crossland, C., and D. C. Hambrick. 2007. "How National Systems Differ in Their Constraints on Corporate Executives: A Study of CEO Effects in Three Countries." *Strategic Management Journal* 28 (8): 767–789. doi:10.1002/smj.610.

Davis-Friedmann, D. 1991. *Long Lives: Chinese Elderly and the Communist Revolution*. Stanford, California, USA: Stanford University Press.

Dibrell, C., and E. Memili. 2019. "A Brief History and A Look to the Future of Family Business Heterogeneity: An Introduction." In *The Palgrave Handbook of Heterogeneity among Family Firms*, edited by Dibrell, C., and E. Memili, 1–15. London, UK: Palgrave Macmillan, Cham

DiMaggio, P. 1997. "Culture and Cognition." *Annual Review of Sociology* 23 (1): 263–287. doi:10.1146/annurev.soc.23.1.263.

Dinh, T. Q., and A. Calabrò. 2019. "Asian Family Firms through Corporate Governance and Institutions: A Systematic Review of the Literature and Agenda for Future Research." *International Journal of Management Reviews* 21 (1): 50–75. doi:10.1111/ijmr.12176.

Dou, J., N. Wang, E. Su, H. Fang, and E. Memili. 2020. "Goal Complexity in Family Firm Diversification: Evidence from China." *Journal of Family Business Strategy* 11 (1): 100310. doi:10.1016/j.jfbs.2019.100310.

Finkelstein, S., and B. K. Boyd. 1998. "How Much Does the CEO Matter? the Role of Managerial Discretion in the Setting of CEO Compensation." *Academy of Management Journal* 41 (2): 179–199.

Fiordelisi, F., and O. Ricci. 2014. "Corporate Culture and CEO Turnover." *Journal of Corporate Finance* 28: 66–82. doi:10.1016/j.jcorpfin.2013.11.009.

Friedman, S. D. 1991. "Sibling Relationships and Intergenerational Succession in Family Firms." *Family Business Review* 4 (1): 3–20. doi:10.1111/j.1741-6248.1991.00003.x.

Gabarro, J. J. 1987. *The Dynamics of Taking Charge*. Boston, USA: Harvard Business Press.

Goel, S., P. Mazzola, P. H. Phan, T. M. Pieper, and R. K. Zachary. 2012. "Strategy, Ownership, Governance, and Socio-psychological Perspectives on Family Businesses from around the World." *Journal of Family Business Strategy* 3 (2): 54–65. doi:10.1016/j.jfbs.2012.03.005.

Greenhalgh, S. 1985. "Sexual Stratification: The Other Side Of" Growth with Equity" in East Asia." *Population and Development Review* 11: 265–314. doi:10.2307/1973489.

Greenhalgh, S. 1994. "De-orientalizing the Chinese Family Firm." *American Ethnologist* 21 (4): 746–775. doi:10.1525/ae.1994.21.4.02a00050.

Gupta, V., and N. Levenburg. 2010. "A Thematic Analysis of Cultural Variations in Family Businesses: The CASE Project." *Family Business Review* 23 (2): 155–169. doi:10.1177/089448651002300205.

Hambrick, D. C., and E. Abrahamson. 1995. "Assessing Managerial Discretion across Industries: A Multimethod Approach." *Academy of Management Journal* 38 (5): 1427–1441.

Hambrick, D. C., and S. Finkelstein. 1987. "Managerial Discretion: A Bridge between Polar Views of Organizational Outcomes." *Research in Organizational Behavior*.

Hambrick, D. C., and G. D. Fukutomi. 1991. "The Seasons of a CEO's Tenure." *Academy of Management Review* 16 (4): 719–742. doi:10.5465/amr.1991.4279621.

Hambrick, D. C., A. Werder, and E. J. Zajac. 2008. "New Directions in Corporate Governance Research." *Organization Science* 19 (3): 381–385.

Hamilton, G. G., and N. W. Biggart. 1988. "Market, Culture, and Authority: A Comparative Analysis of Management and Organization in the Far East." *American Journal of Sociology* 94: S52–S94. doi:10.1086/228942.

Hamilton, G. G., and K. Cheng-Shu. 1990. "» The Institutional Foundations of Chinese Business: The Family Firm in Taiwan «in: Compa-rative Social Research 2, 12: S."

Han, J., A. V. Shipilov, and H. R. Greve. 2017. "Unequal Bedfellows: Gender Role-based Deference in Multiplex Ties between Korean Business Groups." *Academy of Management Journal* 60 (4): 1531–1553.

HanKook Ilbo. 2019. "LG Group Keeps the Succession Rule of First-son over Four Generations."

Hannan, M. T. 1998. "Rethinking Age Dependence in Organizational Mortality: Logical Fromalizations." *American Journal of Sociology* 104 (1): AJSv104p126–164. doi:10.1086/210004.

Hatch, M. J. 2018. *Organization theory: Modern, symbolic, and postmodern perspectives*. Oxford, UK: Oxford university press.

Hoetker, G. 2007. "The Use of Logit and Probit Models in Strategic Management Research: Critical Issues." *Strategic Management Journal* 28 (4): 331–343. doi:10.1002/smj.582.

Hofstede, G. 1993. "Cultural Constraints in Management Theories." *Academy of Management Perspectives* 7 (1): 81–94. doi:10.5465/ame.1993.9409142061.

Hong, S. J. 2010. "Early Recovery from the Global Financial Crisis: South Korea Case." *KDI report*.

Hoskisson, R. E., R. A. Johnson, and D. D. Moesel. 1994. "Corporate Divestiture Intensity in Restructuring Firms: Effects of Governance, Strategy, and Performance." *Academy of Management Journal* 37 (5): 1207–1251.

Huang, X., and E. Van de Vliert. 2003. "Where Intrinsic Job Satisfaction Fails to Work: National Moderators of Intrinsic Motivation." *Journal of Organizational Behavior: The International Journal of Industrial, Occupational and Organizational Psychology and Behavior* 24 (2): 159–179. doi:10.1002/job.186.

Ingram, P., and B. Silverman. 2002. *The New Institutionalism in Strategic Management*. Oxford, UK: Elsevier.

Jacobs, L., G. Goupei, and P. Herbig. 1995. "Confucian Roots in China: A Force For'l 'Oday's Business', {l/fartagemmt Danton 33." *0* 297: 34.

Johnson, C., T. J. Dowd, and C. L. Ridgeway. 2006. "Legitimacy as a Social Process." *Annual Review of Sociology* 32: 53–78. doi:10.1146/annurev.soc.32.061604.123101.

Kane, T., K. R. Holmes, and M. A. O'Grady. 2007. "2007 Index of Economic Freedom."

Katz, D., and R. L. Kahn. 1978. *The Social Psychology of Organizations*. Vol. 2. New York, USA: Wiley New York.

Kim, A. E. 2002. "Characteristics of Religious Life in South Korea: A Sociological Survey." *Review of Religious Research* 43: 291–310. doi:10.2307/3512000.

KyungHyang News. 1999. "Cheabols' Succession." *KyungHyang News*.

Lam, R. C. 2006. "Contradictions between Traditional Chinese Values and the Actual Performance: A Study of the Caregiving Roles of the Modern Sandwich Generation in Hong Kong." *Journal of Comparative Family Studies* 37: 299–313.

Lee, H. 2004. *HanKook Chaebol-sa(The History of Korean Chaebol)*. Seoul, South Korea: DaeMyung.

Lee, K. S., G. H. Lim, and W. S. Lim. 2003. "Family Business Succession: Appropriation Risk and Choice of Successor." *Academy of Management Review* 28 (4): 657–666. doi:10.5465/amr.2003.10899446.

Lu, L.-C., G. M. Rose, and J. G. Blodgett. 1999. "The Effects of Cultural Dimensions on Ethical Decision Making in Marketing: An Exploratory Study." *Journal of Business Ethics* 18 (1): 91–105. doi:10.1023/A:1006038012256.

Markides, C. C. 1992. "Consequences of Corporate Refocusing: Ex Ante Evidence." *Academy of Management Journal* 35 (2): 398–412.

Markides, C. C. 1995. "Diversification, Restructuring and Economic Performance." *Strategic Management Journal* 16 (2): 101–118. doi:10.1002/smj.4250160203.

Meyer, J. W., and B. Rowan. 1977. "Institutionalized Organizations: Formal Structure as Myth and Ceremony." *American Journal of Sociology* 83 (2): 340–363.

Meyer, J. W., and W. R. Scott, eds. 1983. *Centralization and the Legitimacy Problems of Local Government*. Newbury Park, CA: Sage.

Miller, D. 1993. "The Architecture of Simplicity." *Academy of Management Review* 18 (1): 116–138. doi:10.5465/amr.1993.3997509.

Miller, D., and P. H. Friesen. 1980. "Momentum and Revolution in Organizational Adaptation." *Academy of Management Journal* 23 (4): 591–614.

Miller, D., M. Wright, I. L. Breton-Miller, and L. Scholes. 2015. "Resources and Innovation in Family Businesses: The Janus-face of Socioemotional Preferences." *California Management Review* 58 (1): 20–40. doi:10.1525/cmr.2015.58.1.20.

Molly, V., E. Laveren, and M. Deloof. 2010. "Family Business Succession and Its Impact on Financial Structure and Performance." *Family Business Review* 23 (2): 131–147. doi:10.1177/089448651002300203.

North, D. C. 1990. *Institutions, Institutional Change and Economic Performance*. Cambridge, UK: Cambridge university press.

Ocasio, W. 1994. "Political Dynamics and the Circulation of Power: CEO Succession in US Industrial Corporations, 1960-1990." *Administrative Science Quarterly* 39: 285–312. doi:10.2307/2393237.

Ocasio, W., and H. Kim. 1999. "The Circulation of Corporate Control: Selection of Functional Backgrounds of New CEOs in Large US Manufacturing Firms, 1981–1992." *Administrative Science Quarterly* 44 (3): 532–562. doi:10.2307/2666961.

Oh, I., and H.-J. Park. 2001. "Shooting at a Moving Target: Four Theoretical Problems in Explaining the Dynamics of the Chaebol." *Asia Pacific Business Review* 7 (4): 44–69. doi:10.1080/713999115.

Park, C., and S. Kim. 2008. "Corporate Governance, Regulatory Changes, and Corporate Restructuring in Korea, 1993–2004." *Journal of World Business* 43 (1): 66–84. doi:10.1016/j.jwb.2007.10.008.

Perrow, C. 1986. "Economic Theories of Organization." *Theory and Society* 15 (1–2): 11–45. doi:10.1007/BF00156926.

Pfeffer, J. 1981. "Management as Symbolic Action: The Creation and Maintenance of Organizational Paradigm." *Research in Organizational Behavior* 3: 1–52.

Pfeffer, J., and G. R. Salancik. 1978. *The External Control of Organizations: A Resource Dependence Perspective*. Stanford, California, USA: Stanford University Press.

Pomerleano, M., and W. Shaw. 2005. *Corporate Restructuring: Lessons from Experience*. Washington D. C., USA: World Bank.

Powell, W. W., and P. J. DiMaggio. 2012. *The New Institutionalism in Organizational Analysis*. Chicago and London: University of Chicago press.

Quigley, T. J., and D. C. Hambrick. 2012. "When the Former CEO Stays on as Board Chair: Effects on Successor Discretion, Strategic Change, and Performance." *Strategic Management Journal* 33 (7): 834–859. doi:10.1002/smj.1945.

Redding, G. 2004. "The Conditional Relevance of Corporate Governance Advice in the Context of Asian Business Systems." *Asia Pacific Business Review* 10 (3–4): 272–291. doi:10.1080/1360238042000264360.

Rowley, C., and J. Bae. 2004. "Big Business in South Korea: The Reconfiguration Process." *Asia Pacific Business Review* 10 (3–4): 302–323. doi:10.1080/1360238042000264388.

Rowley, C., and M. Warner. 2014. The Changing Contours of Korean Management and Business. *Asia Pacific Business Review* 20 (1): 1–8.

Sakano, T., and A. Y. Lewin. 1999. "Impact of CEO Succession in Japanese Companies: A Coevolutionary Perspective." *Organization Science* 10 (5): 654–671. doi:10.1287/orsc.10.5.654.

Scott, P. 1995. *The Meanings of Mass Higher Education*. Buckingham, UK: McGraw-Hill Education (UK).

Selznick, P. 1957. *Leadership in Administration*. Evanston, Illinois, USA: Peterson.

Selznick, P. 1948. "Foundations of the Theory of Organization." *American Sociological Review* 13 (1): 25–35.

Seoul News Corporation. 2005. *Chaebolga Mak*. Seoul: MooHan.

Shen, W., and T. S. Cho. 2005. "Exploring Involuntary Executive Turnover through a Managerial Discretion Framework." *Academy of Management Review* 30 (4): 843–854. doi:10.5465/amr.2005.18378881.

Shim, J., and S. Park. 2018. "Koo Guangmo Pays 0.9 Bil as Inheritance Tax." *Money today*.

Shinkle, G. A., A. P. Kriauciunas, and G. Hundley. 2013. "Why Pure Strategies May Be Wrong for Transition Economy Firms." *Strategic Management Journal* 34 (10): 1244–1254. doi:10.1002/smj.2060.

Smart, D. L., and M. A. Hitt. 1994. "A Mid-range Theory regarding the Antecedents of Restructuring Types: An Integration of Agency, Upper Echelon and Resource-based Perspectives." *Advances in Strategic Management* 10 (part A): 159–186.

Stevens, J. M., J. M. Beyer, and H. M. Trice. 1978. "Assessing Personal, Role, and Organizational Predictors of Managerial Commitment." *Academy of Management Journal* 21 (3): 380–396.

Stinchcombe, A. L. 1965. *Social Structure and Organizations*. Bingley, UK: Emerald Group Publishing Limited.

Suchman, M. C. 1995. "Managing Legitimacy: Strategic and Institutional Approaches." *Academy of Management Review* 20 (3): 571–610. doi:10.5465/amr.1995.9508080331.

Sundaramurthy, C., and G. E. Kreiner. 2008. "Governing by Managing Identity Boundaries: The Case of Family Businesses." *Entrepreneurship Theory and Practice* 32 (3): 415–436. doi:10.1111/j.1540-6520.2008.00234.x.

Tan, D. S., and S. Akhtar. 1998. "Organizational Commitment and Experienced Burnout: An Exploratory Study from a Chinese Cultural Perspective." *The International Journal of Organizational Analysis* 6: 310–333. doi:10.1108/eb028889.

Therneau, T. M., and S. A. Hamilton. 1997. "rhDNase as an Example of Recurrent Event Analysis." *Statistics in Medicine* 16 (18): 2029–2047. doi:10.1002/(SICI)1097-0258(19970930)16:18<2029::AID-SIM637>3.0.CO;2-H.

Thompson, J. D. 1967. *Organizations in Action: Social Science Bases of Administrative Theory*. New York, USA: Transaction publishers.

Tsu, T. Y. H. 2020. "The Chinese Joint Family as a "White Lie": Competing Visions of the Family in 19th-century Taiwanese Family Division Contracts." *Asian Studies Review* 44 (1): 136–151. doi:10.1080/10357823.2019.1675586.

Tu, W., and W. Du. 1996. *Confucian Traditions in East Asian Modernity: Moral Education and Economic Culture in Japan and the Four Mini-dragons*. Cambridge, Massachusetts and London, England: Harvard University Press.

Tushman, M. L., and E. Romanelli. 1985. "Organizational Evolution: A Metamorphosis Model of Convergence and Reorientation." *Research in Organizational Behavior*.

Villalonga, B., and R. Amit. 2006. "How Do Family Ownership, Control and Management Affect Firm Value?" *Journal of Financial Economics* 80 (2): 385–417. doi:10.1016/j.jfineco.2004.12.005.

Weidenbaum, M. L., and S. Hughes. 1996. *The Bamboo Network: How Expatriate Chinese Entrepreneurs are Creating a New Economic Superpower in Asia*. New York, USA: Simon and Schuster.

Wiersema, M. F. 1995. "Executive Succession as an Antecedent to Corporate Restructuring." *Human Resource Management* 34 (1): 185–202. doi:10.1002/hrm.3930340111.

Wiersema, M. F., and K. A. Bantel. 1993. "Top Management Team Turnover as an Adaptation Mechanism: The Role of the Environment." *Strategic Management Journal* 14 (7): 485–504. doi:10.1002/smj.4250140702.

Yan, J., and R. Sorenson. 2006. "The Effect of Confucian Values on Succession in Family Business." *Family Business Review* 19 (3): 235–250. doi:10.1111/j.1741-6248.2006.00072.x.

Yang, B. 2012. "Confucianism, Socialism, and Capitalism: A Comparison of Cultural Ideologies and Implied Managerial Philosophies and Practices in the PR China." *Human Resource Management Review* 22 (3): 165–178. doi:10.1016/j.hrmr.2012.01.002.

Zajac, E. J., and J. D. Westphal. 1996. "Who Shall Succeed? How CEO/board Preferences and Power Affect the Choice of New CEOs." *Academy of Management Journal* 39 (1): 64–90.

Zheng, W., K. Singh, and C.-N. Chung. 2017. "Ties to Unbind: Political Ties and Firm Sell-offs during Institutional Transition." *Journal of Management* 43 (7): 2005–2036. doi:10.1177/0149206315575553.

Appendix. Business group profile

Business group name	Established year	Successor name(s)	Ratio of family ownership	Ratio of external board
Anam	1956	Joojin Kim	.	.
Bongmyung	1955	Byungmoo Lee	.	.
Bumyang	1966	Seungjoo, Park	.	.
Byucksan	1971	Heechul Kim	.	41.4%
Choongang	1965		.	.
Choongsam	1954	Joonho Lee	.	.
Choyang sangseon	1961	Jaeik Park	.	.
Daehanhaewoon	1968	Jinbang Lee	.	10.5%
Daejeon pihuck	1960		.	.
Daelim	1960	Joonyong Lee	2.2%	41.4%
Daenong	1955		.	.
Daesang	1958	Changwook Lim	7.7%	32.0%
Daeshin	1962	Yeorong Lee	.	.
Daesung	1952	Youngdae Kim	14.5%	38.8%
Daewoo	1967		.	5.6%
Dong-a construction	1957		.	.
Dong-a pharm	1949		.	39.3%
Dongbu	1969		.	38.3%
Dongkuk jekang	1954	Sejoo Chang	8.6%	40.9%
Dongkuk	1965		.	.
Dongmyung	1959		.	.
Dongwon	1969	Samkoo Kim	3.9%	41.4%
Dongyang	1955	Jehyun Hyun	7.2%	39.4%
Doosan	1951	Yongkon Park, Jeongwon Park	.	41.4%
Gaepoong	1954		.	.
Gangwon	1952	Moonwon Cheong	.	0.0%
Haitai	1954	Gunbae Park	.	.
Hanbo	1974		.	.
Hanglass	1953	Youngjeung Choi	.	10.5%
Hanhwa	1952	Seungyeon Kim	0.8%	40.9%
Hanil	1956	Choongwon Kim	.	.
Hanjin	1957	Yangho Cho	3.6%	41.9%
Hwanshin	1947		.	.
Hyosung	1957	Sukrae Cho	9.4%	41.4%
Hyundai	1955	Monghun Chung	2.7%	39.6%
Jinro	1954		.	.
Kapeul	1954	Changho Park	.	
Kia	1959		.	.
Kohap	1966		.	.
Kolong	1957	Woongryul Lee	2.8%	41.4%
Kookje	1950		.	.
Kukdong construction	1953		.	.
Kukdong oil	1964		.	.
Kumho	1954	Seongyong Park, Jeongkoo Park, Samkoo Park	.	41.4%

(Continued)

(Continued).

Business group name	Established year	Successor name(s)	Ratio of family ownership	Ratio of external board
Kypyong	1980		.	.
Kyungbang	1956	Joon Kim	.	34.6%
LG	1953	Bonmoo Koo	.	42.4%
Life	1973		.	.
Lotte	1967	Dongbin Shin	4.1%	40.1%
Newcore	1981		.	.
Samchully	1955	Mandeuk Lee	.	29.2%
Samho	1956		.	.
Samhwan	1952	Yongkwon Choi	.	39.3%
Samlib	1959		.	.
Sammi	1960		.	.
Samsung	1953		9.0%	39.8%
Samyang	1955	Sangha Kim, Yoon Kim	.	37.0%
Shindonga	1962		.	.
Shinho	1971		.	.
SK	1962		.	40.5%
Ssangyong	1962		.	38.3%
Taekwang	1961		14.0%	36.3%
Taepyeong-yang	1959	Kyungbae Seo	.	36.3%
Taihan	1955	Beom Sul	.	41.4%
Wooseong	1966		.	.
Youngpoong group	1949		5.3%	41.4%
Yulsan	1976		.	.

1: We collected information on the year of establishment from business group websites and local newspapers.

2: During our observation period, most business groups experienced a succession event once (except three groups)

3: For the ratio of family ownership, we searched for government website (Fair Trade Commission, https://www.egroup.go.kr/egps/wi/comm/kmbntThemaList.do_) and collected founder families' stake in the group. Please note that as Korean government has released this data on a yearly basis from 2000, we could not collect all yearly data during our observation period. Here, we provide the average ratio of family ownership with available data.

4: For the ratio of outside board members, we searched for Korea government's electronic disclosure system (http://dart.fss.or.kr/) and collected the data on board members in each business group. As Korean government started to mandate public disclosure of management during the Asian crisis, we could not collect the information on board membership before 1997. Here, we provide the average ratio of external board members with available data.

The shadow of a departing CEO: outsider succession and strategic change in a business group

Changsu Kim, Jong-Hun Park, Jiyoon Kim and Youngjoo Lee

ABSTRACT

This study examined the influence of both departing and incoming CEOs on strategic change. Highlighting the importance of taking a business group-level approach in the study of CEO succession in emerging economies, the study investigated the interaction effect of departing and incoming CEOs on strategic change in group-affiliated firms in Korea. We distinguished outsider successors into in-group and group outsiders. Our theory and the evidence from a sample of 304 CEO successions suggests that group outsiders significantly differ from in-group outsiders in their reaction to the shadow of departing CEOs, although both are outsiders at the firm level. The negative CEO retention effect on strategic change was attenuated by new CEOs coming from outside the business group. Our findings regarding moderating effects also show that the strategic change effects of outsiders are stronger in the event of a global financial crisis. Our results reveal the contrasting views relating to the group-level transfer of executives, providing insights for both researchers and practitioners.

Introduction

Outsider succession can serve as a primary method for organizations to overcome resistance to strategic change. Researchers have investigated the contingencies that may influence the ability and willingness of outside successors to enact strategic change. For example, using longitudinal data from US airline and chemical industries between 1972 and 2010, Karaevli and Zajac (2013) showed that, although outsiders were less likely to be selected in relatively stable circumstances (e.g. good firm performance, a long-tenured predecessor CEO, and ordinary succession), once they were selected, they were able to generate a greater degree of strategic change in these contexts. Although such research has been informative, our understanding of outsider succession and strategic change in the more heterogeneous context of emerging economies remains limited, despite its importance (Chung and Luo 2013).

Emerging economies, with their unique corporate governance such as their business group structure, offer an opportunity to extend the literature on outsider succession and strategic change. A business group – a gathering of affiliated firms under the group's control – is a prevalent form of diversified corporation in many emerging economies

(Khanna and Palepu 2010). Compared with its standalone counterparts, a business group from emerging economies is more likely and able to utilize an executive-level workforce through its internal labour market as a sort of strategic resource-sharing (Chang, Cho, and Shin 2007). Thus, an executive succession in a standalone firm results in the outgoing CEO's departure from the firm, whereas in a business group, an executive succession frequently involves executive transfer within a group. Therefore, a business group in an emerging economy is a distinct context in which to examine outsider succession and strategic change.

The research context of this study is business groups in Korea. Business groups in Korea actually encompass both chaebol and non-chaebol groups (Shin et al. 2018). The Korea Fair Trade Commission ranks business groups in terms of the total assets of all group-affiliated firms and identifies the top-tier business groups (i.e. chaebol) for the purpose of cross-shareholding restrictions. A cursory look at our data on Korean business groups indicates that the degree of strategic change is lower in chaebol-affiliates than in non-chaebol affiliates. Perhaps chaebol-affiliates are more likely to show lower strategic changes due to the structural inertia existing in chaebol groups. It seems that, from both theoretical and practical standpoints, a clear need exists to reconsider and extend the concept of outsider succession at the business group level for a better understanding of the strategic change in emerging economies. Therefore, this study provides a more fine-grained distinction between different types of outsider succession. Thus far, the underlying construct and measurement of successor origin is based on a firm-level dichotomy: firm outsiders versus firm insiders. However, in the business group context, outsiders can be divided further into in-group outsiders, who move from other firms but within the same group, and group outsiders, who move into a group from other organizations outside the group. This more refined distinction of successor origin offers a more nuanced implication of the way outsider CEOs lead to strategic change in the business group context.

In addition, there has been little attention paid to the idea that the presence of departing CEOs within a business group might restrict incoming CEOs from taking strategic actions (Nakauchi and Wiersema 2015). This deficiency is at odds with the reality that, in many cases, outgoing CEOs do not fully depart the scene (Quigley and Hambrick 2012). For example, Korean business groups do not typically search and appoint CEOs beyond the group boundary unless they face strong organizational and environmental pressures for change (Song, Lee, and Khanna 2016). Therefore, the typical succession process in a Korean business group results in the outgoing CEO moving to other affiliated firms. In such a context, the retention of an outgoing CEO in a group is conventional and an efficient form of executive resource utilization. However, incoming CEOs who operate in the shadows of their predecessors may have limited leeway in the strategic means at their disposal.

This study examines the influence of both outsider succession and predecessor retention on strategic change, along with the interaction of the two within a business group boundary. Predecessor CEOs who transfer to other affiliated firms may exert implicit and explicit influence on any strategic moves made by their previous organizations. We argue that, in such cases of predecessor retention and influence, the role and responsibility of outsider successors, as a strategic inertia breaker, will become more critical in alleviating the negative effect of predecessor CEO retention on strategic change. This study goes a step further by incorporating contingency factors that can shape the scope of the strategic changes that a CEO can make. The 2008 global financial crisis has been differentiated from typical environmental contingencies in terms of its overarching influential power. Thus, by considering both incoming and departing CEOs simultaneously and by incorporating contingency factors, this study aims to investigate an important yet underestimated effect of outsider succession on strategic change in a business group context.

We organize this article as follows: in the next section, we discuss theory and develop hypotheses. In the subsequent sections, we present the research design and provide the results. We conclude with suggestions for scholarship and practice.

Relevant theory and hypothesis development

This section commences by proposing a social network as a theoretical lens in the study of a business group; it then outlines the different types of outsiders and their effects on strategic change in a business group context. The final discussion in the section investigates the continuing presence and influence of departing CEOs, the contingency factors of the 2008 global financial crisis, and their direct and indirect effects on incoming CEOs' strategic change efforts.

Social networks among upper echelons in a business group

Scholars studying upper echelons have found that executive succession can serve as an important change mechanism (Finkelstein, Hambrick, and Cannella 2009). Although the top management team as a whole is considered to be the firm's upper echelon, the CEO heads this top management team. Studies in this tradition regard top managers, notably the CEO, as an important strategic asset that sets the path for the firm's strategic direction and assume that outsider succession reflects an intent to initiate swift changes (Karaevli and Zajac 2013). However, growing evidence suggests that, beyond deeming the CEO as a standalone agent or resource of the firm, there is another important relational dimension that is largely neglected in the CEO turnover and succession literature. In particular, the effectiveness of a CEO's strategic contributions to the organization is determined by the relationships that the CEO maintains both within and outside the firm, especially in many emerging economies (Cao, Maruping, and Takeuchi 2006).

Business groups in many emerging economies consist of a set of legally independent firms bound together by multiple and stable interfirm ties. The ties range from formal arrangements (e.g. equity cross-holdings and interlocking directorates) to informal interpersonal ties based on identity and trust (Granovetter 1995). Equity cross-holdings among group-affiliated firms create a structure of mutually tied relationships as well as serving as a means for protecting firms from hostile takeovers and buyouts from outsiders (Gerlach 1992). Another mechanism for binding firms together is the interlocking directorate, in which group-affiliated firms have common members on their boards of directors; these members may help coordinate group activities. Yet social networks among upper echelons based on communal identity and interpersonal trust constrain strategic actions and are, in turn, shaped by them. For example, individual executives' interpersonal ties within a Korean business group work not only towards power group formation at the top levels, but also towards the formation of informal relations and cliques (Joh and Jung 2018; Kim and Cannella 2008; Shin et al. 2018).

The central theses of our perspectives are grounded in a view of CEOs as entities embedded within a business group social network. Granovetter described embeddedness as 'the fact that economic action and outcomes, like all social action and outcomes, are affected by actors' dyadic (pairwise) relations and by the structure of the overall network of relations' (1992, 33). Granovetter (1992) illustrates two types of network embeddedness: relational and structural embeddedness. Network researchers have argued that both relational embeddedness (e.g. the characteristics of relationships) and structural embeddedness (e.g. the characteristics of the relational structure) influence the nature and scope of relationships (Burt 1992; Coleman 1988; Uzzi 1996). The current study pays particular attention to the embeddedness discrepancy of incoming and departing CEOs on the basis of their cross-cutting interpersonal ties in a business group boundary (Cao, Maruping, and Takeuchi 2006). In business groups, both becoming CEO and then making strategic changes in the group-affiliated firms are difficult and require the support of those already in the business group. However, new CEOs often find it challenging to find supportive executive members within their new firms. Thus, the impact of CEO succession on strategic change depends on the portfolio of relationships of both the incoming and departing CEOs within a business group network.

Outsider succession and strategic change in a business group

In general, outside CEO successors are selected by the board of directors when a firm has a need for strategic changes, such as when poor performance needs to be improved, whereas inside successors are selected when the firm is pursuing strategic continuity (Finkelstein, Hambrick, and Cannella 2009). According to Finkelstein and Hambrick (1990), CEOs, having bounded rationality, find it difficult to understand and interpret excessive information within a complex environment. Under these circumstances, CEOs cognitively reorganize such complex environmental cues based on their own perspectives. Therefore, CEOs' attributes and characteristics greatly influence firms' major strategic decisions. As strategies determine the allocation of resources within a firm, strategic change implies a strong discontinuity in the patterns of resource allocation (Finkelstein and Hambrick 1990). Among the many CEO characteristics that affect a firm's strategic change, our study focuses on new CEOs' origin (outsider versus insider), as it is related to the willingness to initiate strategic changes. Indeed, the act of appointing an outsider is meant to send signals internally that change is coming and externally that the firm has taken an extraordinary measure in order to break with the past.

As a new strategy can bring significant changes within an organization, there may be some resistance from the incumbent executives and employees. Due to socialization processes inside the firm, long-tenured insiders are more likely to have narrow perspectives and psychological commitment to the status quo (Karaevli 2007). Moreover, due to their entrenched social relationships within firms, inside CEO successors tend not to make the necessary changes once in their new position (Chung and Luo 2013). On the contrary, CEO successors from the outside do not hesitate to pursue new strategic moves, because their social relatedness within the firm may be weaker than that of inside successors. Moreover, as outside successors are less burdened by the status quo, they can make strategic moves relatively easily.

Our sample of Korean business groups was composed of 57.6% firm insiders and 42.4% firm outsiders, which, in turn, was broken down into 21.7% in-group outsiders (from other firms but within a group) and 20.7% group outsiders (from outside a group). The in-group outsider succession (21.7%) consisted of incoming CEOs moving from other group-affiliated firms or from the group headquarters. The selection of a group outsider (20.7%) was a highly charged decision, representing a repudiation of the incumbent's strategic decisions. Group outsiders are normally prized for their fresh perspectives and their prior performance records. Compared with firm insiders, both in-group outsiders and group outsiders are less likely to be socially connected to intra-firm social networks or committed to the status quo.

Therefore, we argue that, compared to inside successors, outside CEO successors including both in-group and group outsiders have greater legitimacy in terms of overcoming strategic inertia, making strategic initiatives, and pursuing strategic redirection.

Hypothesis 1a: In business groups, CEO succession by in-group outsiders is associated with higher subsequent strategic change than succession by firm insiders.

Hypothesis 1b: In business groups, CEO succession by group outsiders is associated with higher subsequent strategic change than succession by firm insiders.

Retaining departing CEOs in a business group

Despite the intuitive appeal of the positive relationship between succession and change, there are countervailing forces that can significantly diminish a new CEO's ability to make such changes. Hambrick and Finkelstein (1987) introduced the concept of managerial discretion, defined as latitude of action, in an effort to explain the degree to which top executives have influence over organizational outcomes. New CEOs typically have strong motivation to initiate strategic changes. However, the magnitude of implemented post-succession strategic change is highly dependent on the new CEOs' discretion for action. Researchers have considered various sources of managerial discretion, stemming mainly from three sets of factors: environmental, organizational, and individual characteristics (Finkelstein, Hambrick, and Cannella 2009). Despite such research on the sources of managerial discretion, little attention has been paid to the idea that powerful parties might restrict a new CEO from making significant changes (Quigley and Hambrick 2012). Among such powerful parties are the predecessor CEOs who remain in a business group.

Quigley and Hambrick's (2012) study of 181 successions in the industries of computer hardware, software, and electronics found that, after succession, the predecessor CEO remained as a board chair in 51% of cases. By the fifth year following succession, 21% of predecessor CEOs (38 out of 181 cases) still remained as a chair. This finding highlights a critical institutional reality in the US: Some incoming CEOs are assuming office while their predecessors remain in the firm as board chairs. This reality is particularly noteworthy in Japan, an institutional context noted for a lack of board independence. A typical succession in Japan involves the CEO stepping down and taking the position of board chair. Moreover, in Japan, the influence of departing CEOs is enormous and significant because, as board chairs, they also hold an executive position on the top management team (Nakauchi and Wiersema 2015). Studies in both the US and Japan indicate that the continuing presence of the prior executive as a board chair restricts a successor's discretion, thereby suppressing his or her ability to make strategic changes. We extended these studies to trace departing and incoming CEOs at the business group level and examine how a predecessor's lingering presence in a business group might affect a new CEO's strategic change initiative.

In our sample of Korean business groups, more than 34% of predecessor CEOs remained in the group. This figure captures only pure retention cases, excluding retention cases in formality such as moving to an advisory position and then retiring a year or two later. The pure retention cases include outgoing CEOs staying in a firm as board members or remaining in the same business groups as CEOs of other affiliated firms. At Samsung, for example, the group system of internal promotion and lateral transfer of top executives facilitates a group-wide utilization of managerial resources and helps inculcate executives' sense of belonging to the Samsung group by creating cross-cutting ties across affiliated firms (Song, Lee, and Khanna 2016). Although such a group-level arrangement has advantages in facilitating resource utilization and group identity, it may have unexpected shortcomings, limiting the adaptive strategic changes that are among the supposed benefits of changing top executives. If outgoing CEOs remain in a group as CEOs of other firms or as board members, it can constrain the new CEO's decision-making power.

For social-political reasons, the continuing presence of the outgoing CEO in a business group constrains an incoming CEO's power to make strategic changes. First, departing CEOs who stay in a group as board members or CEOs of other affiliated firms can be expected to favour the strategies and policies that they have put in place. They are likely to resist any contemplated changes out of a fear that their legacies will be eroded in the event of significant changes (Quigley and Hambrick 2012). Constraints occur not only because of overt power from board members, but also because of an indirect and informal influence associated with the presence of predecessor CEOs in business groups as CEOs of other affiliated firms. The successor may not want to make changes because of a subtle unease associated with undoing the strategies of a predecessor who lingers in a group.

Accordingly, it is proposed that the continuing presence of a predecessor CEO in a business group restricts the new CEO's discretion and thus suppresses the new CEO's strategic change efforts.

Hypothesis 2: The retention of a departing CEO in a business group is negatively associated with the subsequent strategic change of an incoming CEO.

Interaction between departing and incoming CEOs

Before proceeding to our interaction hypothesis involving the departing and incoming CEOs, it is essential to acknowledge that both the departure of an existing CEO and the selection of a new CEO are influenced by a common set of factors – notably, the degree to which the firm believes the change is needed. In other words, predecessors often leave firms in need of some change, while successors often arrive with a strong urge to enact change (Quigley and Hambrick 2012). However, what if old CEOs do not fully depart the scene when new CEOs come from outside to drive strategic changes? What if the lingering old CEO even expressly criticizes the new strategic initiatives proposed by the incoming outside CEO? One might argue that retention of the old CEO generally has a negative effect on a strategic change as hypothesized above; however, outsider succession might have offsetting effects, because externally hired successors are not constrained by the internal social network embeddedness.

CEO turnover and succession mean not only the departure of the old CEO and the selection of a new CEO, but also a change in the social structure in which the departing and incoming CEOs have been embedded. A CEO's intragroup network is composed of his or her connections with other members within the group, such as other top management team members, board members, and executives from other group-affiliated firms. Given this backdrop, we emphasize the strategic importance of the CEO's social networks and develop a hypothesis in order to understand how the combination of the departing CEO retention and the successor CEO's origin leads to strategic changes. Thus, the focus is more on the relative relational positioning of the departing and incoming CEOs within the business group boundary.

Given the retention of predecessor CEOs in business groups, our hypothesis basically compares incoming outsiders with incoming insiders. The combination of the departing CEO retention with insider succession can be characterized by tight coupling. Inside executives have often been selected by predecessors and have close social ties with them; in such conditions, feelings of solidarity and obligation may be strong between the departing and the incoming CEOs and isomorphism within the relationship may decrease diversity (Uzzi 1997). Therefore, such tightly coupled relationships reduce the flow of new ideas into the group, resulting in resistance to change (Adler and Kwon 2002).

On the contrary, the combination of the departing CEO's retention and outsider succession can be characterized by loose coupling. Outsider succession combined with the predecessor's retention will create a relational configuration whereby the internal entrenchment of the predecessor is likely to be counterbalanced by outsider succession. Such a configuration may lead to attenuation or even a reversal of the negative retention effect on strategic change. The predecessor's retention may engender the insulation of a group social network, whereas outsider succession facilitates the flow of new ideas and rejuvenates change imperatives, functioning as an inertia breaker.

Consistent with Hypotheses 1a and 1b in terms of the different outsider types in a business group context, the predecessor retention effect interacts with both in-group outsiders and group outsiders. Moreover, we argue that the negative retention effect in Hypothesis 2 will be attenuated to a greater extent by group outsiders. By and large, the strong strategic inertia developed during predecessors' time in office increases the difficulty of pursuing strategic changes for the incoming outside successors (Shen and Cannella 2002a). Compared to in-group outsiders, group outsiders – because they do not have entrenched social relationships within a group – tend not to be constrained when making the necessary changes in their new firms. Moreover, based on the different knowledge, perspective, and experience outside a group, group outsiders can initiate a strategic move relatively easily in spite of a predecessor's presence in a business group. Accordingly,

Hypothesis 3a: In business groups, the negative effect of the predecessor CEO's retention on a strategic change will be weaker for in-group outsiders than firm insiders.

Hypothesis 3b: In business groups, the negative effect of the predecessor CEO's retention on a strategic change will be weaker for group outsiders than firm insiders.

Hypothesis 3c: In business groups, the negative effect of the predecessor CEO's retention on a strategic change will be weaker for group outsiders than in-group outsiders.

Moderating effect of the global financial crisis

It has long been debated whether or not CEOs are really important in terms of firm strategy and performance (Finkelstein, Hambrick, and Cannella 2009). A breakthrough has come from the concept of managerial discretion, i.e. certain contexts afford CEOs more discretion than others. In other words, a low-discretion context, for instance, the global financial crisis in 2008, permits CEOs marginal discretion over strategic action (Kim, Park, and Kim 2020). The 2008 global financial crisis was catastrophic, affecting various industries as well as countries around the world to different extents. It produced extremely unstable business environments and increased environmental uncertainties globally (Paunov 2012). The global financial crisis created an unfavourable business environment for firms as a whole. Moreover, the crisis imposed pressure on CEOs to avoid bold decisions. When CEOs perceive an environment as threatening or have little confidence, they tend to adopt a defensive stance, leading to a decrease in strategic changes overall.

While acknowledging these constraining effects of crisis on strategic change, we further examined the moderating role of the global financial crisis. To be specific, in the case of crisis and the consequent uncertainty, the managerial discretion of incoming and departing CEOs will be dampened. Thus, in the context of the 2008 global financial crisis, strategic initiatives by CEOs that entailed significant resource allocations would have been restricted. It is, therefore, interesting to compare the period before and after the global financial crisis in order to understand how the strategic change effect of outsider CEOs, as well as departing CEOs' retention effect, changed as a result of the financial crisis.

In general, it is difficult for CEOs to make strategic changes in tumultuous business environments such as the 2008 global financial crisis. However, it is the emergence of crisis where change is badly needed. Therefore, once outside CEO successors are selected, they will not hesitate to pursue new strategic moves, because they have come to the position with an imperative for change. In contrast, the 2008 global financial crisis worked as a constraining moderator for the predecessor retention effect. In general, a predecessor's continuing presence will suppress a new CEO's managerial discretion. However, CEO succession during and after the global financial crisis represented a periodic occasion to realign strategic directions with the change imperatives of the environment, making it difficult for a lingering predecessor to exert explicit and implicit influence. Thus, the global financial crisis tended to dampen the predecessor retention effect, thereby weakening the negative relationship between the predecessor retention and strategic change.

Hypothesis 4: In the post-crisis period, the strategic change effect of the outsider succession has been stronger, whereas the predecessor retention effect on strategic change has been weaker. In other words, Hypotheses 1a and 1b will be more prominent and Hypothesis 2 will be less prominent in the post-crisis period than in the pre-crisis period.

Methods

Data collection and sample

To conduct the empirical analysis of our hypotheses, we compiled a list of the 200 largest companies on the Korea Stock Exchange between 2001 and 2014. We selected larger publicly listed companies for the purpose of data collection. In the wake of the Asian financial crisis in 1998, the Korean government made significant progress in enacting corporate governance reforms in order to increase the transparency of corporate decision-making, particularly in larger publicly listed companies (Chang, Cho, and Shin 2007). Such national regulations have led to larger companies revealing more information to investors than smaller firms. We intentionally focused on manufacturing firms by eliminating financial service companies. Due to different structures in firms' financial statements, the data from financial service companies cannot be integrated with those of manufacturing companies within the same dataset. We further eliminated single companies from our sample, as our study focused on firms that belong to business groups. Through this process, we collected 2,509 observations for the research period, from which we identified 516 CEO turnover cases. After eliminating those CEO turnovers that were related to mandatory retirement, illness, or death, we retained only the non-voluntary CEO turnover cases. Finally, we were able to use only those CEO turnover cases with complete data at the firm-year level for all variables in this study, ending up with a total of 304 turnover cases in our sample.

To collect data for this study, we used the following sources: the Data Analysis, Retrieval and Transfer System (DART) database of Korea's Financial Supervisory Service; the DataGuide database of Korea's FnGuide company; the Korea Integrated News Database System (KINDS); the KIS database of the Korea Investors Service (KIS) company; and the Online Provision Enterprises Information (OPNI) database of the Korea Fair Trade Commission. More specifically, data related to the CEO, board of directors, and company characteristics were obtained from each firm's annual report in the DART database. We defined a firm's CEO as the person who officially signed the cover page of the annual report of the firm available in the DART database. We identified a CEO turnover when the names of the CEOs who signed the annual reports changed in the following year. To keep track of the potential status of both departing and incoming CEOs, we relied on various sources, such as the annual reports of firms and news media articles provided by the

KINDS database. To classify our sample firms as either chaebol or non-chaebol, we relied on the OPNI database of the Korea Fair Trade Commission. Data for firm performance and other financial statements were gathered from the DataGuide and the KIS databases.

Measures

Dependent variable

Conceptually, strategic change indicates the degree to which a firm's strategy varies over time. Building on Finkelstein and Hambrick's (1990) concept, we operationalized subsequent strategic change as the extent to which a firm's strategic resource allocation varies over the three years following a CEO turnover. These resource allocation dimensions included advertising intensity (advertising/sales), research and development intensity (R&D/sales), plant and equipment upgrades (net plant and equipment/gross plant and equipment), overhead efficiency (selling, general, and administrative expenses/sales), inventory levels (inventory/sales), and financial leverage (debt/equity). These six strategic dimensions show the competitive profile of the firm (Westphal, Seidel, and Stewart 2001). Prior research has used these measures because they are important to firm performance and can be controlled by top management. They are also complementary to one another (Haynes and Hillman 2010).

Advertising intensity, R&D intensity, and plant and equipment upgrades were used as indicators of the allocation of firm resources across marketing, innovation, and capacity-expansion activities. Overhead efficiency and inventory levels reflected the structural expenses of the firm whereas financial leverage captured the firm's approach to capital management (Geletkanycz and Hambrick 1997). The data for the six resource allocation dimensions were collected from the DataGuide and the KIS databases. Some of these data were missing in the databases due to a lack of reporting. To mitigate this problem, we used only those firms with complete data for all six resource allocation dimensions.

First, we calculated the variance of a particular resource allocation dimension of a firm over three years and subtracted it from the variance of the industry average value of the resource allocation over the same period. We then computed a composite index of all six resource allocation dimensions in order to form an index of subsequent strategic change. Thus, the greater the composite index of all six resource allocation dimensions following a CEO turnover, the greater the degree to which the firm has undertaken strategic change as a result of CEO change.

Independent variables

Identifying CEO turnovers is a challenging task in succession and governance studies, since firms seldom fully disclose the true reasons behind CEO resignations. Following Wiersema and Zhang (2011), this study took a two-step approach to identify CEO turnovers. We first identified whether and when the sample firms experienced CEO turnovers during the period of 2001–2014. We then assessed the nature of the CEO turnovers in more detail.

Initially, we found 516 CEO succession cases among the 2,509 firm-year observations during the research period based on the DART database. We searched the *KINDS* database for articles on the 516 CEO successions and the subsequent career paths of those involved in the succession cases. We excluded those CEO turnovers that were related to mandatory retirement, illness, or death. For mandatory retirement, we used the age of 64 as a cut-off point following previous research (Shen and Cannella 2002b). We did not find any news release from our content analysis indicating that CEOs had voluntarily left their firms to move to a career path in the public sector. Finally, we collected 304 CEO turnover cases with complete data at the firm-year level for all the variables in our study. With regards to the measurement of CEO successors' origin, an insider CEO successor was defined as one who previously worked for the focal firm for more than two years; if this was not the case, he or she was defined as an outsider CEO successor (Cannella and Lubatkin 1993).

In our sample of 304 CEO turnovers, the origin of incoming CEOs can be divided into firm insiders (n = 175; 57.6% of our sample) versus firm outsiders (n = 129; 42.4%). Firm outsiders can be further divided into in-group outsiders (n = 66; 21.7%) versus group outsiders (n = 63; 20.7%). We measured the in-group outsider variable as a dummy (i.e. 1 if an incoming CEO was a member of any other companies within the business group and 0 otherwise) and did the same with the group outsider variable (i.e. 1 if an incoming CEO was not a member of any companies within the business group and 0 otherwise). Table 1 shows the distribution of incoming CEO origin (i.e. insider, in-group outsider, or group outsider) across the years studied, which was relatively stable during the research period.

Our sample of 304 CEO turnovers can also be classified on the departing CEO side. A large percentage of departing CEOs (n = 104, 34% of our sample) remained within the same business group following the CEO turnover. More specifically, 56 CEOs (18%) remained as a chair or director of the board of directors, and 48 CEOs (16%) became the CEO of other affiliates within the same business group. We measured the retention of the former CEO variable as a dummy: 1 if a departing CEO remained within the same business group following the CEO turnover and 0 otherwise. As shown in Table 1, it appears that the distribution of departing CEO status remained stable during the research period.

Moderating variable

We measured the global financial crisis as a dummy variable: 0 before the crisis (from 2001 to 2008), 1 after the crisis (from 2009 to 2014).

Control variables

Because a variety of factors can influence a firm's subsequent strategic change, we included firm-level, board-level, CEO-level, and year control variables. For the firm-level control variables, we controlled for firm age, firm size, firm profitability, working capital ratio, and chaebol. Firm age was measured as the natural logarithm of years since a firm's year of establishment (Haynes and Hillman 2010). Firm size was measured as the natural logarithm of the total number of employees at the end of the fiscal year, while firm profitability was measured as the return on total assets (Zhang and Rajagopalan 2010). Working capital ratio was measured as working capital divided by total sales. Chaebol was coded as 1 if the firm was affiliated with a chaebol business group listed in the OPNI database of the Korea Fair Trade Commission (Chung and Luo 2013). For the board-level control variables, we controlled for board size and outside director ratio. Board size was measured as the number of board members, and the outside director ratio was measured as the ratio of outside directors to all board members (Shen and Cannella 2002b). For the CEO-level control variables, we controlled for the age and

Table 1. CEO turnover cases across the years from 2001 to 2014.

	2001	2002	2003	2004	2005	2006	2007	2008	2009	2010	2011	2012	2013	2014	Total
Incoming CEO															
Insider	9 (3.0%)[a]	7(2.3%)	15 (4.9%)	19 (6.3%)	11 (3.6%)	17 (5.6%)	9 (3.0%)	11 (3.6%)	9 (3.0%)	14 (4.6%)	11 (3.6%)	22 (7.2%)	11 (3.6%)	10 (3.3%)	175 (57.6%)
In-group outsider	2 (0.7%)	7 (2.3%)	5 (1.6%)	2 (0.7%)	3 (1.0%)	8 (2.6%)	6 (2.0%)	2 (0.7%)	4 (1.3%)	3 (1.0%)	9 (3.0%)	7 (2.3%)	3 (1.0%)	5 (1.6%)	66 (21.7%)
Group outsider	3 (1.0%)	4 (1.3%)	5 (1.6%)	4 (1.3%)	1 (0.3%)	5 (1.6%)	5 (1.6%)	5 (1.6%)	6 (2.0%)	8 (2.6%)	5 (1.6%)	4 (1.3%)	6 (2.0%)	2 (0.7%)	63 (20.7%)
Sum	14 (4.6%)	18 (5.9%)	25 (8.2%)	25 (8.2%)	15 (4.9%)	30 (9.9%)	20 (6.6%)	18 (5.9%)	19 (6.3%)	25 (8.2%)	25 (8.2%)	33 (10.9%)	20 (6.6%)	17 (5.6%)	304 (100%)
Departing CEO															
Remained in BOD	3 (1.0%)	2 (0.7%)	8 (2.6%)	4 (1.3%)	2 (0.7%)	10 (3.3%)	2 (0.7%)	3 (1.0%)	3 (1.0%)	4 (1.3%)	3 (1.0%)	9 (3.0%)	3 (1.0%)	0 (0%)	56 (18.4%)
Remained within the group as the CEO of other affiliates	2 (0.7%)	5 (1.6%)	7 (2.3%)	2 (0.7%)	2 (0.7%)	4 (1.3%)	3 (1.0%)	4 (1.3%)	3 (1.0%)	2 (0.7%)	4 (1.3%)	4 (1.3%)	3 (1.0%)	3 (1.0%)	48 (15.8%)
Departed from the group	9 (3.0%)	11 (3.6%)	10 (3.3%)	19 (6.3%)	11 (3.6%)	16 (5.3%)	15 (4.9%)	11 (3.6%)	13 (4.3%)	19 (6.3%)	18 (5.9%)	20 (6.6%)	14 (4.6%)	14 (4.6%)	200 (65.8%)
Sum	14 (4.6%)	18 (5.9%)	25 (8.2%)	25 (8.2%)	15 (4.9%)	30 (9.9%)	20 (6.6%)	18 (5.9%)	19 (6.3%)	25 (8.2%)	25 (8.2%)	33 (10.9%)	20 (6.6%)	17 (5.6%)	304 (100%)

[a]The numbers in parentheses are the proportion of the CEO turnover cases in our sample.

tenure of the departing CEO. The tenure of the departing CEO was measured as the number of years that he/she had held the position prior to the CEO turnover (Haynes and Hillman 2010). We also controlled for the age and ownership of the incoming CEO. The ownership of the incoming CEO was measured as a dummy: 1 if the CEO was a member of an owning family and 0 otherwise (Shen and Cannella 2002b). Finally, to control for differences in subsequent strategic change due to economic cycles, we included year fixed effects.

Analysis

To examine the causal relationships in the empirical test, we imposed a time lag between the independent and dependent variables. Independent and control variables were measured in year *t*, and the dependent variable was measured from year *t* to year ($t + 2$). We used the generalized least squared (GLS) procedures, which are appropriate for unbalanced panel data analysis, in order to correct for heteroscedasticity and autocorrelated error terms (Lu and Beamish 2004).

Results

Table 2 contains descriptive statistics and correlations among the variables included in this study. To check multicollinearity, this study ran ordinary least squares (OLS) regressions to generate variance inflation factors (VIFs) for all variables. The average VIF value was lower than 2, which is well below the recommended cut-off of 10. Therefore, multicollinearity was not a problem (Chatterjee, Hadi, and Price 2000).

Table 3 provides the results of our analyses. Model 1 of Table 2 is a baseline model consisting of only control variables. We used Model 2 to test Hypotheses 1a and 1b. In Model 2, both in-group outsider and group outsider status had positive and significant effects on subsequent strategic change ($b = .008$, $p < .001$ for in-group outsider; $b = .012$, $p < .001$ for group outsider); these results were relatively stable across the models. These results supported Hypotheses 1a and 1b.

Hypothesis 2 predicted that the retention of a departing CEO in a business group would be negatively associated with a subsequent strategic change. We used Model 3 to test Hypothesis 2. In Model 3, the retention of a former CEO showed a negative and significant effect on a subsequent strategic change ($b = -.005$, $p < .001$). The same result was obtained from Model 4 to Model 6. These results supported Hypothesis 2.

Hypotheses 3a and 3b predicted the interaction effect of the relationship between the retention of the former CEO and the outsider origin on a subsequent strategic change. In Hypotheses 3a and 3b, we predicted that the negative effect of the predecessor CEO's retention on a subsequent strategic change would be weaker for both in-group outsiders and group outsiders compared to firm insiders. We used Model 4 to test Hypotheses 3a and 3b. In Model 4, the interaction between the retention of the former CEO (C) and group outsider (B) had a positive and significant effect on a subsequent strategic change ($b = .018$, $p < .001$), thereby supporting Hypothesis 3b. However, the interaction between the retention of the former CEO (C) and in-group outsider (A) had a positive but insignificant effect ($b = .009$, $p > .05$), failing to support Hypothesis 3a.

Table 2. Descriptive statistics and correlations.

Variables	Mean	Std. Dev	1	2	3	4	5	6	7	8	9	10	11	12	13	14	15
1.Subsequnt strategic change	.023	0.043															
2.Group outsider (incoming CEO)	.207	0.406	.057														
3.In-group outsider (incoming CEO)	.217	0.413	.023	−.269***													
4.Retention of former CEO	.342	0.475	−.026	−.061	.091												
5. Global financial crisis	.457	.499	−.106	.036	.013	−.091											
6.Firm age	42.977	17.679	−.021	−.145*	−.037	−.067	.172**										
7.Firm size	7.609	1.528	.120*	−.031	.009	−.043	.047	.068									
8.Working capital ratio	.042	0.304	−.014	.021	.012	.001	−.011	−.096	−.067								
9.ROA	.007	0.061	.121*	−.070	.069	.029	.112	−.096	.098	−.014							
10.Chaebol	.579	0.495	−.123*	−.238***	.239***	.067	.020	.196***	.222***	−.139*	−.086						
11.Board size	2.104	0.313	.074	−.094	−.032	−.002	−.158**	.012	.241***	−.054	.025	−.046					
12.Outside director ratio	.470	0.259	.049	.023	−.029	.016	.127*	.071	.285***	−.052	.053	.137*	−190***				
13.Age of departing CEO	60.303	4.901	−.077	.002	−.046	−.138*	.186**	.099	.001	−.056	.117*	−.015	.041	−.172*			
14.Tenure of departing CEO	4.373	3.859	.056	−.108	−.103	.123*	−064	−.041	−.133*	.022	.108	−238***	−.029	−.011	.108		
15.Age of incoming CEO	56.855	5.167	−.072	.224***	−.066	−.063	.210***	.128*	.144*	−.127*	−.005	.070	.114*	.053	.144*	−.021	
16.Ownership of incoming CEO	.086	0.280	.038	−.127*	−.047	.052	−.115*	−.024	−.104	−.004	.044	−.049	−.031	−.005	.000	.089	−.434***

n = 304, *$p < .05$; **$p < .01$, ***$p < .001$

In Hypothesis 3 c, we hypothesized that group outsiders would show a stronger interaction effect than in-group outsiders. The Chow test based on Model 4 reveals that the difference in the coefficients between the C*B and C*A variables was positive and significant ($b = .017$, $p < .05$). These results provide support for Hypothesis 3 c.

Hypothesis 4 predicted that the strategic change effect of the outsider succession would be stronger and the predecessor retention effect on strategic change weaker during the post-crisis period. It is worthwhile to note that the global financial crisis was estimated as negative and significant ($b = -.026$, $p < .001$ in Model 5; $b = -.027$, $p < .001$ in Model 6), implying that the level of post-crisis strategic changes has generally been lower than that of pre-crisis changes. Moreover, we found partial support for Hypothesis 4. On one hand, the interaction terms between the global financial crisis and both types of outsiders were estimated as positive and significant ($b = .010$, $p < .001$ for in-group outsider; $b = .011$, $p < .001$ for group outsider in Model 5). On the other hand, the interaction term between the global financial crisis and the retention of a former CEO was estimated as insignificant.

We further examined whether the directions of interaction effects were consistent with Hypotheses 3 and 4. First, the interaction between the origin of the new CEO and the status of the former CEO is illustrated in Figure 1, which is drawn from Model 4 of Table 3. For an insider CEO, the slope of strategic change was estimated as negative (–.008 from .026 to .018), implying there was a negative effect from a former CEO's retention on the strategic changes of an insider CEO. For an in-group outsider CEO, the slope of strategic change was also estimated as negative (–.006 from .032 to .026), but the difference between the two slopes was not significant (.002, $p > .10$). However, for a group outsider CEO, the slope of strategic change became positive and significant (.011 from .026 to .037). These results imply that the negative effect of the predecessor CEO's retention on strategic change becomes weaker for group outsider CEOs than for either insider CEOs or in-group outsider CEOs. Hence, the graphical results in Figure 1 provide support for H3b and H3c.

Furthermore, Figure 2 graphically depicts the moderating effect predicted by Hypothesis 4. Figure 2 shows that the strategic change effects of both types of outsider successions were stronger during the post-crisis period than during the pre-crisis period. By and large, the graphical results in Figure 2 provide partial support for H4.

Supplementary analysis

In order to secure a sufficient sample size for this study, we combined two different cases of former CEO retention: (1) departing CEOs remaining as board members (n = 56), and (2) transfer of departing CEOs to the CEO positions of other affiliate firms within the same business group (n = 48). Although it is not clear which type of former CEO retention has a stronger shadowing power on the incoming CEO, it is possible that the shadowing influences of the former CEO differ between the two types of former CEO retention. Thus, we checked the robustness of our findings by eliminating each type from our sample in turn and then conducting respective supplementary regression analysis. By and large, we found similar results when testing our hypotheses in *both* the sample only including the departing CEOs remaining as board members *and* the sample only including the transfer of departing CEOs to the CEO positions of other affiliate firms. Table 4 provides the

Table 3. Results of regression analysis for subsequent strategic change.

Variables	Model 1	Model 2	Model 3	Model 4	Model 5	Model 6
Constant	.055***	.053***	.044***	.049***	.042***	.045***
Firm age	.000***	.000***	.000***	.000***	.000***	.000***
Firm size	.003***	.003***	.004***	.003***	.003***	.003***
Working capital ratio	−.001	−.001	−.000	−.003**	−.000	−.000
ROA	.079***	.089***	.086***	.067***	.070***	.071***
Chaebol	−.010***	−.010***	−.009***	−.008***	−.008***	−.008***
Board size	.001	.004***	.005***	.002	.003**	.007***
Outside director ratio	.008***	.007***	.006***	.005**	.007***	.010***
Age of departing CEO	−.000***	−.000***	−.000***	−.000***	−.000*	−.000***
Tenure of departing CEO	.000***	.001***	.001***	.001***	.001***	.001***
Age of incoming CEO	−.000***	−.001***	−.001***	−.000***	−.001***	−.001***
Ownership of incoming CEO	.003***	.002*	.001	.000	.000	.001
In-group outsider (A)		.008***	.008***	.006***	.001	−.001
Group outsider (B)		.012***	.012***	.001	.002	−.005***
Retention of former CEO (C)			−.005***	−.007***	−.002**	−.010***
C x A				.001		.005***
C x B				.018***		.020***
Global financial crisis (D)					−.026***	−.027***
D x A					.010***	.011***
D x B					.011***	.017***
D x C					.001	−.000
Wald Chi2	36054.30 ***	15528.53 ***	18634.56 ***	10533.05 ***	764.34 ***	9213.03 ***

n = 304, *p < .05; **p < .01, ***p < .001. Year dummy variables are omitted due to space limit.

supplementary regression analysis for the latter case, confirming that former CEOs can still have a substantial influence even when they move to other affiliate firms within the same business group.

Discussion

This study examined the interaction effect of departing and incoming CEOs on the strategic changes of group-affiliated firms in Korea. We found that both firm-level and group-level outsider successions were significant predictors of strategic change. However, the continuing presence of a departing CEO within a group suppressed the incoming CEO's strategic change initiative. Moreover, we found that group-level outsider succession had a counterbalancing impact on the presence of the departing CEOs within a group, whereas firm-level outsider succession had no impact. These findings not only highlight the importance of taking a business group-level approach when studying the strategic change impact of CEO succession in emerging economies, but also suggest that there are different patterns of interactional dynamics in the influence of outgoing CEOs and the strategic mandates of incoming outsiders.

This study also examined the moderating effect of the 2008 global financial crisis as a contingency variable. We argue that the outsider succession-strategic change relationship depends on the higher-order context of global crisis that can constrain the managerial discretion of a CEO. We found that the strategic change effect of outsider successions was more prominent in the post-crisis period. These results apply for both in-group outsiders and group outsiders. Overall, it was less likely for strategic changes to be made during and after the crisis. Interestingly, however, it was the emergence of the crisis that allowed greater room for outsider CEOs to make post-succession strategic changes.

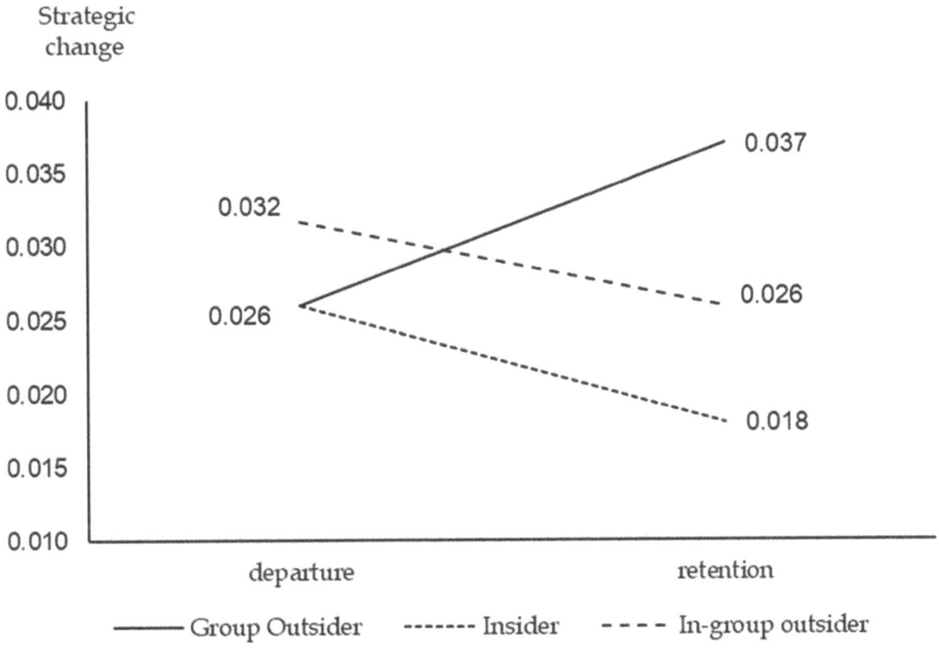

Figure 1. Interaction between the retention of former CEO and the new CEO origin.

Theoretical implication

The evidence supports our proposition that relying solely on firm origin to divide CEO successors into insiders and outsiders neglects prevalent business group structures in emerging economies. Grounded on the business group literature (Chang and Hong 2000; Song, Lee, and Khanna 2016), we distinguished two types of outsider successors – in-group outsiders and group outsiders – according to firm-level versus group-level demarcations. Our findings on the interaction effect (Hypotheses 3a and 3b) show that group outsiders significantly differed from in-group outsiders in their strategic mandates and their reaction to the shadow of departing CEOs, although both were outsiders at the firm level. As the distinction between firm-level outsiders and group-level outsiders is important in the study of business groups from emerging economies, more research is needed regarding the antecedents and consequences of these two types of outsider successors.

In addition, our study has clearly demonstrated that focusing on an incoming CEO alone without considering the departing CEO's status cannot fully or accurately capture the CEO succession effect on strategic change. Our results have corroborated previous findings that a newly appointed CEO's ability to enact strategic change is influenced by whether or not the former CEO stays on as board chair (Nakauchi and Wiersema 2015; Quigley and Hambrick 2012). Our results have also further suggested that the lingering presence of outgoing CEOs within a group as board members or as CEOs of other affiliates hinders the strategic change consequences of CEO succession. However, the weakened negative CEO retention effect caused by new CEOs coming from outside the group is intriguing. Group outsiders are a non-routine case, accounting for only one-fifth of our

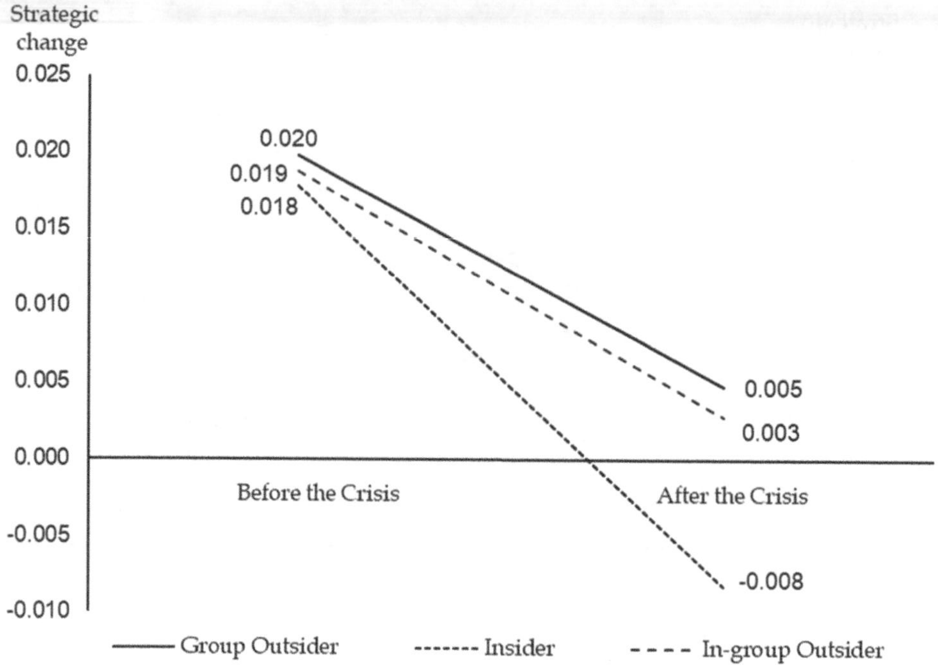

Figure 2. Interaction between the global financial crisis and the new CEO origin.

Table 4. Results of supplementary regression analysis.

Variables	Model 1	Model 2	Model 3	Model 4	Model 5
In-group outsider (A)	.009***	.009***	.005***	−.003**	−.005***
Group outsider (B)	.007***	.008***	−.000	−.001	−.005***
Retention of former CEO (C)		−.008***	−.011***	.001	−.011***
C x A			.009***		.017***
C x B			.042***		.045***
Global financial crisis (D)				−.028***	−.022***
D x A				.019***	.015***
D x B				.016***	.015***
D x C				−.013***	−.011***
Wald Chi2	12870.82 ***	14279.49 ***	2556.09 ***	5619.86 ***	5386.60 ***

n = 248, *p < .05; **p < .01, ***p < .001. Control variables and year dummy variables are omitted due to space limit.

sample. Such cases are infrequent, but when they happen, they have significant ramifications for post-succession strategic change because they are normally accompanied by group-wide support and commitment to strategic redirections.

Practical implication

When a group is committed to a strategic change but a predecessor CEO remains in the group, it is advised that the firm bring on a new CEO from outside the group rather than from within the group in order to gain an outsider's fresh perspective and a CEO with the audacity to break the inertia. Korean business groups are known for their group-level resource sharing and allocations (Chang and Hong 2000). In business groups, particularly where the group headquarters orchestrates strategic directions, the group can evoke constructed crises for group-affiliated firms by bringing on outsider CEOs (Song, Lee, and Khanna 2016). Outsider CEOs can construct an urgency for change in response to poor performance when a firm has lost its competitive standing in the market and in technology. As strategic redirections face strong resistance internally, business groups have to construct crises with external CEOs. Appointing CEOs from outside the group may serve not only as an antidote to inertia but also as a means to shift strategic orientation.

Relatedly, our results have shown the contrasting views on group-level transfers of executives. Korean business groups frequently use executive transfers across group headquarters and group-affiliated firms (Song, Lee, and Khanna 2016), thereby generating resource utilization benefits at the group level. This view is consistent with previous findings that business groups are efficient in minimizing the transaction costs stemming from the market failures prevalent in emerging economies (Khanna and Palepu 2010). Although the system helps inculcate an internal labour market within the group, the internal transfer of executives apparently has a downside (Bidwell and Keller 2014). Our results also showed the constraining effect of the predecessor CEO's retention on strategic change. In other words, as long as the predecessor is on the scene, the new CEO must put a host of actions on hold even when eager to enact some changes (Quigley and Hambrick 2012). If such a scenario occurs, business groups, as a whole, will have difficulties staying nimble and flexible in strategy execution. Our study has highlighted the benefits of hiring CEOs from outside the group in such circumstances.

Limitations

This study has several limitations. Given our focus on advancing a more nuanced framework for understanding the outsider succession–strategic change relationships in the presence of the predecessor CEO in a group, we did not address the performance implications of this relationship. Future research should investigate how outsider CEO succession, predecessor CEO retention, and the interplay of the two affect other executive changes and firm performance. Another related limitation is that, like other large sample and longitudinal studies of CEO succession, our study did not directly observe the interactional dynamics between new outsider CEOs and the lingering predecessor CEOs. Do retained predecessors exert an indirect influence on new CEOs? Do outsider successors hold back certain change initiatives in order not to offend their predecessors? It might be fruitful to examine how new outsider CEOs work around the implicit constraints imposed by their retained predecessors.

Finally, although this study focuses on the impact of CEO succession on strategic change, strategic change momentum may in turn lead to CEO turnover in both the firm and the business group as a whole. Future studies should address the complex nature of recursive relationships between CEO succession and strategic change.

Conclusion

Our study has provided empirical evidence of the restrictive effects of a predecessor's retention on strategic change. By showing that successors from outside the group still undertake strategic changes even in the presence of predecessors in the group, we have presented an interplay between departing and incoming CEOs, providing insights for both researchers and practitioners. Our study also points to the need to consider not only firm-level but also group-level boundary conditions when studying CEO succession in emerging economies.

Acknowledgements

We wish to thank Naon Park at KCGS (Korea Corporate Governance Service) for help with data collection. We also acknowledge the insightful comments and suggestions of three anonymous reviewers and the guidance of Ingyu Oh, Associate Editor of *Asia Pacific Business Review*.

Funding

This work was supported by the Ministry of Education of the Republic of Korea and the National Research Foundation of Korea [NRF-2020S1A5A2A01047075].

References

Adler, P. S., and S.-W. Kwon. 2002. "Social Capital: Prospects for a New Concept." *Academy of Management Review* 27: 17–41. doi:10.5465/amr.2002.5922314.

Bidwell, M., and J. R. Keller. 2014. "Within or Without? How Firms Combine Internal and External Labor Markets to Fill Jobs." *Academy of Management Journal* 57 (4): 1035–1055. doi:10.5465/amj.2012.0119.

Burt, R. S. 1992. *Structural Holes: The Social Structure of Competition*. Cambridge: Harvard University Press.

Cannella, A. A., and M. Lubatkin. 1993. "Succession as a Sociopolitical Process: Internal Impediments to Outsider Selection." *Academy of Management Journal* 36 (4): 763–793.

Cao, Q., L. M. Maruping, and R. Takeuchi. 2006. "Disentangling the Effects of CEO Turnover and Succession on Organizational Capabilities: A Social Network Perspective." *Organization Science* 17 (5): 563–576. doi:10.1287/orsc.1060.0201.

Chang, J. J., Y. J. Cho, and H. H. Shin. 2007. "The Change in Corporate Transparency of Korean Firms after the Asian Financial Crisis: An Analysis Using Analysts' Forecast Data." *Corporate Governance: An International Review* 15 (6): 1144–1167. doi:10.1111/j.1467-8683.2007.00637.x.

Chang, S. J., and J. Hong. 2000. "Economic Performance of Group-affiliated Companies in Korea: Intragroup Resource Sharing and Internal Business Transactions." *Academy of Management Journal* 43 (3): 429–448.

Chatterjee, S., A. S. Hadi, and B. Price. 2000. *Regression Analysis by Examples*. NY: Wiley.

Chung, C.-N., and S. R. Luo. 2013. "Leadership Succession and Firm Performance in an Emerging Economy: Successor Origin, Relational Embeddedness, and Legitimacy." *Strategic Management Journal* 34: 338–357. doi:10.1002/smj.2011.

Coleman, J. S. 1988. "Social Capital in the Creation of Human Capital." *American Journal of Sociology* 94: 95–120. doi:10.1086/228943.

Finkelstein, S., and D. C. Hambrick. 1990. "Top-management-team Tenure and Organizational Outcomes: The Moderating Role of Managerial Discretion." *Administrative Science Quarterly* 35 (3): 484–503. doi:10.2307/2393314.

Finkelstein, S., D. C. Hambrick, and A. A. Cannella. 2009. *Strategic Leadership: Theory and Research on Executives, Top Management Teams, and Boards*. Strategic Management Series. New York: Oxford University Press.

Geletkanycz, M. A., and D. C. Hambrick. 1997. "The External Ties of Top Executives: Implications for Strategic Choice and Performance." *Administrative Science Quarterly* 42: 654–681. doi:10.2307/2393653.

Gerlach, M. L. 1992. "The Japanese Corporate Network: A Blockmodel Analysis." *Administrative Science Quarterly* 37: 105–139. doi:10.2307/2393535.

Granovetter, M. 1992. "Problems of Explanation in Economic Sociology." In *Networks and Organizations: Structure, Form and Action*, edited by N. Nohria and R. G. Eccles, 25–56. Boston: Harvard Business School Press.

Granovetter, M. 1995. "Coase Revisited: Business Groups in the Modern Economy." *Industrial and Corporate Change* 4 (1): 93–140. doi:10.1093/icc/4.1.93.

Hambrick, D. C., and S. Finkelstein. 1987. "Managerial Discretion: A Bridge between Polar Views of Organizational Outcomes." *Research in Organizational Behavior* 9: 369–406.

Haynes, K. T., and A. Hillman. 2010. "The Effect of Board Capital and CEO Power on Strategic Change." *Strategic Management Journal* 31 (11): 1145–1163. doi:10.1002/smj.859.

Joh, S. W., and J.-Y. Jung. 2018. "When Do Firms Benefit from Affiliated outside Directors? Evidence from Korea." *Corporate Governance International Review* 26 (6): 397–413. doi:10.1111/corg.12224.

Karaevli, A. 2007. "Performance Consequences of New CEO 'Outsiderness': Moderating Effects of Pre-and Post-succession Contexts." *Strategic Management Journal* 28: 681–706. doi:10.1002/smj.589.

Karaevli, A., and E. J. Zajac. 2013. "When Do Outsider CEOs Generate Strategic Change? The Enabling Role of Corporate Stability." *Journal of Management Studies* 50 (7): 1267–1294. doi:10.1111/joms.12046.

Khanna, T., and K. Palepu. 2010. *Winning in Emerging Markets*. Boston, MA: Harvard Business Press.

Kim, J., J.-H. Park, and C. Kim. 2020. "CEO Overseas Experience and Firm Internationalization: Before and after the Global Financial Crisis." *Journal of Korea Trade* 24 (7): 54–72.

Kim, Y., and A. A. Cannella. 2008. "Social Capital among Corporate Upper Echelons and Its Impacts on Executive Promotion in Korea." *Journal of World Business* 43 (1): 85–96. doi:10.1016/j.jwb.2007.10.009.

Lu, J. W., and P. W. Beamish. 2004. "International Diversification and Firm Performance: The S-curve Hypothesis." *Academy of Management Journal* 47 (4): 598–609.

Nakauchi, M., and M. F. Wiersema. 2015. "Executive Succession and Strategic Change in Japan." *Strategic Management Journal* 36 (2): 298–306. doi:10.1002/smj.2255.

Paunov, C. 2012. "The Global Crisis and Firms Investments in Innovation." *Research Policy* 41 (1): 24–35. doi:10.1016/j.respol.2011.07.007.

Quigley, T. J., and D. C. Hambrick. 2012. "When the Former CEO Stays on as Board Chair: Effects on Successor Discretion, Strategic Change, and Performance." *Strategic Management Journal* 33 (7): 834–859. doi:10.1002/smj.1945.

Shen, W., and A. A. Cannella. 2002a. "Revisiting the Performance Consequences of CEO Succession: The Impacts of Successor Type, Postsuccession Senior Executive Turnover, and Departing CEO Tenure." *Academy of Management Journal* 45 (4): 717–733.

Shen, W., and A. A. Cannella. 2002b. "Power Dynamics within Top Management and Their Impacts on CEO Dismissal Followed by inside Succession." *Academy of Management Journal* 45 (6): 1195–1206.

Shin, J. Y., J.-H. Hyun, S. Oh, and H. Yang. 2018. "The Effects of Politically Connected outside Directors on Firm Performance: Evidence from Korean Chaebol Firms." *Corporate Governance: An International Review* 26: 23–44. doi:10.1111/corg.12203.

Song, J., K. Lee, and T. Khanna. 2016. "Dynamic Capabilities at Samsung: Optimizing Internal Co-opetition." *California Management Review* 58 (4): 118–140. doi:10.1525/cmr.2016.58.4.118.

Uzzi, B. 1996. "The Sources and Consequences of Embeddedness for the Economic Performance of Organizations: The Network Effects." *American Sociological Review* 61: 674–698. doi:10.2307/2096399.

Uzzi, B. 1997. "Social Structure and Competition in Interfirm Networks: The Paradox of Embeddedness." *Administrative Science Quarterly* 42: 35–67. doi:10.2307/2393808.

Westphal, J. D., M. D. L. Seidel, and K. J. Stewart. 2001. "Second-order Imitation: Uncovering Latent Effects of Board Network Ties." *Administrative Science Quarterly* 46 (4): 717–747. doi:10.2307/3094829.

Wiersema, M. F., and Y. A. N. Zhang. 2011. "CEO Dismissal: The Role of Investment Analysts." *Strategic Management Journal* 32 (11): 1161–1182. doi:10.1002/smj.932.

Zhang, Y., and N. Rajagopalan. 2010. "Once an Outsider, Always an Outsider? CEO Origin, Strategic Change, and Firm Performance." *Strategic Management Journal* 31 (3): 334–346. doi:10.1002/smj.812.

Remains on the board: outside directors' behaviour and their survival chance in Korean firms

Taeyoung Yoo and Yunsung Koh

ABSTRACT

Korean firms, often represented by a business group or chaebol, have adopted and increased outside directors owing to the government's initiative for corporate governance reform. However, their monitoring role has been criticized as rubber-stamping. This study extends the literature, which explains outside directors' ineffectiveness in terms of their focus on advising roles over monitoring ones, by pitting these directors' behaviours against their roles. It argues that their behavioural characteristics, i.e. proactive versus conformist, affect their chance of survival on the board and subsequently influence firm performance. Analysing both survey and accounting data on 157 outside directors in Korean listed firms, this study finds that outside directors have a lower survival chance when they proactively perform their roles regardless of whether this involves monitoring or advising. However, when they survive, their proactive behaviour increases Tobin's q. This study further investigates how to improve the lower survival chance for proactive outside directors, and sheds light on the moderating roles of power such as foreign ownership (for firms with higher growth opportunities) and outside directors' valuable knowledge and experience such as elite MBA degrees (for firms with lower growth opportunity). This study discusses the theoretical and practical implications for outside directors' behaviour and firm performance as a result of corporate governance reform in Korean firms.

Introduction

Studies on corporate governance have emphasized the importance of outside directors' monitoring role to firm performance (Deutsch, Keil, and Laamanen 2011; Huang and Chan 2018; Lim and McCann 2013). Subsequently, South Korean (hereafter Korean) firms have increased their number of outside directors since 1998, as part of the corporate governance reform initiated by the government (Yoo and Rhee 2013). However, as illustrated by corporate scandals during the 2000 s, it is difficult to say that outside directors satisfactorily fulfil their monitoring roles (Yoo 2017; Yoo and Jung 2015). Some studies have even reported that outside directors who hold similar positions in other firms cause shareholder discontent with regard to monitoring (Hillman et al. 2011).

Faced with the gap between theoretical expectations and firm practices, extant studies have focused on outside directors' roles (Bolino et al. 2008; Westphal and Stern 2007) and their sociopolitical connections (Carcello et al. 2011). For instance, those who focus on monitoring roles are less likely to be (re)appointed on the board than those who assume advisory roles. Furthermore, outside directors' personal connections on the board drive them to support and approve managerial decisions rather than monitor and refute them. These explanations indicate that firms (i.e. members such as CEOs who appoint outside directors) generally prefer outside directors to hold supporting roles rather than monitoring ones, and consequently attenuate the agency theory's expectation for monitoring (Udueni 1999).

Nevertheless, the current studies still have some limitations in terms of understanding the unsatisfactory performance of outside directors: 1) incomplete analysis of behavioural characteristics in comparative terms regarding roles; 2) insufficient implication of behavioural characteristics for firm performance; and 3) limited suggestion for effective mechanisms for outside directors to implement their expected roles. First, the critical issue in conducting expected roles might not be the firms' preference for advisory roles. Outside directors' rubber-stamping behaviour, i.e. their unconditional support for managerial decisions without any scrutiny (Herman 1981), matters regardless of whether they are in monitoring or advisory roles. Second, as a performance outcome of the first issue, if a board comprises outside directors who largely conduct their roles through supporting behaviour, the focal firm's performance might suffer. Third, we should alternatively draw on sustainable mechanisms that will help outside directors to implement their expected roles even under specific behavioural characteristics or the influence of CEOs.

This study proposes that behavioural characteristics are divided into two types: proactive and conformist. Proactive outside directors might often collide with CEOs and managers, and hence are less likely to survive on the board. The lower survival chance for proactive outside directors, who will improve firm performance if they can survive, might be an important reason for the disappointing performance of outside directors in Korean firms' corporate governance reform. This study investigates the mechanisms that will help proactive outside directors to survive on their board. External mechanisms, such as foreign investors who are less likely to be affected by managerial power, and indigenous resources, such as those with the valuable experiences and knowledge indispensable for CEOs' performance, could improve the survival chance for outside directors who proactively conduct their roles.

To conduct an empirical analysis, this study has employed both survey and accounting data on 157 outside directors who worked at publicly trading firms in Korea during the 2000–2013 period. Since the mid-1990 s, the Korean government has enforced corporate governance reform, and firms have adopted outside directors on their boards. Nevertheless, the contributions of outside directors are controversial. This might be because Korean firms choose outside directors in order to align with their own interests. For instance, they might (re)appoint outside directors who are conformist rather than proactive in conducting their roles. Furthermore, outside directors in Korean firms tend to have strong personal connections to CEOs or other board members in the focal firm, such as having studied at university together. This phenomenon provides a valuable opportunity for investigating the effects of outside directors' behavioural characteristics (proactive vs. conformist) on their survival and on the firm's subsequent performance in comparative terms regarding their expected roles (monitoring vs. advising).

The rest of this paper is organized as follows. The second section reviews the literature on outside directors and their behavioural characteristics and develops the hypotheses. The next two sections describe the data and methodology and report the empirical outcomes. The concluding section features a discussion of the theoretical and practical implications for effective outside directorships, with remarks on directions for future research.

Theoretical background and hypotheses

Outside directors' expected roles and actual practices

Agency theory explains that the separation of ownership and control in modern firms indispensably leads to conflicting interests between shareholders and managers; it thus calls for consolidation of monitoring mechanisms (Jensen 2001). Enhanced monitoring mechanisms will control the improper behaviour of managers and improve shareholders' wealth. For this reason, regulatory practices, such as the Sarbanes-Oxley Act in the US and the Commercial Act in Korea, have emphasized the roles of outside directors. As non-management members of the board (Johnson, Daily, and Ellstrand 1996), outside directors have substantially increased in number in Korea, as well as in the US (Gordon 2007), Germany and Japan (Yoshikawa, Tsui-Auch, and McGuire 2007).

The literature has suggested that outside directors critically affect firms' decision making and performance, such as their investment decisions and Tobin's q (Barnhart, Marr, and Rosenstein 1994; Gillette, Noe, and Rebello 2008; Hillman, Nicholson, and Shropshire 2008). Outside directors' independence helps them to evaluate corporate decision-making separately from corporate routines and obsession with short-term outcomes, thus contributing to firm performance. Furthermore, given that outside directors have accumulated valuable experiences and knowledge from their services to other firms or other industries, their role in acquiring relevant resources is critical (Hillman and Dalziel 2003) and their network ties expedite knowledge transfer (Westphal, Seidel, and Stewart 2001). The expansion of a firm's boundaries through outside directors also helps the firm to fundraise efficiently and to improve the learning experience for innovation (Yoo and Sung 2015).

However, the effects of outside directors on performance are not conclusive (Adams, Hermalin, and Weisbach 2010; Dalton et al. 1998; de Andrés, Arranz-Aperte, and Rodriguez-Sanz 2017). In the US, outside directors' role is often criticized as rubber-stamping (Herman 1981). Their appointment is a result of personal connections and ingratiation (Westphal and Stern 2007). The gap between outside directors' expected roles and actual practices is also prevalent in Korean firms. Outside directors have connections with CEOs or controlling family members of the focal firms and consequently do not conduct effective monitoring roles (Biz 2020; Weekly Donga 2015). They are negatively or not significantly related to firm performance indicators such as ROA, Tobin's q and shareholder returns (Yoo and Jung 2015).

Outside directors' ineffectiveness and role-based explanations

Regarding outside directors' unsatisfactory performance, previous studies have distinguished their roles: while they are expected to conduct both monitoring and advisory roles, those who focus on the latter are more likely to receive additional board appointments (Westphal and Stern 2007). This implies that outside directors' inclination towards advisory roles rather than monitoring roles leads to a higher chance of survival on the board. Outside directors' personal and sociopolitical connections with their appointers is another cause of their unsatisfactory performance (Khatri, Tsang, and Begley 2006). Those with such connections are called grey directors (Klein 1998), as the connections obscure the identity of the outside directors, placing them somewhere between vigilant monitors and friendly colleagues (Golden-Biddle and Rao 1997). These connections subsequently constrain their independence and limit the fulfilment of their monitoring role.

While the literature explains the causes of outside directors' ineffectiveness, it still has some limitations in terms of understanding the behavioural characteristics of outside directors when conducting monitoring roles: the preference of advisory roles to monitoring roles could imply that CEOs will distance themselves from those who try to constrain their discretions, regardless of whether the outside directors are inclined towards monitoring or advisory roles. An empirical analysis suggests that CEOs offer personal and professional favours to security analysts who provide positive ratings for their firms, while retaliating against those who report negative information (Westphal and Clement 2008). Furthermore, the analysis shows that analysts who are aware of their peers' loss of favour from CEOs restrain themselves from downgrading the firms.

CEOs' preference for conformity and the self-restraint of analysts can be explained by the lens of reciprocity (Herman 1981; Ma and Khanna 2016; Wade, O'Reilly, and Chandratat 1990). Reciprocity explains why outside directors avoid constraining CEOs when conducting their expected roles, regardless of whether they are monitoring or advisory. Such constraints could harm the exchange relationship between the outside directors and the appointers, who tend to be CEOs or controlling family members of the focal firms. If an outside director constrains a CEO, the CEO will deprive him of something valuable such as his directorship. Therefore, outside directors are likely to endorse whatever the firm or CEO requests, regardless of whether their role is advisory or monitoring. This indicates that outside directors might not even be effective in conducting advisory roles. The implication of behavioural characteristics, such as constraining or conforming, for advisory roles further encourages us to investigate behaviour in comparative terms regarding roles.

Behaviour vs. role on the board

The discussion above suggests two critical issues regarding the behavioural characteristics of outside directors on the board. First, these behavioural characteristics (proactive vs. conformist) could overwhelm the effects of their expected roles (monitoring vs. advising) in terms of predicting who will survive on the board. By definition, proactive characteristics indicate energetic and somewhat aggressive participation, constraining or enforcing, while conformist ones denote a willingness to act together for the common benefit and consequently to provide favourable actions in an unquestioning manner, such as granting whatever is desired by CEOs. In other words, appointers such as CEOs might deliberately reappoint those who display unquestioningly supporting behaviours rather than those who proactively participate in decision processes, regardless of whether their roles are monitoring or advising. In this case, monitoring roles conducted in a conformist way will positively affect outside directors' chance of survival on the board, while advisory roles implemented in a proactive way will have a negative impact on their survival chance.

Second, and consequently, those who do not want to lose their places on the board will restrain themselves from behaving proactively, as proactive behaviour could be interpreted as aggressive or even constraining or enforcing (Lorsch and MacIver 1989; Molm 2003). A previous study suggests that ingratiation and flattery are a noteworthy behaviour used by outside directors to maintain their places on the board (Stern and Westphal 2010). In this study, however, outside directors' behavioural characteristics, whether proactive or conformist, do not have to reach the level of value consensus (ingratiation) or complimentary remarks (flattery). Ingratiation and flattery are interpreted as vigorous and intentional acts, deliberately used when aiming for success. In contrast, conformist behaviour (e.g. granting whatever is desired by CEOs) is a relatively passive act, and thus can be generally applicable to the behavioural characteristics of outside directors on the board.

It is notable that outside directors' self-interested restraint from proactive behaviours can occur in both monitoring and advising roles. Recent empirical studies have highlighted the two issues: human beings are presupposed to show punitive reactions to negative or uncooperative behaviour (Carpenter, Matthews, and Ong'ong'a 2004; Friedman and Singh 2004), which could be greater than expected when economic interests are involved (Fehr and Gachter 2000). CEOs may feel that outside directors' active participation is restrictive, rather than supportive of their decision-making. With advisory roles, for instance, they may see suggestions for alternative ideas and more comments than requested as a constraining pressure rather than a friendly endorsement. Furthermore, CEOs benefit from the merciless sacking of uncooperative exchange partners (outside directors in this study), because this kind of retaliatory action or the mere possibility of it may encourage more favourable behaviour in the future among other uncooperative exchange partners (Crombag, Rassin, and Horselenberg 2003; McCullough 2008).

Outside directors' behavioural characteristics mean that those who are conformist rather than proactive will dominate the board, regardless of whether they fulfil monitoring or advisory roles. This study thus raises the following hypotheses:

H1a: Proactive behaviour by outside directors will have a negative effect on their chance of survival on the board, regardless of whether they are in monitoring or advisory roles.

H1b: Conformist behaviour by outside directors will have a positive effect on their chance of survival on the board, regardless of whether they are in monitoring or advisory roles.

Outside directors' behavioural characteristics and firm performance

Both monitoring and advisory roles carried out by outside directors are critical for improving firm performance. Monitoring roles discipline CEOs' and other managers' self-interested decision-making against diverse stakeholders, while advisory roles provide valuable resources for idea shaping and strategy implementation (Kemp 2006). However, if the outside directors' behavioural characteristics are not sufficient to perform their expected roles, e.g. if they simply provide unquestioning consent or consolidate friendship ties, then their role implementation will hardly contribute to firm performance, regardless of whether they focus on advisory or monitoring roles.

This scepticism indicates that outside directors' rubber-stamping behaviour will support managerial decisions without scrutinizing them (Herman 1981). A moderate approach describes these behavioural characteristics as ingratiatory, comprising subtle forms of flattery and opinion conformity (Stern and Westphal 2010). It is notable that such behavioural characteristics are related to the fulfilment of outside directors' expected roles in terms of firm performance. This study thus proposes the following hypotheses:

H2a: The effect of proactive behaviour by outside directors on firm performance will be positive, particularly if they survive on the board, regardless of whether they conduct monitoring or advisory roles.

H2b: The effect of conformist behaviour by outside directors on firm performance will be negative, regardless of whether they conduct monitoring or advisory roles.

Sustainable mechanisms for outside directors' proactive behaviour

Previous studies have suggested some contingent mechanisms for promoting outside directors' role implementation: compensation schemes such as stock options (Lim and McCann 2013); social and organizational identities (Hillman, Nicholson, and Shropshire 2008); and status (Veltrop et al. 2017).

First, the incentive scheme indicates that stock options are effective in compromising the self-serving interests of outside directors in terms of performing their expected roles (Deutsch, Keil, and Laamanen 2011). Outside directors with stock options will increase firms' risk taking, measured by Tobin's q and R&D investment. In particular, relative stock options that positively depart from the prior option grant are critical in incentivizing outside directors to support risky investment (Lim and McCann 2013). Second, the suggestions of social and organizational identities highlight that those who develop and utilize multiple identities can effectively perform their monitoring and advisory roles by alternating their identities according to functional contexts. Outside directors can simultaneously maintain their monitoring roles and friendship ties on the board by managing their required identities in this way. Third, the status of outside directors, which accrues from their personal assets or the corporate and social entities that they serve, affects the extent to which they can uphold independence. Outside directors with high status can resist pressures from other stakeholders and initiate strategic changes that constrain corporate routines and CEOs' discretion.

Nevertheless, there are a couple of limitations in the suggestions: they are easily affected by other factors, such as controlling shareholders (chaebol in this study) and powerful CEOs. Ownership concentration and powerful CEOs with large stock options weaken the effects of outside directors' stock ownership on risk-taking (Lim and McCann 2013). In addition, incentive schemes might not be attractive for capable outside directors; alternatively, they might promote unethical behaviours by outside directors and eventually harm various stakeholders in the firm (Certo et al. 2008). Social and organizational identities could also contradict the theoretical expectation. A study has reported that government officials who serve on firm boards show different behaviours in their monitoring roles: they are active in private firms, but not active in state-owned firms (Zhu and Yoshikawa 2016). This implies that consistent implementation of monitoring role is not an easy task. Furthermore, outside directors with high status will not join firms in trouble, since such behaviours could leave them isolated in their professional communities (Diestre, Rajagopalan, and Dutta 2015).

In contrast, some extant studies on the effectiveness of corporate governance have emphasized the mechanisms that provide relative power against controlling shareholders or CEOs (Anderson and Reeb 2004). This study thus calls for a focus on additional mechanisms that could discourage conformist behaviour among outside directors or facilitate their proactive behaviour. Given that some mechanisms, such as foreign ownership and valuable experiences and knowledge on the part of outside directors, are relatively sustainable vis-à-vis the power of controlling shareholders and CEOs, they will help proactive outside directors to maintain their places on the board.

First, foreign ownership functions as an influential shareholder because it often consists of institutional rather than individual investors (Aggarwal, Klapper, and Wysocki 2005). Foreign ownership is accompanied by significant voting rights, though these may not constitute controlling power; it also upholds shareholder-oriented values, such as returns on investment, and can effectively challenge the self-serving behaviour of controlling shareholders or CEOs (Bradshaw, Bushee, and Miller 2004). Thus, foreign ownership adjusts the power imbalance between outside directors and controlling shareholders or CEOs, regardless of whether the preference is to sell shares in invested firms or maintain them (Yoo and Rhee 2013).

Another point to note is that foreign ownership is relatively free from the social connections that underpin the tacit compliance between outside directors and CEOs/other stakeholders (Ferreira and Matos 2008). With strong incentives to monitor CEOs' behaviour in order to achieve investment returns (Desender et al. 2016), foreign shareholders' weak social connections help them maintain a distance from the influence of controlling shareholders. The information asymmetry faced by foreign ownership, due to cultural and institutional barriers and difficulties in accessing internal corporate information, is another element encouraging outside directors to be proactive in their roles (Yoo and Koh 2014).

Motivations and disadvantages will encourage foreign shareholders to take tougher positions in monitoring and supporting outside directors' proactive behaviour. Given that foreign investors are more positively associated with strategic investments when growth opportunities are present than when they are absent (David et al. 2006), foreign shareholders' tough stance in monitoring is particularly strong when firms show high growth opportunity, i.e. a high level of investment risk, which puts the investment at a critical point. Therefore, this study explores the following hypothesis:

H3a: Foreign ownership will moderate (increase) the survival chance of outside directors who show proactive behaviour and (decrease) that of outside directors who show conformist behaviour, particularly in firms with high growth opportunity.

Another mechanism for proactivity in outside directors is constituted by the valuable resources that are indispensable to a firm's or CEO's performance (Hambrick, Misangyi, and Park 2015). CEOs who have power or interlocked ties with high-status firms will override other directors' opinion (Zhu and Chen 2015). However, opportunism decreases when resource complementarity and symmetric dependence are constructed among business partners (Ali and Larimo 2016). If outside directors can provide intangible experiences and knowledge that cannot be easily substituted, even powerful CEOs will realize the need to utilize these intellectual assets and tolerate the proactive behaviour and constraints on their discretion. This is particularly effective for firms that are experiencing stagnant growth and thus need to utilize external resources in order to escape turbulent contexts (Villanueva-Villar, Rivo-López, and Lago-Peñas 2016). In such cases, outside directors do not have to exploit 'ingratiation comprising flattery, opinion conformity, and favour-rendering' (Westphal and Stern 2006, 169) in order to maintain their places on the board. Therefore, although the motivation to punish those who behave proactively and somewhat aggressively may still be stronger than the motivation to reward those who show helpful behaviour (Charness and Rabin 2000; Westphal and Clement 2008, 879), outside directors who provide valuable resources will improve their chance of survival on the board despite their proactive behaviours. This study thus suggests the following hypothesis:

H3b: Outside directors' valuable experiences and knowledge will moderate (increase) their survival chance if they show proactive behaviour and decrease it if they show conformist behaviour, particularly in firms with low growth opportunity.

Methods

Sample and data collection

The dataset in this study consists of primary (survey) and secondary (personal and accounting) data. The survey data, collected from November 2013 to September 2014, comprises outside directors at Korean listed firms. Since 2000, large Korean firms have been obliged to appoint outside directors in more than half of the positions on their boards. According to commercial law, outside directors cannot work for more than two firms at a time; this rule has been in effect since April 2013. Therefore, the list of outside directors from 2000 to 2013 was constructed from the DART (data analysis, retrieval and transfer) system of the Financial Supervisory Service. Due to contact information availability, a survey questionnaire was sent to 723 outside directors via email, with a courtesy letter that did not explain the purpose of the survey. The final respondent sample comprised 157 outside directors (response rate 21.7%). The years of data for each outside director were different, since they had served for different periods. Their socio-demographic details, such as gender, age, and elite MBA degrees, are presented in Table 1. To test sample representation, this study performed mean t-tests to assess the difference between respondents and non-respondents in terms of socio-demographic variables. The results showed that respondents were not significantly different from non-respondents.

The secondary data comprises outside directors' personal information and the accounting information of the firms where they had worked or were working. Due to the different working periods of the directors, the time window of the data spans from 2000 to 2013. The accounting data were collected from the databases of KISVALUE (www.kisvalue.com) and FnGuide (www.fnguide.com), which provide firm-level information based on the annual reports and audit results of each company. Personal information,

Table 1. Socio-demographic statistics of respondents.

Items	Observable conditions N = 157 (%)
Gender	
Female	2 (1.3)
Male	155 (98.7)
Age mean	56.2
Between 30 ~ 39	3 (1.9)
Between 40 ~ 49	14 (8.9)
Between 50 ~ 59	92 (58.6)
Over 60s	48 (30.6)
Elite undergraduate	
Yes	113 (72.0)
No	44 (28.0)
Elite MBA	
Yes	17 (10.8)
No	140 (89.2)
Industries	
High-tech	29 (18.5)
Medium high-tech	39 (24.8)
Medium low-tech	20 (12.7)
Others	69 (44.0)

such as age, gender, and academic backgrounds, were also collected from the database of the Korea Listed Companies Association (KLCA).

Measures

The dependent variable was measured by *whether an outside director stayed on the board* after her/his term was up. The variable was a dummy, set to 1 if a focal director stayed on the board for another year after her/his term was up and 0 otherwise. The data were hand-calculated from the data source, KLCA.

The independent variables were measured by survey data. Referring to the literature (Stern and Westphal 2010; Westphal and Stern 2007), the questionnaires on outside directors' behavioural characteristics were constructed following face-to-face interviews with three outside directors and three professors and finalized by a ten-person pilot test. Outside directors assume two basic roles: monitoring and advising. These roles can be conducted in a proactive or conformist way. In different situations, the roles can be conducted in different ways. Thus, this study used four independent variables.

Three questions were asked to capture each variable. (1) *Proactive monitoring*: 1) 'When examining agendas, I request that the person in charge be present and explain them in detail'; 2) 'I request that the focal firm report how they implemented the board decisions and the outcomes'; and 3) 'I request that the focal firm provide relevant information in advance of board meetings'. (2) *Conformist monitoring*: 1) 'When examining agendas, I respect the focal firm's intention as a priority'; 2) 'When examining agendas, I consider the business schedule set by the focal firm to be best'; and 3) 'I make sure my monitoring role does not collide with the business strategy of the focal firm'. (3) *Proactive advising*: 1) 'I try to provide alternative suggestions that the managers have not considered'; 2) 'I try to comment as often as possible'; and 3) 'I often suggest critical perspectives'. (4) *Conformist advising*: 1) 'I try my best to provide harmonious suggestions when requested'; 2) 'I provide advice from an early stage in order to avoid conflict'; and 3) 'I ask the focal firm whether it needs my advice'. All the items were measured on a 5-point Likert-type scale, ranging from 1 (strongly disagree) to 5 (strongly agree).

The second group of independent variables comprised sustainable mechanisms for proactive outside directors: *foreign ownership* and *elite MBA degree*. Foreign ownership was measured by the proportion of shares owned by foreign investors, which will show the change of ownership structure in a firm (Yoo and Koh 2014). Another moderating variable, outside directors' valuable experiences and knowledge, was measured by whether the outside director held an elite MBA degree. Previous studies, e.g. Westphal and Stern (2006), treated elite MBA degrees as social networks, which acted to reduce social uncertainty on the board. However, this study focuses on the dimensions of their resources and status (Akerlof 1970). Such a degree indicates that the holder passed competitive exams, was trained in appropriate business and management knowledge and has credentials in terms of career and experience. Thus, elite MBA degrees in this study were measured as those from Korea's top three schools, Yonsei University, Seoul National University and Korea University, and from the Ivy League schools in the US, MIT and Stanford University. Their experiences and subsequently their implicit capacity for higher professional positions were separately controlled as shown below.

The control variables were measured according to the literature (Carcello et al. 2011; Westphal and Clement 2008; Westphal and Stern 2007). The following items were included: outside directors' *social interactions and academic connections on the board, higher position in a previous or current profession, elite undergraduate degree, gender, age(log), and profession*; and the focal firm's *cash flow, ROA, leverage, size(log), age(log), controlling shareholders' ownership, and industry*. Some data were transformed into natural logarithm due to skewness.

Outside directors' social interactions on the board were measured by the following three items on a 5-point Likert-type scale in the survey: 1) 'I have had a personal relationship with the focal firm's CEO or managing directors before appointment on the board'; 2) I have frequent informal contact, such as telephone conversations, with the focal firm's CEO or managing directors"; and 3) 'I have frequent informal meetings with the focal firm's CEO or managing directors.'

Outside directors' academic connections on the board were identified using the information collected from KLCA. They were coded as a dummy, set to 1 if they attended the same school at undergraduate or graduate level in one of these three categories: 1) academic connections with CEO or chairman; 2) academic connections with managing directors on the board; or 3) academic connections with other outside directors on the board. The dummy was set to 0 otherwise. However, the correlations among the three items were almost 1 and thus the three items were merged into a single variable relating to academic connections on the board: academic connections with the CEO, chairman, managing directors, or other outside directors on the board.

A higher position in a previous or current profession was coded 1 for those who held such positions as deputy attorney general, dean of department, director of a governmental office, or higher. The elite undergraduate degree was measured by the same standard applied to the elite MBA degree. Gender, age(log), and profession (the seven categories included lawyers, professors, public officers, businesspeople, accountants, researchers, and other) were obtained from KLCA.

Unlike previous studies, such as those of Westphal and Clement (2008) and Westphal and Stern (2007), this study also included a variety of firm-related data, since they could affect a focal firm's decision-making. For instance, high-performing firms might not change their directors as frequently. Thus, cash flow from operations and ROA (return on assets) were included: cash flow was scaled by sales, while ROA was measured by net income divided by total assets. Leverage was calculated by the ratio of debt to total assets. Firm size, measured by total assets(log) and age(log), were obtained from DART. Controlling shareholders' ownership was measured by the proportion of stakes held by the largest shareholder of a firm's outstanding shares. The controlling shareholders' ownership reflected this study's Korean context, in which business group (chaebol) and family influence are still a factor despite corporate governance reform by the government.

Industry dummies were measured using the two-digit Standard Industrial Classification codes of Korea and categorized into four groups using the definition from the Organization for Economic Co-operation and Development (OECD) (2005): high, medium-high, medium-low and low technology industries.

Analysis

An exploratory factor analysis was performed using principal-component factors extraction, rotated with a varimax rotation. It was further investigated whether the factors selected above had sufficient validity, as well as whether there were any problems with the common method variance.

For all regressions, robust standard errors were applied by clustering each firm, since correlation among error terms could bias the empirical results. To test the relative relationships between outside directors' chance of survival on the board and the four explanatory variables, i.e. proactive monitoring, conformist monitoring, proactive advising, and conformist advising, this study used maximum-likelihood probit regression analysis (see Table 3). To measure the effect of outside directors' survival on focal firms' performance, OLS regression was adopted with the dependent variable of Tobin's q, which represents market responses to a firm's current activities and future performance (see Table 4). It was measured by the following formula: (book value of total assets – book value of equity + market value of equity)/book value of total assets. In this study, Tobin's q was also used as an indicator of a firm's growth opportunity, since it functions as a broader measure of investment decisions in terms of both the external factors and internal capabilities of a firm (David et al. 2006).

In addition, using maximum-likelihood probit regression, this study examined the moderating effect of foreign ownership and elite MBA degrees on the relationship between outside directors' behavioural characteristics and their survival (see Table 5).

Results

The exploratory factor analysis provided 15 principal factors, but only 5 factors with eigenvalues over 1 were selected: 'proactive monitoring', 'conformist monitoring', 'proactive advising', 'conformist advising', and 'social interaction'. The items with factor loadings over 0.6 were included in each variable.

The results of a confirmatory factor analysis using STATA software (version 13.1) supported the selection of these five factors. The model with the five latent constructs achieved a good fit, as indicated by the CFI (Comparative Fix Index) value (.9642) and the RMSEA (Root Mean Square Error of Approximation) value (.0418). The TLI (Tucker-Lewis Index) value was 0.9514. Moreover, no interfactor correlation was above the recommended level of .65 (Tabachnick and Fidell 1996). Thus, there was statistical support for the discriminant validity of the five constructs. For each of the five variables, a composite measure was constructed based on the factor loadings. To test the reliability and internal consistency of each of the five factors, Cronbach's alpha estimates were used. The Cronbach's alpha estimates were above the standard of 0.7 (George and Mallery 2003).

Table 2 presents the summary statistics, showing the means, standard deviations, and correlations of the variables in this study. Proactive and conformist monitoring were negatively correlated, as anticipated. However, it appears absurd that the correlation between proactive and conformist advising was positive. It is hard for outside directors to show behavioural inconsistency in conducting monitoring roles, even in different situations. However, they could relatively easily show different behavioural characteristics in advisory roles, depending on the context. Regarding this issue, the multicollinearity in the regression was checked. The VIFs (variance inflation factors) of all the independent variables in Table 2 were much lower than 10, indicating that the coefficient estimates were stable (Stevens 1996).

Table 3 illustrates the results of the maximum-likelihood probit regression. Hypotheses 1a and 1b state that the effect of outside directors' proactive behaviour on their chance of survival will be negative, while that of conformist behaviour will be positive, regardless of whether they are performing monitoring or advisory roles. Models 3, 4, and 5 of Table 3 generally support this hypothesis. Conformist monitoring increased the chance of survival on the board ($p < 0.05$ or 0.1). While proactive advising decreased the chance ($p < 0.05$]), conformist advising increased it ($p < 0.1$). Regarding effect size on survival, the effect of conformist monitoring was larger than that of proactive monitoring by 0.338 ([CI_{95} = 0.115, 0.560]). The effect of conformist advising was larger than that of proactive advising by 0.097 ([CI_{95} = −0.125, 0.318]). Among the control variables, academic connections and a higher position in a previous or current profession strongly increased the chance of survival.

Hypotheses 2a and 2b suggest that the effect of outside directors' proactive behaviour on firm performance will be positive, while that of conformist behaviour will be negative, regardless of whether they conduct monitoring or advisory roles. Table 4 partially supports these hypotheses. Models 3 and 4 in Table 4 illustrate that outside directors' proactive monitoring ($p < 0.05$) and advisory ($p < 0.1$) roles improve Tobin's q. However, the effect of conformist behaviour on firm performance does not show statistical significance.

Hypotheses 3a and 3b posit the moderating effects of foreign ownership and outside directors' valuable experience and knowledge on the relationship between behavioural characteristics and survival. In Table 5, models 1 and 2 represent the outcomes for hypothesis 3a, while models 3 and 4 display the outcomes for hypothesis 3b. The outcomes partially support the two hypotheses. The first two models in Table 5 illustrate that in firms with high growth opportunity (Tobin's $q > 1$), foreign ownership decreased the survival chance of outside directors conducting conformist monitoring ($p < 0.1$) or advising ($p < 0.05$). In contrast, its moderating effect for proactive behaviour was not statistically significant. Models 3 and 4 of Table 5 show that in firms with low growth opportunity (Tobin's $q \leq 1$), an elite MBA degree increased the survival chance of outside

Table 2. Summary statistics and correlations of variables.

Variables	Ob.	Mean	S. Dv.	1	2	3	4	5	6	7	8	9	10
1.stay as outside directors	157	.6369427	0.482420	1.0000									
2.monitoring_proactive	157	3.81104	0.750379	−0.0077	1.0000								
3.monitoring_conformist	157	3.490446	0.625389	0.2257*	−0.2384*	1.0000							
4.advising_proactive	157	3.575372	0.565650	−0.0204	0.3518*	−0.3780*	1.0000						
5.advising_ conformist	157	2.824841	0.757159	0.0442	0.2667*	−0.0272	0.2194*	1.0000					
6.social interaction	157	2.613588	0.754389	−0.0298	−0.1449	0.2503*	−0.1667*	0.1071	1.0000				
7.academic connections	157	.3184713	0.467374	0.2602*	0.0996	−0.0188	0.1511	−0.0316	−0.0245	1.0000			
8.elite undergraduate	157	.7197452	0.450561	−0.0287	0.0636	−0.0399	0.0080	−0.1072	−0.0252	0.2135*	1.0000		
9.elite MBA	157	.1082803	0.311728	−0.0779	−0.0216	−0.0221	0.1897*	0.0130	−0.0844	0.0258	0.1718*	1.0000	
10.higher position	157	.3248408	0.469814	0.1843*	0.1631*	0.0434	0.1364	−0.0733	−0.0957	0.1097	−0.0214	−0.1542	
11.gender	157	.9872611	0.112504	0.1505	0.0979	−0.0321	0.0823	0.0113	−0.0584	0.0777	0.0556	0.0396	1.0000
12.age(log)	157	4.023114	0.109639	−0.1900*	0.1323	−0.0487	0.0242	0.0240	−0.0448	−0.0455	−0.0076	−0.0832	0.0788
13.tobin q(t + 1)	157	1.226564	0.677434	0.1945*	0.0639	0.0283	0.2339*	0.0515	−0.0920	0.0351	−0.0150	0.0271	0.2834*
14.cash flow/sales	156	.0377731	1.178365	0.1454	−0.0476	0.0345	−0.0251	0.0300	−0.0012	0.0875	0.0014	0.0820	0.1402
15.ROA	156	.0345109	0.194307	0.1471	−0.0702	0.1278	0.0271	−0.0443	−0.1276	−0.0120	0.0675	−0.0047	−0.0951
16.leverage	156	.4524994	0.228341	−0.2011*	0.1708*	−0.1087	0.0280	−0.0021	−0.0612	0.0163	−0.0921	−0.1762*	0.1838*
17.firm size(log)	156	8.971779	0.805681	0.0408	0.2950*	−0.0566	0.2544*	0.0555	−0.2398*	0.3567*	0.1055	0.1502	0.0932
18.foreign ownership	156	.1514769	0.163389	0.0979	0.1706*	0.0642	0.1248	0.0315	−0.1372	0.2502*	0.1171	0.1825*	0.2517*
19.firm age(log)	157	1.480785	0.346049	−0.0456	−0.0097	0.1234	−0.1671*	−0.0314	−0.0455	−0.0609	−0.1363	−0.2331*	0.1661*
20.controlling shareholder	156	.408259	0.182933	0.0374	−0.1827*	−0.0053	−0.1505	−0.0409	0.0613	−0.1467	0.0210	0.0152	−0.0234

Variables	11	12	13	14	15	16	17	18	19	20
11.gender	1.0000									
12.age(log)	0.0294	1.0000								
13.tobin q(t + 1)	0.0276	−0.0963	1.0000							
14.cash flow/sales	−0.0035	−0.0512	−0.0396	1.0000						
15.ROA	−0.0197	−0.1507	0.2105*	0.0550	1.0000					
16.leverage	0.1561	0.1433	−0.0664	−0.1742*	−0.1269	1.0000				
17.firm size(log)	0.1276	0.2465*	0.0586	0.1109	0.1543	0.1824*	1.0000			
18.foreign ownership	0.0112	0.1314	0.2574*	0.1357	0.2319*	−0.2731*	0.6401*			
19.firm age(log)	−0.0262	0.0981	−0.1552	−0.0147	−0.0446	0.1024	−0.0305	1.0000	1.0000	
20.controlling shareholder	−0.0279	−0.0581	−0.1808*	0.0542	0.1388	−0.0835	−0.2081*	−0.2091*	0.0560	1.0000

* $p < 0.05$.

Table 3. Probit regression for outside director's proactive behaviour.

Dependent variable	Stay as outside director				
Explanatory variables	Model1	Model2	Model3	Model4	Model5
Monitoring_proactive			−0.045		−0.073
			(0.172)		(0.186)
Monitoring_conformist			**0.479***		**0.404+**
			(0.208)		(0.223)
Advising_proactive				**−0.522***	−0.338
				(0.230)	(0.252)
Advising_conformist				**0.257+**	**0.271+**
				(0.159)	(0.161)
Social interaction		0.053	−0.100	−0.024	−0.152
		(0.158)	(0.161)	(0.160)	(0.160)
Academic connections		1.298***	1.340***	1.416***	1.415***
		(0.353)	(0.367)	(0.362)	(0.369)
Elite undergraduate	−0.174	−0.469	−0.444	−0.469	−0.408
	(0.268)	(0.301)	(0.301)	(0.317)	(0.311)
Elite MBA	−0.812+	−0.772+	−0.884*	−0.718+	−0.856*
	(0.419)	(0.408)	(0.422)	(0.389)	(0.414)
Higher position	0.872**	0.913**	0.866**	1.059***	0.992**
	(0.307)	(0.314)	(0.315)	(0.325)	(0.324)
Age(log)	−5.365***	−5.408***	−4.950***	−5.728***	−5.312***
	(1.297)	(1.330)	(1.258)	(1.394)	(1.301)
Cash flow/sales	1.032+	1.420+	1.502*	1.741*	1.729*
	(0.604)	(0.742)	(0.728)	(0.800)	(0.765)
ROA	0.165	0.382	0.134	0.026	−0.089
	(1.055)	(1.169)	(1.094)	(1.047)	(1.041)
Leverage	−1.259+	−1.248	−1.186	−1.290	−1.202
	(0.695)	(0.767)	(0.765)	(0.793)	(0.789)
Firm size(log)	0.060	−0.195	−0.156	−0.137	−0.126
	(0.232)	(0.256)	(0.266)	(0.262)	(0.273)
Foreign ownership	0.142	−0.011	−0.289	−0.329	−0.453
	(1.177)	(1.190)	(1.220)	(1.211)	(1.243)
Firm age(log)	0.124	0.333	0.047	0.203	0.036
	(0.355)	(0.372)	(0.376)	(0.368)	(0.371)
Controlling shareholder	0.725	1.132	0.993	1.092	0.994
	(0.808)	(0.808)	(0.792)	(0.809)	(0.786)
Constant	21.885***	23.748***	21.026***	26.173***	23.232***
	(5.300)	(5.562)	(5.511)	(5.907)	(5.707)
Industry & profession	Included	Included	Included	Included	Included
Observations	151	151	151	151	151
Wald chi2	37.90**	51.20***	50.73***	59.24***	58.39***
Pseudo R2	0.2131	0.2963	0.3233	0.3215	0.3384

Robust standard errors in parentheses, clustered by firms; + $p < 0.1$, * $p < 0.05$, ** $p < 0.01$, *** $p < 0.001$.

directors conducting proactive monitoring ($p < 0.01$) and advising ($p < 0.001$), while it decreased the survival chance of those conducting conformist monitoring ($p < 0.05$).

Figures 1 and 2 illustrate the moderating effects of foreign ownership and elite MBA degrees, respectively, on survival chance.

Robustness test

This study examined the relative effects of outside directors' behavioural characteristics and roles on their chance of survival, with a joint test of coefficients to check whether the effect of proactive monitoring on survival was any different from that of proactive advising. The joint test result confirms they had a similar effect, at a 99% significance

Table 4. OLS regression for the effects of outside directors on firm performance.

Dependent variable	Tobin Q (t + 1)					
	All samples		Sub-sample (stay = 1)		Sub-sample (stay = 0)	
Explanatory variables	Model1	Model2	Model3	Model4	Model5	Model6
Monitoring_proactive	0.058		**0.302***		−0.056	
	(0.090)		(0.124)		(0.135)	
Monitoring_conformist	−0.012		−0.223		−0.016	
	(0.076)		(0.167)		(0.093)	
Advising_proactive		**0.258***		**0.351+**		0.184
		(0.118)		(0.183)		(0.159)
Advising_conformist		0.040		0.043		0.055
		(0.071)		(0.122)		(0.070)
Social interaction	−0.041	−0.037	−0.148	−0.133	0.038	0.035
	(0.087)	(0.078)	(0.119)	(0.116)	(0.116)	(0.088)
Academic connections	0.011	−0.016	−0.164	−0.220	−0.063	−0.093
	(0.121)	(0.120)	(0.162)	(0.158)	(0.134)	(0.133)
Elite undergraduate	−0.042	−0.005	0.146	0.155	−0.106	−0.138
	(0.118)	(0.111)	(0.174)	(0.177)	(0.119)	(0.108)
Elite MBA	−0.018	−0.102	−0.497	−0.529	0.353	0.357
	(0.225)	(0.199)	(0.398)	(0.369)	(0.295)	(0.234)
Higher position	0.172	0.152	0.124	0.102	−0.039	−0.033
	(0.140)	(0.136)	(0.193)	(0.193)	(0.114)	(0.120)
Foreign ownership	1.321+	1.540*	1.220	1.715+	0.964	1.310
	(0.725)	(0.676)	(0.953)	(0.982)	(1.056)	(1.128)
Constant	6.054*	5.281*	4.494	3.214	3.834	5.773
	(2.516)	(2.489)	(2.985)	(3.026)	(4.269)	(3.538)
All other variables in Table 3	Included	Included	Included	Included	Included	Included
Observations	155	155	98	98	57	57
F	1.47+	1.96**	1.65*	1.60+	5.73***	8.49***
R2	0.2240	0.2626	0.3774	0.3668	0.3960	0.4338

Robust standard errors in parentheses, clustered by firms; + $p < 0.1$, * $p < 0.05$, ** $p < 0.01$, *** $p < 0.001$.

level ($Chi^2 = 4.30$). The joint test on conformist monitoring and conformist advising shows the same result ($Chi^2 = 7.80$).

Regarding the endogeneity concern, this study used a year-lagged dependent variable for performance, Tobin's q (t + 1). For the relationship between behavioural characteristics and survival following the term, the questionnaire specifically asked the respondents to evaluate their behaviour during their service on the board. Survival or lack of it was coded by secondary information, i.e. the outcomes following the term period.

This study also used two alternative dependent variables: unwilling resignation from the board and frequency of appointment on the board. To measure 'unwilling resignation', a questionnaire item was included in the survey: 'I resigned from the board due to the expiration of my contract'. It was measured with a 5-point Likert-type scale – 1 (strongly disagree) to 5 (strongly agree) – instead of a binary yes or no question. This was because the reasons for resignation could be complex. Therefore, those who were not serving on the board at the time of the survey and responded to the question with 1, 2 or 3 were coded 1 for unwilling resignation; otherwise they were coded 0. Another dependent variable, frequency of appointment, was measured by the number of appointments on the board for each outside director at a focal firm. The regression results in Table 6 generally move in the same direction, although not completely consistently, as those reported in Table 3. Those who performed conformist monitoring showed lower unwilling resignation ($p < 0.001$, model 3) and a higher frequency of appointment ($p < 0.05$, model 7). In contrast, those who conducted proactive advising displayed a lower frequency of appointment ($p < 0.05$, model 8).

Table 5. Probit regression for the moderating effects of foreign ownership and elite MBA degree.

Dependent variable	Stay as outside director			
	Growth opportunity is high (Tobin q > 1)		Growth opportunity is low (Tobin q ≤ 1)	
Explanatory variables	Model1	Model2	Model3	Model4
Monitoring_proactive	0.734 (0.500)		−3.466** (1.173)	
Monitoring_conformist	1.031+ (0.543)		3.161** (1.083)	
Moni_proactiv * foreig. owner	0.490 (2.080)			
Moni_confor * foreign owner	**−4.192+** (2.534)			
Moni_proactiv * elite MBA			**6.409**** (2.052)	
Moni_confor * elite MBA			**−4.536*** (2.069)	
Advising_proactive		−0.655 (0.867)		−1.791*** (0.551)
Advising_conformist		1.257*** (0.372)		0.085 (0.405)
Adv_proactiv * foreign owner		2.494 (3.015)		
Adv_confor * foreign owner		**−4.831*** (2.075)		
Adv_proactiv * elite MBA				**2.289***** (0.652)
Adv_confor * elite MBA				0.003 (0.113)
Social interaction	0.109 (0.363)	−0.269 (0.379)	−2.377** (0.886)	−0.349 (0.286)
Academic connections	0.987 (0.671)	0.723 (0.612)	11.447** (3.805)	3.711*** (1.044)
Elite undergraduate	0.019 (0.619)	0.284 (0.601)	0.201 (0.514)	−0.606 (0.506)
Elite MBA	−1.420* (0.608)	−1.784* (0.809)	−7.687 (5.935)	−8.951*** (13.487)
Higher position	0.988+ (0.518)	1.105* (0.542)	5.347*** (1.208)	2.160* (0.887)
Foreign ownership	15.139 (13.223)	5.741 (12.245)	−10.977** (4.041)	−3.111 (2.047)
Constant	11.715 (8.983)	17.061* (8.060)	134.089*** (41.900)	64.947*** (21.993)
All other variables in Table 3	Included	Included	Included	Included
Observations	65	65	82	82
Wald chi2	43.57**	39.81*	71.01***	35.04+
Pseudo R2	0.3655	0.3808	0.7532	0.5030

Robust standard errors in parentheses, clustered by firms; + $p < 0.1$, * $p < 0.05$, ** $p < 0.01$, *** $p < 0.001$.

Discussion

Korean large firms, represented by chaebol, have adopted and increased their numbers of outside directors due to the government's initiative for corporate governance reform. However, according to the empirical findings of this study, the term duration (and possibly the selection) of outside directors is strongly influenced by their academic connections and higher positions in previous or current professions. This phenomenon illustrates that controlling families still maintain their influence and obstruct corporate governance reform to suit their own interests. Given the organizational characteristics of Korean firms set out above, this study has examined the unsatisfactory performance of

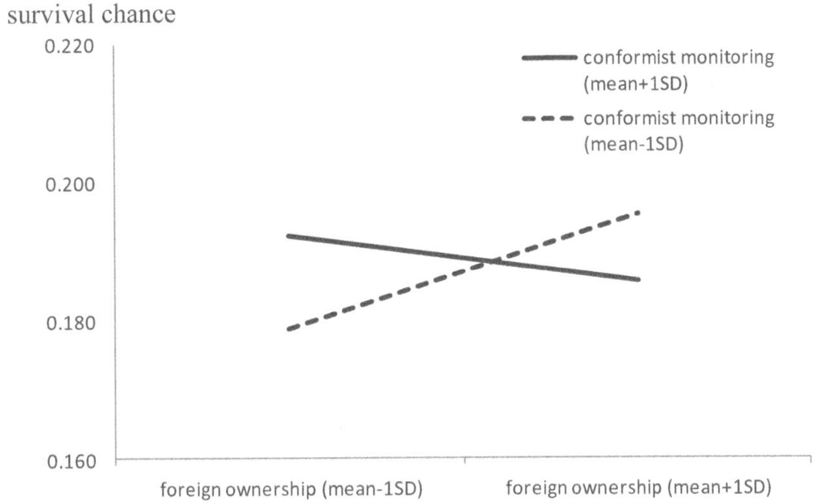

Figure 1. The moderating effects of foreign ownership on the relationship between conformist monitoring and survival chance.

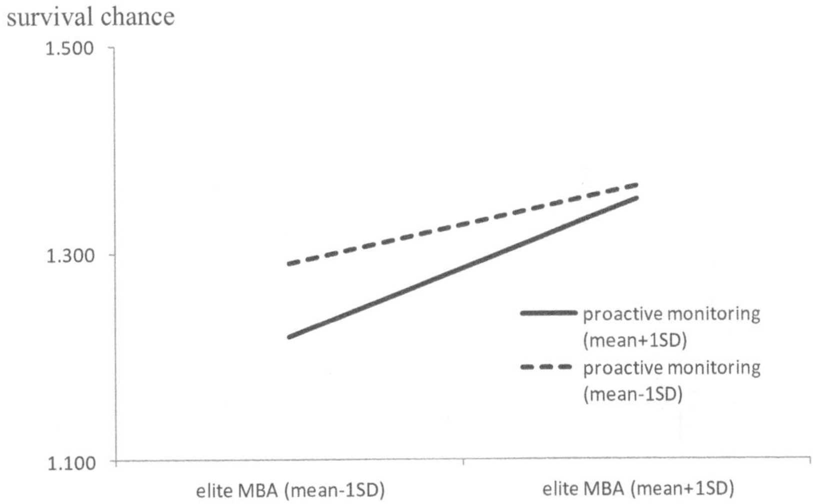

Figure 2. The moderating effects of elite MBA degree on the relationship between proactive monitoring and survival chance.

outside directors in terms of their behavioural characteristics, i.e. proactive vs. conformist, and has extended the literature that draws on outside directors' roles and their socio-political connections. The findings clarify that outside directors' proactive or conformist behaviours affect their chance of survival on the board, regardless of whether their roles are monitoring or advisory. Regarding firm performance, those who conduct proactive behaviour, if they survive on the board, improve Tobin's q. It is also noteworthy that the variables of foreign ownership and outside directors' valuable experiences and knowledge moderate the relationship between behavioural characteristics and survival chance, depending on the focal firm's business context.

Table 6. Robustness tests for outside directors' proactive behaviour.

Dependent variables	Unwilling resignation (probit)				Frequency of appointment (OLS)			
Explanatory variables	Model1	Model2	Model3	Model4	Model5	Model6	Model7	Model8
Monitoring_proactive			−0.266				0.002	
			(0.221)				(0.110)	
Monitoring_conformist			**−0.855*****				**0.305***	
			(0.251)				(0.155)	
Advising_proactive				−0.072				**−0.347***
				(0.295)				(0.172)
Advising_conformist				−0.034				0.024
				(0.218)				(0.111)
Social interaction		−0.354	−0.169	−0.353		0.194+	0.114	0.166
		(0.274)	(0.307)	(0.273)		(0.117)	(0.128)	(0.120)
Academic connections		0.157	−0.120	0.169		0.212	0.209	0.252
		(0.459)	(0.449)	(0.449)		(0.243)	(0.243)	(0.247)
Elite undergraduate	−0.438	−0.452	−0.405	−0.468	0.093	0.058	0.066	0.033
	(0.395)	(0.404)	(0.411)	(0.404)	(0.184)	(0.206)	(0.203)	(0.213)
Elite MBA	1.942***	1.980***	2.210***	1.981***	0.387	0.451	0.439	0.551+
	(0.505)	(0.519)	(0.582)	(0.487)	(0.322)	(0.332)	(0.346)	(0.334)
Higher position	−0.572+	−0.663+	−0.722*	−0.672*	0.259	0.260	0.221	0.310
	(0.334)	(0.347)	(0.348)	(0.342)	(0.228)	(0.224)	(0.229)	(0.230)
Constant	−26.227**	−26.600**	−21.157*	−26.764**	−1.225	−1.925	−3.238	−0.797
	(9.298)	(9.832)	(8.942)	(9.710)	(2.810)	(2.800)	(2.962)	(2.830)
All other variables in Table 3	Included	Included	Included	Included	Included	Included	Included	Included
Observations	137	137	137	137	155	155	155	155
(Wald chi2) F	(46.43)***	(42.87)***	(54.63)***	(44.71)**	4.78***	4.05***	3.42***	5.68***
(Pseudo R2) R2	(0.2903)	(0.3106)	(0.3969)	(0.3113)	0.1440	0.1675	0.1935	0.1933

Robust standard errors in parentheses, clustered by firms; + $p < 0.1$, * $p < 0.05$, ** $p < 0.01$, *** $p < 0.001$.

Implications

For theoretical development

First, the findings help us to reconsider the effectiveness of monitoring roles in agency theory. Outside directors, as emphasized in corporate governance reforms such as the Sarbanes-Oxley Act, are a representative mechanism for monitoring and controlling the self-serving behaviour of CEOs and managers. However, the empirical outcomes of this study illustrate that those who perform their roles proactively are less likely to survive on the board. This implies that outside directors face unfavourable environments in terms of implementing their expected roles, which could result in unsatisfactory firm performance. We thus need to consider moderating mechanisms in order to enable outside directors to conduct their expected roles. In this study, those who had enough power, such as foreign ownership and/or valuable resources that were indispensable for CEOs' performance, were effective examples of role implementation by outside directors. More discussion is provided below regarding the practical implications.

This study also advances the role-based explanations for the unsatisfactory performance of outside directors. The literature argues that some outside directors are more likely to survive on the board than others or to enjoy additional appointments in other firms. It identifies the phenomenon according to the specific roles assumed by outside directors, i.e. monitoring vs. advising. However, the literature does not consider the instances where expected roles are performed with particular behavioural characteristics, which could be a critical factor in outside directors' chance of survival on the board and subsequent role performance. That is, even monitoring roles might be conducted in a conformist manner by unquestioningly approving or consenting to CEOs' or managers' decision-making, although these roles do not reach the level of ingratiation. This type of monitoring is not what is expected by agency theory and role-based explanations. At the same time, those who perform advisory roles are more likely to be sacked when they proactively perform the roles. Proactive advising includes suggestion of alternative ideas and discussion of the negative dimensions of the agenda on the table, which might consequentially remove, transform, or at least delay the agenda at hand. Although this process will make the final decision-making process more deliberate and robust, the empirical outcomes of this study indicate that those who perform their roles proactively, regardless of whether they involve monitoring or advising, are less likely to survive on the board.

Regarding the relationship between outside directors and firm performance, the findings of this study imply that the frequent corporate scandals could be the result of the unsatisfactory fulfilment of outside directors' expected roles and that this is caused by their behavioural characteristics, i.e. a preference for conformist behaviours over proactive ones in role implementation. Although the conformist behaviours may not go as far as ingratiation, outside directors who unquestioningly support and endorse CEOs' decisions could dominate the board. These conformist behaviours illustrate that human beings tend to respond positively to favour-rendering (Crombag, Rassin, and Horselenberg 2003; McCullough 2008). By examining outside directors' behavioural characteristics, such as proactive versus conformist behaviours, this study identifies why monitoring mechanisms on the board are often unsatisfactory. The board might comprise outside directors who are inclined to support and endorse, while those who proactively perform their roles are less likely to survive on the board.

For readers and business and management practice

Regarding corporate governance reform, this study calls for a focus on new ways for outside directors to implement their expected roles. The suggestions in the extant studies are categorized into two approaches: economic (agency cost) and sociological (identity and status). Economic approaches suggest compensation schemes in order to align the interests of outside directors with those of shareholders. A stock option is an effective mechanism for outside directors to promote risky investment by firms. However, this effectiveness is limited, since it is substitutable with CEOs' stock options (Deutsch, Keil, and Laamanen 2011) and weakened by powerful CEOs (Lim and McCann 2013). Furthermore, stock options for CEOs are more popular than those for outside directors.

Sociological approaches emphasize identity and status. When outside directors develop and manage multiple identities, they can engage in both monitoring and advisory roles (Hillman, Nicholson, and Shropshire 2008). Outside directors with high status will not adopt conformist behaviour in order to survive on the board (Veltrop et al. 2017). Nevertheless, outside directors experience conflicts in managing their contradictory identities, e.g. monitoring versus friendship, and face intra-role clashes (Golden-Biddle and Rao 1997). High-status directors are not willing to join firms that require active monitoring or advising, such as firms with financial restatement (Diestre, Rajagopalan, and Dutta 2015), or to leave them facing a crisis (Withers, Corley, and Hillman 2012).

Alternatively, this study emphasizes that effective power or valuable resources can sustainably promote the likelihood of outside directors performing their expected roles in corporate governance reform. The unconditional adoption of outside directors without taking the organizational characteristics of a country into consideration may lead to inefficiencies. The conflicts between government pressures for corporate governance reform and firms' attempts to avoid it do matter. However, even under controlling families in Korean firms, foreign owners can enjoy independent power against controlling shareholders due to their investment interest and independence from the focal firm's sociopolitics. Elite MBA degrees represent valuable knowledge and experiences and even denote status including social capital. It is noteworthy that the alternative mechanisms in this study are more sustainable than those suggested by the literature. CEOs easily override compensation schemes. The societal dimension relies upon an individual's discretion. In contrast, foreign ownership is structural, and could be pitted against CEOs' influence. Those with elite MBA degrees enjoy relatively high mobility, possibly owing to their valuable resources and status, and thus could speak independently against the intentions of CEOs and controlling shareholders.

Limitations and future research

To generalize the findings of this study in the Korean context, it would be useful to employ a comparative study across countries, since different sociocultural backgrounds affect outside directors' behavioural characteristics. In addition, extending the time window of the analysis could help investigate the possible change in behavioural characteristics over time. Furthermore, other dimensions of human characteristics, including psychological traits and personality, could provide additional findings to help understand outside directors' role implementation.

Conclusion

This study has analysed both survey and accounting data on 157 outside directors in large Korean firms regarding the corporate governance reform initiated by the government. The paper's key contribution is to extend the literature by pitting outside directors' behaviours against their roles and to argue that their behavioural characteristics, i.e. proactive versus conformist, affect their chance of survival on the board and subsequently influence firm performance. In terms of practical implications, this study sheds light on the moderating roles of power, e.g. foreign ownership (for firms with higher growth opportunity), and outside directors' valuable knowledge and experience, e.g. elite MBA degrees (for firms with lower growth opportunity).

Disclosure statement

No potential conflict of interest was reported by the author(s).

Funding

This work was supported by the Hankuk University of Foreign Studies Research Fund of 2021.

References

Adams, R., B. Hermalin, and M. Weisbach. 2010. "The Role of Boards of Directors in Corporate Governance: A Conceptual Framework and Survey." *Journal of Economic Literature* 48 (1): 58–107. doi:10.1257/jel.48.1.58.

Aggarwal, R., L. Klapper, and P. Wysocki. 2005. "Portfolio Preferences of Foreign Institutional Investors." *Journal of Banking & Finance* 29 (12): 2919–2946. doi:10.1016/j.jbankfin.2004.09.008.

Akerlof, G. 1970. "The Market for "Lemons": Quality Uncertainty and the Market Mechanism." *Quarterly Journal of Economics* 84 (3): 488–500. doi:10.2307/1879431.

Ali, T., and J. Larimo. 2016. "Managing Opportunism in International Joint Ventures: The Role of Structural and Social Mechanisms." *Scandinavian Journal of Management* 32 (2): 86–96. doi:10.1016/j.scaman.2016.03.002.

Anderson, R., and D. Reeb. 2004. "Board Composition: Balancing Family Influence in S&P 500 Firms." *Administrative Science Quarterly* 49 (2): 209–237.

Barnhart, S., W. Marr, and S. Rosenstein. 1994. "Firm Performance and Board Composition: Some New Evidence." *Managerial Decision Economics* 15 (4): 329–340. doi:10.1002/mde.4090150407.

Biz, C. 2020. "Outside Directors of Chaebol Firms are Still Rubber-Stamper." Accessed 3 June 2021. https://biz.chosun.com/site/data/html_dir/2020/04/05/2020040500309.html

Bolino, M., M. Kacmar, W. Turnley, and J. Gilstrap. 2008. "A Multi-Level Review of Impression Management Motives and Behaviours." *Journal of Management* 34 (6): 1080–1109. doi:10.1177/0149206308324325.

Bradshaw, M., B. Bushee, and G. Miller. 2004. "Accounting Choice, Home Bias, and US Investment in Non-US Firms." *Journal of Accounting Research* 42 (5): 795–841. doi:10.1111/j.1475-679X.2004.00157.x.

Carcello, J., T. Neal, Z. Palmrose, and S. Scholz. 2011. "CEO Involvement in Selecting Board Members, Audit Committee Effectiveness, and Restatements." *Contemporary Accounting Research* 28 (2): 396–430. doi:10.1111/j.1911-3846.2010.01052.x.

Carpenter, J., P. Matthews, and O. Ong'ong'a. 2004. "Why Punish? Social Reciprocity and the Enforcement of Prosocial Norms." *Journal of Evolutionary Economics* 14 (4): 407–429. doi:10.1007/s00191-004-0212-1.

Certo, S., C. Dalton, D. Dalton, and R. Lester. 2008. "Boards of Directors' Self-Interest: Expanding for Pay in Corporate Acquisitions?" *Journal of Business Ethics* 77 (2): 219–230. doi:10.1007/s10551-006-9345-5.

Charness, G., and M. Rabin. 2000. *Social Preferences: Some Simple Tests and a New Model*. Berkeley: Institute of Business and Economics Research.

Crombag, H., E. Rassin, and R. Horselenberg. 2003. "On Vengeance." *Psychology, Crime, and Law* 9 (4): 333–344. doi:10.1080/1068316031000068647.

Dalton, D., C. Daily, A. Ellstrand, and J. Johnson. 1998. "Meta-Analytic Review of Board Composition, Leadership Structure, and Financial Performance." *Strategic Management Journal* 19 (3): 269–290. doi:10.1002/(SICI)1097-0266(199803)19:3<269::AID-SMJ950>3.0.CO;2-K.

David, P., T. Yoshikawa, M. Chari, and A. Rasheed. 2006. "Strategic Investments in Japanese Corporations: Do Foreign Portfolio Owners Foster Underinvestment or Appropriate Investment?" *Strategic Management Journal* 27 (6): 591–600. doi:10.1002/smj.523.

de Andrés, P., L. Arranz-Aperte, and J. Rodriguez-Sanz. 2017. "Independent versus Non-Independent outside Directors in European Companies: Who Has a Say on CEO Compensation?" *Business Research Quarterly* 20 (2): 79–95.

Desender, K., R. Aguilera, M. Lópezpuertas-Lamy, and R. Crespi. 2016. "A Clash of Governance Logics: Foreign Ownership and Board Monitoring." *Strategic Management Journal* 37 (2): 349–369. doi:10.1002/smj.2344.

Deutsch, Y., T. Keil, and T. Laamanen. 2011. "A Dual Agency View of Board Compensation: The Joint Effects of outside Director and CEO Stock Options on Firm Risk." *Strategic Management Journal* 32 (2): 212–227. doi:10.1002/smj.876.

Diestre, L., N. Rajagopalan, and S. Dutta. 2015. "Constraints in Acquiring and Utilizing Directors' Experience: An Empirical Study of New-Market Entry in the Pharmaceutical Industry." *Strategic Management Journal* 36 (3): 339–359. doi:10.1002/smj.2215.

Fehr, E., and S. Gachter. 2000. "Fairness and Retaliation: The Economics of Reciprocity." *Journal of Economic Perspectives* 14 (3): 159–181. doi:10.1257/jep.14.3.159.

Ferreira, M., and P. Matos. 2008. "The Colors of Investors' Money: The Role of Institutional Investors around the World." *Journal of Financial Economics* 88 (3): 499–533. doi:10.1016/j.jfineco.2007.07.003.

Friedman, D., and N. Singh. 2004. "Negative Reciprocity and the Coevolution of Memes and Genes." *Evolution and Human Behaviour* 25 (3): 155–173. doi:10.1016/j.evolhumbehav.2004.03.002.

George, D., and P. Mallery. 2003. *SPSS for Windows Step by Step: A Simple Guide and Reference, 11.0 Update*. 4th ed. Boston: Allyn & Bacon.

Gillette, A., T. Noe, and M. Rebello. 2008. "Board Structures around the World: An Experimental Investigation." *Review of Finance* 12 (1): 93–140. doi:10.1093/rof/rfm027.

Golden-Biddle, K., and H. Rao. 1997. "Breaches in the Boardroom: Organizational Identity and Conflicts of Commitment in a Nonprofit Organization." *Organization Science* 8 (6): 593–611. doi:10.1287/orsc.8.6.593.

Gordon, J. 2007. "The Rise of Independent Directors in the United States, 1950–2005: Of Shareholder Value and Stock Market Prices." *Stanford Law Review* 59 (6): 1465–1568.

Hambrick, D., V. Misangyi, and C. Park. 2015. "The Quad Model for Identifying a Corporate Director's Potential for Effective Monitoring: Toward a New Theory of Board Sufficiency." *Academy of Management Review* 40 (3): 323–344. doi:10.5465/amr.2014.0066.

Herman, E. 1981. *Corporate Control, Corporate Power*. New York: Cambridge University Press.

Hillman, A., and T. Dalziel. 2003. "Boards of Directors and Firm Performance: Integrating Agency and Resource Dependence Perspectives." *Academy of Management Review* 28 (3): 383–396. doi:10.2307/30040728.

Hillman, A., G. Nicholson, and C. Shropshire. 2008. "Directors' Multiple Identities, Identification, and Board Monitoring and Resource Provision." *Organization Science* 19 (3): 441–456. doi:10.1287/orsc.1080.0355.

Hillman, A., C. Shropshire, T. Certo, D. Dalton, and C. Dalton. 2011. "What I like about You: A Multilevel Study of Shareholder Discontent with Director Monitoring." *Organization Science* 22 (3): 675–687. doi:10.1287/orsc.1100.0542.

Huang, H., and C. Chan. 2018. "Firms' Performance following the Initial Resignation of Independent Directors: Evidence from Taiwan." *Asia Pacific Business Review* 24 (5): 714–729. doi:10.1080/13602381.2018.1423721.

Jensen, M. 2001. "Value Maximization, Stakeholder Theory, and the Corporate Objective Function." *Journal of Applied Corporate Finance* 14 (3): 8–21. doi:10.1111/j.1745-6622.2001.tb00434.x.

Johnson, J., C. Daily, and A. Ellstrand. 1996. "Boards of Directors: A Review and Research Agenda." *Journal of Management* 22 (3): 409–438. doi:10.1177/014920639602200303.

Kemp, S. 2006. "In the Driver's Seat or Rubber Stamp? The Role of the Board in Providing Strategic Guidance in Australian Boardrooms." *Management Decision* 44 (1): 56–73. doi:10.1108/00251740610641463.

Khatri, N., E. Tsang, and T. Begley. 2006. "Cronyism: A Cross-Cultural Analysis." *Journal of International Business Studies* 37 (1): 61–75. doi:10.1057/palgrave.jibs.8400171.

Klein, A. 1998. "Firm Performance and Board Committee Structure." *Journal of Law and Economics* 41 (1): 275–303. doi:10.1086/467391.

Lim, E., and B. McCann. 2013. "The Influence of Relative Values of outside Director Stock Options on Firm Strategic Risk from a Multiagent Perspective." *Strategic Management Journal* 34 (13): 1568–1590. doi:10.1002/smj.2088.

Lorsch, J., and E. MacIver. 1989. *Pawns and Potentates: The Reality of America's Corporate Boards*. Boston, MA: Harvard Business School Press.

Ma, J., and T. Khanna. 2016. "Independent Directors' Dissent on Boards: Evidence from Listed Companies in China." *Strategic Management Journal* 37 (8): 1547–1557. doi:10.1002/smj.2421.

McCullough, M. 2008. *Beyond Revenge*. San Francisco: Jossey-Bass.

Molm, L. 2003. "Theoretical Comparisons of Forms of Exchange." *Sociological Theory* 21 (1): 1–7. doi:10.1111/1467-9558.00171.

OECD. 2005. *OECD Science, Technology and Industry Scoreboard 2005: Towards a Knowledge-Based Economy*. Paris: OECD.

Stern, I., and J. Westphal. 2010. "Stealthy Footsteps to the Boardroom: Executives' Backgrounds, Sophisticated Interpersonal Influence Behaviour, and Board Appointments." *Administrative Science Quarterly* 55 (2): 278–319. doi:10.2189/asqu.2010.55.2.278.

Stevens, J. 1996. *Applied Multivariate Statistics for the Social Sciences*. 3rd ed. Hillsdale: Lawrence Erlbaum.

Tabachnick, B., and L. Fidell. 1996. *Using Multivariate Statistics*. New York: Harper Collins.

Udueni, H. 1999. "Power Dimensions in the Board and outside Director Independence: Evidence from Large Industrial UK Firms." *Corporate Governance: An International Review* 7 (1): 62–72. doi:10.1002/mde.3311.

Veltrop, D., E. Molleman, R. Hooghiemstra, and H. van Ees. 2017. "Who's the Boss at the Top? A Micro-Level Analysis of Director Expertise, Status and Conformity within Boards." *Journal of Management Studies* 54 (7): 1079–1110. doi:10.1111/joms.12276.

Villanueva-Villar, M., E. Rivo-López, and S. Lago-Peñas. 2016. "On the Relationship between Corporate Governance and Value Creation in an Economic Crisis: Empirical Evidence for the Spanish Case." *Business Research Quarterly* 19 (4): 233–245.

Wade, J., C. O'Reilly, and I. Chandratat. 1990. "Golden Parachutes: CEOs and the Exercise of Social Influence." *Administrative Science Quarterly* 35 (4): 587–603. doi:10.2307/2393510.

Weekly Donga. 2015. "Impractical outside Directors in Korea." Accessed 3 June 2021. https://www.donga.com/news/Economy/article/all/20151124/74988406/1

Westphal, J., and M. Clement. 2008. "Sociopolitical Dynamics in Relations between Top Managers and Security Analysis: Favor Rendering, Reciprocity, and Analyst Stock Recommendations." *Academy of Management Journal* 51 (5): 873–897. doi:10.5465/amj.2008.34789647.

Westphal, J., M. Seidel, and K. Stewart. 2001. "Second-Order Imitation: Uncovering Latent Effects of Board Network Ties." *Administrative Science Quarterly* 46 (4): 717–747. doi:10.2307/3094829.

Westphal, J., and I. Stern. 2006. "Interpersonal Influence Behaviour as a Substitute for Elite Credentials and Majority Status in Obtaining Board Appointments." *Administrative Science Quarterly* 51 (2): 169–204. doi:10.2189/asqu.51.2.169.

Westphal, J., and I. Stern. 2007. "Flattery Will Get You Everywhere (Especially if You are a Male Caucasian): How Ingratiation, Boardroom Behaviour, and Demographic Minority Status Affect Additional Board Appointments at U.S. Companies." *Academy of Management Journal* 50 (2): 267–288. doi:10.5465/amj.2007.24634434.

Withers, M., K. Corley, and A. Hillman. 2012. "Stay or Leave: Director Identities and Voluntary Exit from the Board during Organizational Crisis." *Organization Science* 23 (3): 835–850. doi:10.1287/orsc.1110.0660.

Yoo, T. 2017. "The Performance Dimension in Symbolic Management Revisited: The Functional Role of Traditional Mechanisms in Large Korean Firms." *Asia Pacific Business Review* 23 (1): 116–134. doi:10.1080/13602381.2015.1120418.

Yoo, T., and D. Jung. 2015. "Corporate Governance Change and Performance: The Roles of Traditional Mechanisms in France and South Korea." *Scandinavian Journal of Management* 31 (1): 40–53. doi:10.1016/j.scaman.2014.08.005.

Yoo, T., and Y. Koh. 2014. "Agent or Structure for Principal-Principal Conflicts? Audit Firms versus Foreign Ownership in the Asian Context." *Asian Business & Management* 13 (4): 309–332. doi:10.1057/abm.2014.11.

Yoo, T., and M. Rhee. 2013. "Agency Theory and the Context for R&D Investment: Evidence from Korea." *Asian Business & Management* 12 (2): 227–252. doi:10.1057/abm.2013.2.

Yoo, T., and T. Sung. 2015. "How outside Directors Facilitate Corporate R&D Investment? Evidence from Large Korean Firms." *Journal of Business Research* 68 (6): 1251–1260. doi:10.1016/j.jbusres.2014.11.005.

Yoshikawa, T., L. Tsui-Auch, and J. McGuire. 2007. "Corporate Governance Reform as Institutional Innovation: The Case of Japan." *Organization Science* 18 (6): 973–988. doi:10.1287/orsc.1070.0290.

Zhu, D., and G. Chen. 2015. "CEO Narcissism and the Impact of Prior Board Experience on Corporate Strategy." *Administrative Science Quarterly* 60 (1): 31–65. doi:10.1177/0001839214554989.

Zhu, H., and T. Yoshikawa. 2016. "Contingent Value of Director Identification: The Role of Government Directors in Monitoring and Resource Provision in an Emerging Economy." *Strategic Management Journal* 37 (8): 1787–1807. doi:10.1002/smj.2408.

OPEN ACCESS

Transforming Korean business? Foreign acquisition, governance and management after the 1997 Asian crisis

Robert Fitzgerald and Ji Woong Kang

ABSTRACT

The surge in cross-border acquisitions of Korean businesses, following the 1997 Asian Crisis, raised strong debates about the strategic motivations of foreign investors and the failings of selling firms. This article assesses their impact on the governance, management, and competitiveness of the resulting joint ventures and newly-formed enterprises. Contrary to local perceptions, 'fire-sales' and financial opportunism had not motivated foreign buyers, which sought to transform their acquisitions. Nor does government pressure to reform or poor liquidity fully explain the strategies of their Korean counterparts. Through case studies, the article provides insights into the long-term development of governance and management in Korean business.

Introduction: ownership and governance in Korea after 1997

The government and domestic opinion joined the International Monetary Fund in placing blame for the 1997 Asian Crisis and its impact with the *chaebols*, the business groups that dominated the South Korean economy. In this interpretation, the ownership and governance of these *chaebols*, and their affinity for foreign finance, high debts and unrelated diversification explained the economic difficulties facing the country. The government imposed, as a result, governance reforms on indigenous large-scale firms, yet there exists little research on their long-term effects. Moreover, one important component of its change programme was the loosening of inward FDI controls, which allowed foreign acquisitions of Korean businesses. Multinational joint ventures and wholly-owned enterprises would, it was assumed, lead to the transfer of international best-practice management, and act as a source of competition and change. We know little about the *chaebol* subsidiaries whose ownership was transferred to foreign multinationals, and the extent to which they transformed their management practices and core competences. This article explores a number of former *chaebol* affiliates, and analyses the neglected strategic motivations of both the seller and the acquirer. These goals provide insights into the Asian Crisis, and for repercussions on long-term organizational change. We ask to what extent governance, management and capabilities changed in foreign-owned multinational subsidiaries after 1997, and if they differed fundamentally in the short and long-term from Korean-controlled firms.

Literature review: managerial transformation and inward investment

Known as Korea Inc., the nexus of state, banks and *chaebol* business groups oversaw South Korea's industrialization from the 1960s onwards (Jeong 2004; Rohwer 1995; Shin and Chang 2003). While the state set development objectives, it relied heavily on the *chaebols*. Korea's economic success was grounded on indigenous ownership and control. Political and financial networks, as a result, strongly shaped the strategies of the *chaebol*, and the governance, organization and capabilities of affiliate companies (Chang 2006, 2009; Kim 1997; Amsden 1989; Gerschenkron 1962; Haggard 1990; Kohli 2004; Wade 2003). To promote industrialization and the growth of large-scale businesses, the government agreed preferential policy loans, favourable tax rates, and subsidies for the *chaebols*, and introduced protectionism, controlled prices, the licensing of imported technologies, and export goals for preferred firms (Cho 1994; Chen 1995). It allocated the greatest share of financial resources to the largest *chaebols*, for whom sales growth and market share were higher strategic objectives than profitability. The top twenty groups accounted for 7.1% of GDP in 1973, and 14% by 1978 (Jones 1987; Song 1990). The five largest became responsible for 34.8% of manufacturing by 1995, and 45% by 1999, and they were characterized by high levels of diversification through rapid and opportunistic growth (Euh and Rhee 2007; Kang 1989; Lee and Yoo 1987; Rhee 1994). Investments, frequently in unrelated sectors, were not based on thorough risk assessments or profit projections. Circular shareholdings connected the *chaebol* affiliates, and owner-chairmen and their families could control the group with minimal equity. Debts to international lenders, via banks, fuelled the growth of the *chaebols*, notably in the 1990s (Thurbon and Weiss 2006). Between 1990 and 1998, borrowing by the largest thirty rose by 341%. Their average debt-to-equity ratio reached 524% in 1997, the year in which Korea's external debt amounted to US$167bn or 31.4% of GDP (Jeong 2004).

The Asian Crisis of 1997 converted a once-admired business system into the subject of international and domestic criticism. Commercial and merchant banks in Korea encountered liquidity problems, and the won went into freefall (Park and Choi 2004). The Hanbo, Sammi, Jinro, Kia, Haitai and New-Core groups all declared bankruptcy. In December 1997, Korea received a US$58 billion bailout loan from the International Monetary Fund (IMF) on the condition that it agreed to a wide-ranging restructure programme (Hwang 2007). Furthermore, President-elect Kim Dae Jung decided to make the *chaebols* the main target of reform, citing their strategic and organizational weaknesses (*Maeil*, 23 February 1998). Cross-border mergers and acquisitions bringing best global practice in business governance and management would be the main policy instrument. While public opinion was highly critical of the *chaebols*, it perceived M&A as a foreign invasion and as a fire-sale. While especially suspicious of hedge funds, it opposed all inward investors as purely motivated by asset stripping, high returns, and short-term profits (Park 2003; Stoever 2005; Interview #10, #16, #27). Such 'invaders' would not, it followed, invest in the organization and capabilities of their acquisitions, and could not fulfil the government's reform agenda (Zhan and Ozawa 2001). With the *chaebols* being reluctant to reform, and to reduce their grip on the Korean economy, the government imposed targets: the *chaebols* had to reduce debt-to-equity ratios to 200% by 1999, and implement over US$25bn of divestments, including profitable core businesses, by 2000 (Yoon and Kim 1998).

Critics of the Korean business system pointed to the debts of the *chaebols* and crony capitalism as structural deficiencies (Corsetti, Pesenti, and Roubini 1999; Fischer 1998; Goldstein 1998; Hahm and Mishkin 2000). Other voices argued that profit-orientation and the risk calculations associated with market mechanisms could not have achieved rapid industrialization, and that the developmental state model and the government-bank-industry nexus explained Korea's economic achievements. What differentiated 1997 from similar crises in 1970s and 1980s was highly volatile international financial markets creating a self-fulfilling panic. The origins of the Crisis lay not with state activism or the nexus of government, banks and *chaebols*, but with the decontrol of cross-border capital movements and the banking sector (Feldstein 1998; Chang 1998; Chang, Park, and Yoo 1998; Kalinowski 2008; Crotty and Lee 2005; Zheng 2010). Deregulation had begun in the early 1980s, but the pursuit of *segyehwa*, mixing globalization and Anglo-American management practices, by President Kim Young Sam's government during 1993–98 was a turning-point (Seo 2003; Pirie 2006; Kirk 2000; Amsden 1994). The *chaebols* had been allowed to obtain shareholdings in national and regional commercial banks formerly owned by the state, Although these banks were the main source of *chaebol* finance and expansion, the governance implications received little scrutiny (Fields 1995). Large-scale business also invested in 'non-bank financial institutions', the second largest provider of finance, and the regulation of NBFIs was weaker than in the case of the banks. By 1997, the total debt held by the largest thirty *chaebols* was 133,776 billion won, split 55.2 and 42.8% between commercial banks and NBFIs. Short-term low-interest international loans, used to finance long-term *chaebol* investments, increased the risk to the system. The shock when it occurred in 1997 exposed a vulnerable financial structure (Amess & Demetriades, 2010).

Prompted by the IMF, the Kim Dae Jung administration set a high price for bailing out bankrupt banks and businesses, and sought to loosen the grip of the *chaebols* on the economy (Cherry 2003, 2007; Kalinowski 2008; Lee 2001; Lee and Lee 2008; Yu and Choi 1999; Yu and Lee 2000). In their place, it envisaged 'minimum' state intervention, a private capital market committed to prioritising risk assessments and profitability, shorter-term commercial goals, Anglo-American corporate governance, and inward foreign investment (Jun, Sheldon, and Rhee 2010; Jeong 2004; Shin and Chang 2003). The government more clearly codified the accountability and obligations of *chaebol* owners, and stipulated greater protection for minority and independent shareholders. It tightened rules on cross-subsidy between business group affiliates. In addition, it liberalized international mergers and acquisitions and inward FDI (Shin and Chang 2003). Under IMF pressure, in January 1998, President Kim imposed the Five-Point Accord on the five largest *chaebols*, namely Hyundai, Samsung, Daewoo, LG, and SK, and obliged them to focus around three to five core businesses. Uncompetitive affiliates of one group, moreover, would merge with competitive counterparts from another group. The remaining top thirty largest *chaebols* agreed, one month later, to similar restructuring proposals (*Maeil*, 13 January 1998, 24 December 1998, 12 January 1999; Emery 2001; Samsung Economic Research Institute 1998). Inward FDI would replenish foreign currency reserves, and, through M&As, reduce the debt-to-equity ratios of the *chaebols* (Kim and Lee 2007). By driving corporate restructuring and efficiency improvements, it would over the long-term stimulate economic growth (Korea Institute for Industrial Economics & Trade 2001). The threat of hostile acquisition, it was hoped, would impose market discipline on the family-owned *chaebol*, and intensify competition (Cherry 2007; Emery 2001; Thurbon and Weiss 2006). The Korean government passed the Foreign Investment Promotion Act in November 1998, and set ambitious goals of US$20 billion of inward FDI and joining the world's top ten recipients by 2002 (Cherry 2007; Lee, Kim, and Choi 2004; Thurbon and Weiss 2006). By 1999, total IFDI reached US$15.5 billion, with 33% of the sum committed to M&As (*Maeil*, 20 February 2007).

One description of Korean firms in 1997 views them as disadvantaged by exceptional international circumstances, and, subsequently, as unduly pressured by the IMF and their own government into fire-sales of benefit to foreign asset-strippers. Yet we know that some acquired businesses encountered liquidity and capital shortages before the Asian Crisis, and lacked core competencies for long-term competitiveness. Samsung's hypermarket and automobile subsidiaries, Homeplus and Samsung Motor Industries, were examples, as struggling recently-founded firms. In these cases, the Crisis cannot by itself explain the strategic decision of the *chaebols* to divest. The existence of commercial difficulties influenced the priorities of post-acquisition restructuring, and counters the emphasis on unwanted fire-sales. Acquirers bought their new subsidiaries cognisant of the managerial challenges, and aware of which resources and capabilities they needed to transfer and strengthen their investments. Some multinationals had a track-record in international expansion and experience of transforming local enterprises. They sought cross-border synergies that might benefit their operations both in Korea and worldwide (Zhan and Ozawa 2001). For others, acquisitions offered rapid entry into Korea's domestic market, or added prominent Korean exporters to their global production chains. Multinationals focused, too, on buying technology and know-how, and, here, capability transfers could potentially be from the subsidiary to the parent or two-way. Nonetheless, the popular Korean view that foreign acquisitions consistently led to the loss or denuding of key industrial assets was unfounded. Multinational subsidiaries did become less risk-adverse and more focused on profitability and financial outcomes over corporate objectives such as growth, a trend regarded with suspicion by local employees. A corollary was performance-related pay and, potentially, greater job insecurity. The new multinational owners curbed top-down, hierarchical and personal management and decision-making in favour of flatter organizations, inter-departmental coordination, and more collective procedures (Interview #16). This article investigates the implications and the effectiveness of these changes to the management of Korean business, and provides cases and insights into the multinational subsidiaries created as a result of the 1997 Crisis.

Methodology and research questions

Research was principally based on a series of semi-structured interviews with the business executives of leading *chaebol* affiliates acquired by foreign multinationals as a result of the 1997 Asian Crisis. Open-ended questions enabled full exploration of relevant interacting factors, including acquirer motivation, *chaebol* strategic objectives, the resources and capabilities of the parent firm and the subsidiary, and changes in governance and managerial decision-making. Supplemented by company documents, and business newspaper and industry reports, the interviews enabled the in-depth longitudinal analysis of relevant firms, and the semi-structured approach additionally allowed the comparison of businesses and the major factors shaping the outcomes of foreign ownership. With the chosen methodology, the context of the case firms as well as internal developments were explored, and industry and product market characteristics were considered alongside the changing national and international background. Each selected case was shaped by heterogeneous, constantly changing contexts, such as economic conditions, their competitive situation in specific markets, and the different strategies, resources, and capabilities of the firm. Case selection measured the consequences of cross-border acquisitions across various industries, improving the generalisability of the research findings. A total of 48 interviews were conducted, of which 36 are cited in this article.

Using the data provided, the research addressed a number of questions:

- Firstly, to what extent did acquisition by a foreign multinational as a result of the 1997 Asian Crisis transform the governance and management of *chaebol* affiliates, and which factors determined the outcomes?
- Secondly, were changes in governance and management within foreign-owned multinational subsidiaries fundamentally different to developments in Korean-controlled *chaebol* affiliates?
- Thirdly, following the change to foreign ownership, did the capabilities and long-term competitiveness of the acquired *chaebol* affiliates increase or diminish?

Foreign acquisitions and strategic motivations

In the crisis period after 1997, the overriding motive of the *chaebols* was to improve liquidity and to cut debt-to-equity ratios. Some of the businesses sold were profitable, and so provided support for claims of fire-sales. But, given the aim of refocusing and reducing debt, they were regarded as non-strategic by the divesting group: examples, between 1998–2000, included Samsung Electronics, which sold its power device company to Fairchild Semiconductor International; LG Chemicals, which passed its carbon black operation to Degussa; and LG Building Systems, which created a joint venture with Otis Elevator (*Korea Economic Daily*, 19 November 1998). Fairchild Korea Semiconductor and Korea Carbon Black (KCB) were fully-owned multinational subsidiaries at the outset, and Otis Elevator Korea adopted the same ownership and governance arrangements after a short period. Samsung Electronics, in 2002, sold its non-core controller division to Rockwell Automation.

Severe financial difficulties also brought about the sale of core businesses. Samsung, for example, sold its Homeplus hypermarkets and other retailers, which it had intended to develop into a core business. The group affiliate and trading company, Samsung Corporation, had founded Homeplus in 1994. The acquirer was Tesco, the British multinational, which initially preferred a joint venture. It proved able to transfer the financial, managerial, organisational, and operational resources clearly required by Homeplus, which was controlled by the newly-established Samsung Tesco. Samsung Motors Incorporated (SMI) was the second of the group's new ventures in the 1990s, and Korea's most prominent example of governance and business failure. With its global strategic partner Nissan, Renault purchased SMI, which was so obviously short of key technological, managerial and operational capabilities. Samsung's chairman, Lee Kun Hee, had wanted to establish automobile production as core to his *chaebol*, but the haemorrhaging of cash by the new venture became unsustainable. It was the first company in the history of Samsung Group to apply for court receivership. Entry into automobile production was a strategic mistake, following a decision made by the chairman to satisfy his personal obsession for cars (Interview #23). The first vehicle, launched at the outbreak of the Crisis, brought collapsing consumer confidence (Interview #35; Lee and Lee 2007). In 2000, Renault Samsung Motors (RSM) was formed as a joint venture, 70.1% owned by Renault, 19.9% by Samsung, and 10% by 17 creditor banks (Renault, *Annual Report*, 2001; RSM, internal finance document, November 2005). In 2006, Renault increased its holdings in RSM to 80.1% (RSM, *Financial Report*, 2006).

While Homeplus and SMI's difficulties predated 1997, the Asian Crisis did undermine Korean firms with established competitive advantages. By the end of 1998, Lafarge had purchased the plasterboard businesses of Dongbu Hannong Chemical and Byucksan Corporation, founding Lafarge Gypsum Korea Co. Ltd (*Maeil*, 20, 25 September 2000, 29 May 2002; 30 June 2005). Interbrew, in September 1998, bought the majority of Oriental Brewing, with its huge 73% of the Korean beer market, and created a joint venture. The seller, the highly diverse Doosan Group, had been implementing a restructuring programme since 1995 in response to liquidity problems, and, as a result, had sold business to or created joint ventures with Nestle, 3M, Kodak, Seagram, and Coca Cola. During the Asian Crisis, Doosan was consequently financially stronger than most *chaebols*, and, with the sale of Oriental Brewery, it embarked on a series of new but more focused acquisitions. During 1998, it reorganized its remaining 23 affiliates into four companies (*Maeil Business*, 7 April 2009; *Korea Economic Daily*, 30 October 2002, 29 March 2005; Interview #2, #23).

Rapid entry and growth were primary long-term objectives for Tesco, Renault, Otis, Interbrew, and Lafarge. Fairchild and Degussa gained the access they needed to the existing large customers of divesting firms, while Interbrew, Lafarge, and Renault set out to buy local distribution networks, as well as manufacturing facilities. Samsung Tesco's Homeplus, RSM, Oriental Brewery and Otis Korea were originally joint ventures, assuaging local perceptions of asset-stripping, and allowing acquirers to learn more effectively about their new subsidiaries and customers. Over time, they all moved towards full foreign ownership. Most of the multinationals purchasing Korean businesses after 1997 had experience of international acquisitions. They were, therefore, continuing with their global expansion drive, and, sought further synergies across their cross-border operations (Interview #2, #22, #23, #36).

Governance and managerial decision-making

Within the *chaebols*, the affiliate CEO personally made operational decisions, while the group chairman, usually from the founding family, decided group-wide strategic issues. Decision-making was top-down and based on personal authority, and formal consultation procedures were not prominent. Through complex shareholding arrangements, the chairman and the founding family exercised decision-making powers significantly greater than their ownership stakes across the group (Interview #36; *Financial Times*, 22 April 2008). With the Asian Crisis being attributed in part to Korean corporate governance failures, the case firms had to address pressing organizational issues around top-down personal decision-making. The consequences were creating greater coordination and more collectively-inclined processes, establishing an emphasis on financial performance, and transforming the embedded attitudes and practices of employees (Interview #22).

At RSM, formal organizational structures remained largely unchanged, as was the pattern at Otis Elevator and KCB. But all three firms introduced management committees to oversee the subsidiary president or CEO, and inculcated more collectively-inclined practices. Within each *chaebol* affiliate, the performance of the president and directors was typically associated with their ability to implement the policies of the group owner-chairman. The owners and managers of the Samsung Group, in establishing SMI, had ignored the automotive experts they had employed directly from rivals. Given projected returns, their specialists had strongly opposed the levels of investment, and the scale of the Busan factory and its production facilities. The chairman's wish to build the 'best' car meant that Samsung bought the highest standard of equipment and components possible. There was also the question of 'face': how the new venture was perceived was important, and this attitude led to high expenditure on plant, arguably to the detriment of the product (Interview #3, #26).

Top management at Samsung and SMI lacked the knowledge and experience a competitive automaker needed. One manager explained how he was simply expected to follow the decisions of the group's top management, despite his relatively senior position. To transform its new subsidiary, Renault sent over 30 expatriates, who included the CEO, CFO, the heads of R&D and Design, and various specialist managers in procurement, engineering, and manufacturing. As a result, it enhanced local capabilities, ensured greater cross-border coordination and synergies with global operations, and facilitated the production, development and launch of vehicles. Renault introduced an executive committee in which consultations and discussions on all key issues occurred once a week between the leaders of business functions. While all Korean companies have an executive meeting, the cross-functional activity is highlighted at RSM (Interview #23). Without such a committee system, there was a danger that executives would compete against each other for the attention of a new foreign CEO. Renault's emphasis on consultation and coordination between different business functions led to the emergence of other committees at the lower levels of hierarchy (Interview #2, #18, #23). The new decision-making system is rooted in the Renault's business concept of 'organisation with no wall'. In a multinational including Renault, Nissan and RSM, the group requires effective decision-making processes that 'persuade' everyone to move in the same direction (Interview #18, #23). The new system had other benefits: it was effective in building consensus throughout the organisation, and motivating employees. In other words, employees, regardless of business function, could accept and work for organisational goals. Previously, it was possible for each function or individual to pursue their own objectives (Interview, #18).

At Otis Elevator, the management committee required agreement among department heads, included technical input, and sought consensus throughout the subsidiary, in the hope of reaching sound outcomes (Interview, #9, #29, #35, #36). But managers expressed their belief that the business suffered commercially from a lack of local decision-making authority. Obtaining approval from the Asian regional headquarters on a wide range of issues caused frustration. The powers of the president, it was argued, became notably limited, affecting negotiations and decisions on bids for large installation projects. An expatriate CFO, who would be promoted to president in 2008, helped to safeguard performance targets, but increased the scope for unfamiliar internal disagreements (Interview #7, #8). Interestingly, managers at KCB reported that the tradition of speedy decision-making continued, largely due to a foreign CEO who understood Korean management and, furthermore, effectively handled relations between the subsidiary and the Degussa headquarters (Interview #7). All the acquired businesses adopted similar management committee systems, and, in most cases, transformed internal organization by introducing functional departments.

Tesco retained its Korean CEO, which led to instances of arbitrary and top-down outcomes, but the appointment of expatriates and the formalization of decision-making instigated a process of change. Initially, Tesco appointed expatriates to head three of the six newly-created divisions, and it transferred some 30 specialists from its headquarters to lead business functions deemed to lack know-how, including Finance & Strategy, Property Management, Customer Insight, Operations, and Commercial Grocery or procurement. The marketing director was a local, as no expatriate could have adequate understanding of the Korean hypermarket industry (Interview, #1, #13, #19, #28; 'Our Talent – Homeplus People', Samsung Tesco, internal HR document, May 2006). Tesco introduced a flatter organisational structure based on specialised functional units, and its 'Work Level System' reduced hierarchy levels from 11 to 6 in the interests of faster decision-making. A management committee coordinated between different functions (Interview, #14, #28). The CEO chaired the committee, composed of department heads, usually a Vice-President. With the emphasis on cooperation and agreement, the VPs were given wide decision-making powers, in contrast to the complete authority of the CEO or President found in more traditional Korean management. Samsung Tesco, in addition, initiated committee meetings below the VP grade, so that specialists from different functional departments could share ideas and implement policies. Korean-style decision-making, being top-down and swift, risked inadequate technical input and low levels of consensus. At Samsung Tesco, expansion planning and the opening of new stores improved, as former unstructured discussions and lack of experience had led to each outlet taking 2–3 years to open. Samsung Tesco submitted investment proposals, prepared by both the Marketing and Finance Departments, to the parent multinational for approval. A proposal required a high degree of cross-functional coordination. Alongside market and competitor analysis, return on investment (ROI) and net present value (NPV) calculations determined final approval. The subsidiary's business focus, as a result, shifted to profitability and efficiency improvements (Interview #2, #11, #14, #19). The subsidiary opened 71 hypermarkets and 232 express stores between 2000 to 2010 (Interview #14). It would, by 2005, purchase two major supermarket chains in order to expand within a saturated market and in regions where it had little coverage (*Korea Herald*, 21 January 2005; Tesco, *Annual Report*, 2006). The directors of Samsung Tesco directors adopted the 'Tesco way', the three principles of decision-making being 'better for customer, simpler for staff, and cheaper for the company' (Interview, #1, #4).

Fairchild Korea Semiconductor and Rockwell Samsung Automation created clearly defined functional organisations, based around manufacturing, sales, product, finance, or administration, and appointed a head to each unit. Departmental leads formed a management committee chaired by the subsidiary president or CEO (FSI, *Annual Report*, 2011; Interview, #35). The new organisational structures radically changed internal procedures, and introduced open policy arguments and disputes quite untypical in

Korean firms. At both businesses, managers commented how processes became slower and more complex. Critically, they also came to be more deliberative, getting inputs from each department and enhancing coordination over decisions and plans (Interview #9, #29, #35, #36). Managers at Fairchild Korea believed that the authority and decisiveness of Samsung's chairman had brought first mover advantages and, to a large extent, explained the *chaebol*'s success in semiconductors. With huge investment on a continuous basis, and with products having a very short life cycle, the economic environment had favoured bold fast decisions (*Korea Economic Daily*, 11 December 2005). Fairchild Korea vice-presidents, as heads of department, had enhanced authority, which, in turn, reduced the powers that a president would normally exercise within Korean firms. Their three year appointments heightened concerns about short-termism, and communication problems with expatriates and the parent headquarters were noted. Fairchild Korea employed an expatriate CFO, who ensured that the multinational parent's financial targets were met. As at Otis Korea, with authority passing both upwards to the multinational parent and downwards to the vice-presidents, the decision-making authority of the president at Fairchild Korea and Rockwell Samsung in Korea appeared comparatively constrained. In the latter case, furthermore, the regional or main multinational headquarters made all major strategic decisions (Interview, #7, #8, #10). Interbrew and Lafarge, too, transformed their acquired businesses by introducing functional departments, capped by a coordinating management committee. Oriental Brewery retained a Korean CEO, who could have the knowledge needed of its key domestic consumer market, but it did import two departmental heads. Lafarge, by contrast, sent an expatriate CEO. Interbrew established five functional departments at Oriental Brewery, covering human resources, finance, production, sales, and marketing. A VP, with increased decision-making authority, headed each department and sat on the subsidiary's management committee. Most VPs at Oriental Brewery did not understand why agreement and consultation with other departments were necessary. They argued that their colleagues did not have the information to understand other functions. VPs would confront each other to avoid their department being blamed for failure, and opted for low risk outcomes. They would consequently pass on difficult decisions to the Interbrew headquarters, a process that slowed speed of action (Interview #12, #23, #33). Eventually, Interbrew began appointing expatriate CEOs to Oriental Brewery for short periods of two to three years, an approach viewed as increasing the emphasis on financial performance and short-termism (Interview #6).

Most of the case firms experienced initial integration problems. As the post-acquisition transformation at Oriental Brewery and Lafarge Korea was limited, the majority of their employees were receptive to the changes introduced, but viewed the 'foreign' emphasis on profitability over expansion with suspicion. At Lafarge Korea, existing employees in general found it difficult to accept the move away from the established management system towards one founded on individual performance. They preferred promotion based on length of service and life-time job security. Integrating four groups – expatriates from Lafarge, personnel from former rival firms Dongbu and Byucksan, and those recruited after acquisition – aggravated the human resource difficulties. Rockwell Samsung mitigated resistance through training, cross-functional operations, and integration programmes (Interview #2, #5, #22, #23, #30, #36).

Resource and capability transfers

Resource and capability transfers to the subsidiary generally necessitated the appointment and higher use of expatriate executives with the requisite skills and experience, and these managers brought the capacity to coordinate effectively with the parent firm on a range of issues. Strong local capabilities or significant domestic sales led to greater reliance on indigenous or existing managers with core product, production or marketing knowledge. Samsung's Homeplus was a strategic opportunity for Tesco to establish itself in Korea's highly competitive hyper- and supermarket industries. The British retailer had identified its prospective subsidiary's organizational weaknesses, and perceived the business as well-suited to receiving its internationally recognised know-how. Therefore, to fulfil its strategic objectives in Korea, Tesco sent specialists to embed capabilities in property management, finance, and operations, but, as we have noted, it appointed an indigenous marketing director who understood Korean retailing and local consumers. Homeplus had been short of expertise in property management and store expansion, with the result that it had operated inefficiently and grown the business slowly. Tesco prioritized the strengthening of this function, introducing its personnel and tested systems, and instigating training schemes, sometimes on-the-job in Thailand or the UK. It followed a similar approach to supply chain management, market analysis, customer insight surveys, and stock management. The Customer Insight Unit facilitated discussions with the parent firm, and spearheaded the conversion of Samsung Tesco into a customer-centred business. The Supply Chain Management (SCM) Unit would improve stock management at every store. The Customer Plan and Family Card schemes were copies of Tesco's Clubcard loyalty scheme, and the data it provided assisted the formulation and implementation of policies. The UK marketing department regularly provided advice to Samsung Tesco (*Maeil*, 12 July 2001; Interview #21, #28). Overall, the multinational followed the approach it had successfully adopted in Thailand, one of gradual integration and 'glocalisation'. Given differences in retailing, consumer preferences, and Samsung Tesco's corporate culture, it introduced its global standards selectively, recognizing where necessary essential local strengths and skills, but setting the strategic direction in Korea and globally (Interview #2, #14, #19; Suh and Howard 2009).

Given that SMI had only one vehicle at the time of acquisition, Renault's priority was to build a strong portfolio of models. To do so, it owned the financial resources, engineering and management know-how and operational expertise required at RSM, and it addressed the other key issue of human resources and enhanced training schemes (Interview #2, #18). Renault and particularly Nissan transferred their most advanced automotive technologies and production methods. Employees underwent on-the-job training at both Renault and Nissan's headquarters and at their R&D centres, and, likewise, engineers from the French and Japanese companies visited RSM. The subsidiary's R&D function was substantially strengthened, with staff numbers growing from 400 in 2000 to 1,260 by 2010. The Busan factory, having been equipped by Nissan, fitted fortuitously into Renault-Nissan systems, and quickly achieved cross-border operational synergies (Renault, press release, 13 June 2000). Further capital investment was not forthcoming, due to Samsung's overinvestment and substantial spare production capacity. Employee numbers increased from 2,000 in 2000 to 5,500 in 2011 in line with output. As well as manufacturing for the Korean market, the subsidiary exported through Renault-Nissan's global distribution network. As a member of the Renault-Nissan alliance, RSM could buy the most advanced vehicle technology from Renault and Nissan at cost prices, and joint international procurement brought efficiencies (Interview #23). Profits were reinvested in the business, funding vehicle development, R&D, and the Renault Samsung Technical Center (RSTC) at Giehung (Renault, press release, 24 November 2005; Interview #2, #3, #16, #23).

Interbrew wanted, undoubtedly, to change the main strategic aim of Oriental Brewery from expanding sales through heavy debt-financed marketing expenditure towards short-term profitability. It restrained budget increases, cut costs and especially marketing expenditure, and focused on efficiency targets such as labour costs per unit or return on assets. The Doosan Group sold its affiliate to off-load a loss-making business, and to reduce debt burdens. Oriental Brewery, nonetheless, owned brands with wide popular appeal in Korea, and produced beers of high quality. Interbrew had no need to invest in plant or manufacturing skills, and retained the existing training structures. Marketing, founded on local conditions, remained with indigenous managers at the subsidiary. With Koreans showing little interest in Interbrew brands, procurement was the only cross-border synergy of substance (Interview #6, #12, #23, #31, #32, #34). As one manager reported, Interbrew did not transform Oriental Brewery on the lines witnessed at Samsung Tesco or RSM (Interview #12). As had Interbrew, Lafarge had bought from debt-laden Korean businesses, and immediately imposed financial controls, tight budgets, and profit targets. Similarly, because the subsidiary's products had a high reputation, and Korean managers oversaw local customer networks, matters of product, production and marketing remained unchanged (Interview #5, #12, #33).

The Asian Crisis enabled Degussa to establish a presence in Korea, and to gain established access to local buyers. As at RSM, KCB exported goods produced in Korea through Degussa's global distribution network. Transfer of technological know-how was limited, as the subsidiary was well-regarded in this core competence. Reflecting the cases of Interbrew and Lafarge, Degussa largely maintained organizational practices, including training systems. On the other hand, it introduced global standards in IT, finance and foreign currency, risk management, environmental standards, and social responsibility (Interview, #7). Otis Korea began by expanding the maintenance unit and gaining a greater share of Korea's elevator service market. However, to do so, it sold off production facilities and laid off workers in the unprofitable manufacturing division in Korea. Otis did introduce global standards in finance, safety, and ethics. But, as with Interbrew, Lafarge, and Degussa, it retained the majority of the subsidiary's systems and practices. To cut production costs, Otis Korea began to produce more at its factory in Dalian, China, than in Korea (Interview #8).

Fairchild had been attracted to Korea's large semiconductor market, and it acquired access to Samsung's distribution and customer network. It hoped that the subsidiary's acknowledged technological leadership would create a more diversified and advanced product portfolio. In the event, these capabilities led to production being relocated to Korea, and the parent firm made small contribution to capability levels at Fairchild Korea. Fairchild invested substantially in capital projects, but a combination of poor planning and deteriorating market conditions led to major losses (Interview #17, #29). Rockwell was equally attracted by the existence of major customers in Korea, and by operational synergies. Domestic sales rose notably, and exports from the subsidiary improved impressively by a factor of ten between 2002 to 2005. With both parent and subsidiary having distinctive technological capabilities, transfers occurred in both directions through personnel exchange, rotation, and training programmes (Interview #10, #36).

Discussion

Before the 1997 Crisis, the *chaebols* routinely pursued debt-driven growth and market share with inadequate attention to risk-assessment and profitability. The owning families and the appointed chairmen exercised control of these influential business groups significantly greater than their equity, and could transfer value from minority shareholders. With the encouragement of the IMF, the Korean government saw inward FDI and acquisition by foreign multinationals as tools for reducing the debts and the scale of the *chaebols* and believed that international best practice could transform the governance, management and competitive capabilities of both acquired firms and the wider economy. These plans supported the refocusing of the highly-diversified conglomerates that dominated the economy, and programmes to improve corporate transparency and the rights of minority shareholders. To align managerial objectives with the need for sustainability and profitability, and to enhance shareholder value, businesses acknowledged performance based pay, as opposed to seniority-based pay and bonuses.

Undoubtedly, the 1997 Crisis transformed Korean businesses, moving structures and decision-making from an orientation founded on hierarchy, top-down personal authority, a functional focus, rapid growth, and seniority pay and bonuses, which were all associated with a domestic management style. Evidence detects a general shift towards more horizontal and consultative processes, profitability, performance-based decision-making, and professionalism, all connected with international standards and practices (Rowley and Park 2009: 54–62, 125–6). To what extent, therefore, did acquisition by a foreign multinational contribute to the transformation of the governance and management of *chaebol* affiliates? Which factors, international or domestic, determined the outcomes? While each case inevitably shows variations, we can see a clear pattern in the imposition of profit and performance targets that determined investment and operations, as a result of a change in ownership and control. In many cases, the appointment of an expatriate CEO or CFO reinforced the redirection of strategic objectives. Nonetheless, internal debates on the advantages of quick decision-making, risk-taking and long-termism versus short-term profitability and financial sustainability continued. A Bank of Korea report investigated the financial performance of over one hundred majority or fully foreign-owned manufacturing firms, and concluded they were on average more profitable than domestically-controlled firms (Kim and Kim 2008).

Some of the cases witnessed organizational and departmental restructuring, with Samsung Tesco being the most prominent example. Technological leadership, competitive capabilities, and profitability levels largely determined differences in the level of post-acquisition reorganization. On this point, RSM was an exception, because its organization and operational systems, far from being extant and established, needed to be created. The introduction of management committees and interdepartmental coordination in all the multinational subsidiaries studies indicated a strong commitment to horizontal procedures and to the curtailment of top-down personal management. The greater authority of department heads and Vice-Presidents and the control exercised by the parent multinational diminished, bar exceptional circumstances, the role of the CEO or President. Forced to accept horizontal coordination, and interference in their own function or department, subsidiary Vice-Presidents often felt uncomfortable with the change towards consultative procedures, and no doubt attachment to traditional Korean management generally held back acceptance of international practices. The management committee and other coordinating bodies did facilitate technical input, and supported professional processes over the more familiar authoritarian and personal style. Training schemes were introduced or enhanced to improve human resource competence and to increase greater understanding of the multinational's management systems, particularly where cross-borders synergies or capability transfers were paramount.

Were changes in governance and management within foreign-owned multinational subsidiaries fundamentally different to developments in Korean-controlled *chaebol* affiliates? All of the changes in governance and decision-making within multinational subsidiaries located in South Korea had parallels in businesses that remained indigenously owned, mostly because they resulted out of the Crisis and financial necessity. They show the impact of internationalization and global standards on Korea during this period. But they emphasize, too, the importance of ownership on governance, because the case evidence suggests that managerial change in multinational subsidiaries proved comparatively more extensive, deeper and durable.

Lastly, following the change to foreign ownership, did the capabilities and long-term competitiveness of the acquired *chaebol* affiliates increase or diminish? The Korean government enabled inward FDI and international M&A on the grounds it would boost the performance of acquired subsidiaries, and, by example, transform the economy more widely. The case evidence strongly counters public fears that foreign multinationals came after 1997 as opportunistic exploiters of fire-sales and as financially-orientated asset strippers. Wholly-owned subsidiaries in Korea proved better able, when strategically motivated, at transferring resources and capabilities than in identified examples of international joint ventures . But the extent the multinationals invested in their subsidiaries or transferred resources and capabilities varied significantly. Where subsidiaries were bought for their technological leadership, or for their existing domestic and export competitiveness, the transfer of resources and capabilities was more limited. The cases of Fairchild Korea and Rockwell Samsung indicate how capability transfers from subsidiary to parent were important. There is, furthermore, a shortage of evidence to prove that the example of multinational subsidiaries incentivized change in Korean-controlled rivals. The cases underscore the point about ownership and especially international ownership having detectable determinant consequences for governance.

The effects of outside directors on Korean-controlled firms have been debated, and sceptics have highlighted *chaebol* affiliates for low levels of reform compared to privatized or non-*chaebol* firms (Kim and Kim 2008). But this block to change was not relevant in the case of foreign-owned subsidiaries. The established owners of business groups, moreover, increased circulatory share ownership as a means of maintaining control, and prosecutions revealed notorious breaches of transparency and accountability. With the cap on foreign investment in any firm lifted in 1997, inward FDI rose from 1.1 trn won to 11 trn by 2002 (Rowley and Park 2009: 125). The LG chaebol is cited as a model reform example, due to its decision to form an accountable holding-company in 2003, and for splitting into two focused groups in 2005. Holding companies joined foreign-subsidiaries as potential takeover targets, and both categories posed questions about government policy. Korean business assets became vulnerable to international hedge and wealth funds, which, unlike our multinational cases, correctly or incorrectly, did have reputations as financially-orientated asset strippers. Degussa was acquired by Evonik in 2006, and, mainly for strategic reasons connected to its UK home economy, Tesco divested from Korea in 2015. Hedge funds bought and restructured Interbrew along with AnheuserBusch during 2009. All were a cause of uncertainty within their host country operations (Coe, Lee, and Wood 2017). On the other hand, hostile take-overs in Korea have been relatively rare, a fact that challenges claims of incentivizing governance and managerial reform (Kim and Kim 2008; Rowley and Park, 34–5, 106, 140–6).

Implications

Theoretical implications

The cases raise issues about the corporate strategic objectives of inward FDI, and formative influences on the control and management of multinational subsidiaries. Cross-border integration, capability transfer, and the appointment of expatriates strongly enforced the aims of profitability, management and investment processes, and formal decision-making procedures. Full ownership of the subsidiary, at the outset or following acquisition, gave the investing multinational the necessary leverage to implement change. Each case had unique circumstances, yet the need to transfer capabilities to the subsidiary, reliance on expatriate managers, and degrees of cross-border integration were all influential. Reliance on indigenous managers, who needed some freedom of operation to deal with clients and consumers, decreased the need. This localization trend was exampled by Lafarge Korea and Otis Korea, and specifically within sales and marketing at the greatly-changed Homeplus under Samsung Tesco. Nonetheless, we can also detect isomorphic regulatory and institutional pressures in the wake of the 1997 Crisis in improving profitability, increasing transparency, and implementing new governance rules in Korean business generally.

Practical implications

The article raises questions about government policy towards international M&A, governance rules, and enhanced managerial and competitive capabilities. While inward FDI and international M&A undoubtedly helped reduce the debt, scale and industry diversity of leading *chaebols*, evidence on the transfer of best global practice is mixed. Integration within Renault-Nissan's global operations and access to its resources undoubtedly transformed Samsung's failing automobile division to identifiable beneficial effect. Tesco had the retailing expertise and international experience to contribute significantly to the Homeplus brand. But its forced withdrawal from Korea, after many years of operation, posed questions about how host country governments might reassess the value of each inward investment and ownership change to fulfil the public good. The issue was reflected in Evonik's takeover of Degussa and KCB, and, most controversially, by the dissolution of Interbrew and control over Oriental Brewery. Otis Korea and Lafarge Korea were successful enterprises that gave foreign multinationals access to clients, and international resource and capability transfer are less apparent. Technology and knowledge exchange between Fairchild and Rockwell parent and subsidiary firms was two-way, and it was also mutually, if not equally, beneficial. We can see improvements in decision-making, professional management, technical input, long-term planning and profitability within our multinational subsidiaries cases, but scant evidence that their example changed *chaebol* governance more widely. With their ownership less transformed than privatized enterprises or multinational subsidiaries, and more able than non-group firms to resist greater regulatory pressure, *chaebol* affiliates retained many important elements of traditional Korean management.

Limitations

The cases provided are diverse in terms of industry, and comparisons enable greater analytical depth and scope. Although international M&A was intended to spearhead wider change, we explore only a limited number of cases. Further research on foreign owned subsidiaries in Korea would be useful. Moreover, we need to know more about the mechanics of asset and knowledge transfers, and how, over the long term, new resources and capabilities were integrated and systemized alongside existing systems in pursuit of sustainable differentiated competitive advantage. Alternatively, it would be interesting to investigate where such processes failed to improve or led to decreasing competitive advantage. The results could supply insights into the consequences of differing ownership and governance. Hopefully, also, they might generate a clearer debate about the seizing of rapid growth and first mover advantage under guided state development and personal management, and if greater profitability, lower debt leverage and greater shareholder power provided equally successful alternative corporate goals.

Conclusion

Detailed analysis of the multinational acquirers of *chaebol* affiliates after 1997 demonstrates that they had had long-term strategic motivations, contrary to the widely-held view of financial opportunism and 'fire sales'. Businesses with complementary resources and capabilities were the primary target, and multinationals invested in and transferred advanced resources and capabilities to their subsidiaries. Chaebols divested core businesses to avoid the group-wide bankruptcy or, if over-diversified, to facilitate their refocusing. While the *chaebols* came under government pressure, they also had their own strategic reasons for divesting. The policy objectives of transforming acquired *chaebol* affiliates, and drawing investment and knowledge transfer to Korea through international M&A were achieved in the years immediately following 1997. But the transformation proved limited to these cases, and less extensive changes to governance and management elsewhere had a range of other causes. Moreover, foreign ownership did over time create public concern over acquisitions, and raised later debates about asset stripping and the control of vital commercial assets.

References

Amess, K., and P. Demetriades. 2010. "Financial Liberalisation and the South Korean Financial Crisis: An Analysis of Expert Opinion." *World Economy* 33 (2): 212–238. doi:10.1111/j.1467-9701.2009.01225.x.

Amsden, A. 1989. *Asia's Next Giant: South Korea and Late Industrialization*. Oxford: Oxford University Press.

Amsden, A. 1994. "The Specter of Anglo-Saxonization Is Haunting South Korea." In *Korea's Political Economy: An Institutional Perspective*, edited by L. Cho and Y. H. Kim, 87–126. Boulder, CO: Westview Press.

Chang, D. O. 2009. *Capitalist Development in Korea: Labour, Capital, and the Myth of the Developmental State*. New York: Routledge.

Chang, H. J. 1998. "South Korea: The Misunderstood Crisis." In *Tigers in Trouble*, edited by K. S. Jomo, 223–231. London: Zed Books.

Chang, H. J. 2006. *The East Asian Development Experience: The Miracle, the Crisis and the Future*. New York: Zed Books.

Chang, H. J., H. J. Park, and G. C. Yoo. 1998. "Interpreting the Korean Crisis: Financial Liberalization, Industrial Policy and Corporate Governance." *Cambridge Journal of Economics* 22 (6): 735–746. doi:10.1093/cje/22.6.735.

Chen, M. 1995. *Asian Management Systems: Chinese, Japanese and Korean Styles of Business*. London: Routledge.

Cherry, J. 2003. "The 'Big Deals' and Hynix Semiconductor: State-Business Relations in Post-Crisis Korea." *Asia Pacific Business Review* 10 (2): 178–198. doi:10.1080/13602380410001677209.

Cherry, J. 2007. *Foreign Direct Investment in Post-crisis Korea: European Investors and 'Mismatched Globalization'*. Oxford: Routledge.

Cho, S. 1994. *The Dynamics of Korean Economic Development*. Washington, DC: Institute for International Economics.

Coe, N. M., Y. S. Lee, and S. Wood. 2017. "Conceptualizing Contemporary Retail Divestment: Tesco's Departure from South Korea." *Environment and Planning A* 49 (12): 2739–2761. doi:10.1177/0308518X17733265.

Corsetti, G., P. Pesenti, and N. Roubini. 1999. "What Caused the Asian Currency and Financial Crisis?." *Japan and the World Economy* 11 (3): 305–373. doi:10.1016/S0922-1425(99)00019-5.

Crotty, J., and K. K. Lee. 2005. "From East Asian "Miracle" to Neo-liberal "Mediocrity": The Effects of Liberalization and Financial Opening on the Post-crisis Korean Economy." *Global Economic Review* 34 (4): 415–434. doi:10.1080/12265080500441388.

Emery, R. 2001. *Korean Economic Reform: Before and since the 1997 Crisis*. Aldershot: Ashgate.

Euh, Y. D., and J. H. Rhee. 2007. "Lessons from the Korean Crisis: Policy and Managerial Implications." *Long Range Planning* 40 (4/5): 431–445. doi:10.1016/j.lrp.2007.06.005.

Fairchild Semiconductor International. 2011. *Annual Report*, Sunnyvale, California.

Feldstein, M. 1998. "Refocusing the IMF." *Foreign Affairs* 77: 20–33. doi:10.2307/20048786.

Fields, K. 1995. *Enterprise and the State in Korea and Taiwan*. Ithaca, NY: Cornell University Press.

Financial Times, as dates cited.

Fischer, S. 1998. "In Defense of the IMF: Specialized Tools for a Specialized Task." *Foreign Affairs* 77: 103–106. doi:10.2307/20048970.

Gerschenkron, A. 1962. *Economic Backwardness in Historical Perspective*. Cambridge, MA: Harvard University Press.

Goldstein, M. 1998. *The Asian Financial Crisis: Causes, Cures, and Systematic Implications*. Washington, DC: Institute for International Economics.

Haggard, S. 1990. *Pathways from the Periphery: The Politics of Growth in the Newly Industrializing Countries*. Ithaca, NY: Cornell University Press.

Hahm, J. H., and F. Mishkin. 2000. "The Korean Financial Crisis: An Asymmetric Information Perspective." *Emerging Markets Review* 1 (1): 21–52. doi:10.1016/S1566-0141(00)00003-0.

Hwang, I. S. 2007. "'Korean Currency Crisis in 1997: Assessment and Tasks a Decade Later', Samsung Economic Research Institute (SERI)." *Korea Economic Trends* 12 (45): 10–14.

Jeong, S. I. 2004. *Crisis and Restructuring in East Asia: The Case of the Korean Chaebol and the Automotive Industry*. Hampshire, UK: Palgrave Macmillan.

Jones, L. P. 1987. "Jaebul and the Concentration of Economic Power in Korean Development: Issues, Evidence and Alternatives." In *Macroeconomic Policy and Industrial Development*, edited by I. Sakong, 256–284. Seoul: Korea Development Institute (KDI).

Jun, I., P. Sheldon, and J. H. Rhee. 2010. "Business Groups and Regulatory Institutions: Korea's Chaebols, Cross-company Shareholding and the East Asian Crisis." *Asian Business & Management* 9 (4): 499–523. doi:10.1057/abm.2010.26.

Kalinowski, T. 2008. "Korea's Recovery since the 1997/98 Financial Crisis: The Last Stage of the Developmental State." *New Political Economy* 13 (4): 447–462. doi:10.1080/13563460802436616.

Kang, T. W. 1989. *Is Korea the Next Japan?: Understanding the Structure, Strategy, and Tactics of America's Next Competitor*. New York: Free Press.

Kim, E. H., and W. Kim. 2008. "Changes in Korean Corporate Governance: A Response to Crisis." *Journal of Applied Corporate Finance* 20 (1): 46–58. doi:10.1111/j.1745-6622.2008.00168.x.

Kim, E. M. 1997. *Big Businesses, Strong State: Collusion and Conflict in South Korean Development, 1960-1990*. New York: State University of New York Press.

Kim, W. S., and Y. I. Lee. 2007. "Challenges of Korea's Foreign Direct Investment-Led Globalization: Multinational Corporations' Perceptions." *Asia Pacific Business Review* 13 (2): 163–181. doi:10.1080/13602380701223001.

Kirk, D. 2000. *Korean Crisis: Unraveling of the Miracle in the IMF Era*. London: Macmillan.

Kohli, A. 2004. *State-directed Development: Political Power and Industrialization in the Global Periphery*. Cambridge: Cambridge University Press.

Korea Economic Daily, dates as cited.

Korea Herald, dates as cited.

Korea Institute for Industrial Economics & Trade. 2001. *(In Korean) Analysis of the Five Benefits Gained from FDI*. Seoul: KIET.

Lee, J. 2001. "Korea's Financial Crisis: The Crisis of a Development Model?." In *From Crisis to Recovery: East Asia Rising Again?*, edited by T. Yu and D. Xu, 101–140. London: World Scientific.

Lee, K., and C. H. Lee. 2008. "The Miracle to Crisis and the Mirage of the Postcrisis Reform in Korea: Assessment after Ten Years." *Journal of Asian Economics* 19 (5–6): 425–437. doi:10.1016/j.asieco.2008.09.003.

Lee, S. B., J. D. Kim, and N. G. Choi. 2004. "Republic of Korea." In *Managing FDI in a Globalizing Economy: Asian Experiences*, edited by D. Brooks and H. Hill, 153–187. Hampshire: Palgrave Macmillan.

Lee, S. M., and S. J. Yoo. 1987. "Management Style and Practice of Korean Chaebols." *California Management Review* 95: 95–110.

Lee, W., and N. S. Lee. 2007. "Understanding Samsung's Diversification Strategy: The Case of Samsung Motors Incorporated." *Long Range Planning* 40: 488–504. doi:10.1016/j.lrp.2007.06.011.

Maeil, Business Newspaper, dates as cited.

Park, W. A., and G. Choi. 2004. "What Caused the Crisis? A Post Mortem." In *The Korean Economy beyond the Crisis*, edited by D. K. Chung and B. Eichengreen, 48–68. Cheltenham, UK: Edward Elgar.

Park, Y. S. 2003. "FDI into Korea: The past as Prologue." In *Raising the Bar: Korea as a Global Economic Player*, edited by J. Lister, 25–46. Washington, DC: Korea Economic Institute.

Pirie, I. 2006. "Economic Crisis and the Construction of a Neo-Liberal Regulatory Regime in Korea." *Competition & Change* 10 (1): 49–71. doi:10.1179/102452906X92000.
Renault. 2001. *Annual Report.*
Renault Samsung Motors (RSM). 2006. *Financial Report.*
Rhee, J. C. 1994. *The State and Industry in South Korea: The Limits of the Authoritarian State.* London: Routledge.
Rohwer, J. 1995. *Asia Rising.* New York: Simon & Schuster.
Rowley, C., and Y. Park. 2009. *The Changing Face of Korean Management.* Oxford: Routledge.
Samsung Economic Research Institute. 1998. "Drastic Restructuring Has Been Agreed upon by the Government and the Five Largest Conglomerates." *Korean Economic Trends* 2 (38): 4–6.
Seo, J. S. 2003. "Real Exchange Rate and Inward FDI in Crisis-ridden Korea." In *The Korean Economy at the Crossroads*, edited by M. J. Tcha and C. S. Suh, 153–164. London: RoutledgeCurzon.
Shin, J. S., and H. J. Chang. 2003. *Restructuring Korea Inc.* London: RoutledgeCurzon.
Song, B. N. 1990. *The Rise of the Korean Economy.* Oxford: Oxford University Press.
Stoever, W. 2005. "Restructuring FDI Policy in Emerging Economies: The Republic of Korea Case." *Thunderbird International Business Review* 47 (5): 555–574. doi:10.1002/tie.20067.
Suh, Y. G., and E. Howard. 2009. "Restructuring Retailing in Korea: The Case of Samsung Tesco." *Asia Pacific Business Review* 15 (1): 29–40. doi:10.1080/13602380802399312.
Tesco. 2006. *Annual Report.*
Thurbon, E., and L. Weiss. 2006. "Investing in Openness: The Evolution of FDI Strategy in South Korea and Taiwan." *New Political Economy* 11 (1): 1–22. doi:10.1080/13563460500494784.
Wade, R. 2003. *Governing the Market: Economic Theory and the Role of Government in East Asian Industrialization.* Princeton, NJ: Princeton University Press.
Yoon, J. U., and J. H. Kim 1998. "(in Korean) 'The Industry Trend since IMF Bailout'." Samsung Economic Research Institute (SERI), CEO Information: 132.
Yu, Y. J., and I. C. Choi 1999. "(In Korean) 'Two Years after the IMF Bailout: A Review of the Transformation of the Korean Economy and Society'." Samsung Economic Research Institute (SERI), CEO Information: 219.
Yu, Y. J., and G. S. Lee 2000. "(In Korea) 'Three Years after the IMF Bailout: A Review of the Transformation of the Korean Economy'." Samsung Economic Research Institute (SERI), CEO Information: 271.
Zhan, J., and T. Ozawa. 2001. *Business Restructuring In Asia.* Copenhagen: Copenhagen Business School Press.
Zheng, X. 2010. "Global Forces and Corporate Relations in South Korea." *International Political Science Review* 31 (1): 59–76. doi:10.1177/0192512109354472.

Interviews

#1 Executive Director, Express Group, Samsung Tesco, 8 May 2006.
#2 Equity Research Analyst (Automobile Sector), Hyundai Securities, 1 December 2011.
#3 Assistant Manager, Purchasing Division (Body Trim Team), Renault Samsung Motors, 22 December 2011.
#4 Team Leader, Strategic Planning Team, Samsung Tesco, 9 May 2006.
#5 Manager, Human Resources Division, Lafarge Plasterboard Korea, 15 May 2006.
#6 Equity Research Analyst (Brewery Sector), Hyundai Securities, 13 December 2011.
#7 Vice President, Finance & Administration, Evonik Carbon Black Korea, 9 December 2005.
#8 Director, Communications & Government Affairs Team, Otis Elevator Korea, 3 May 2006.
#9 Assistant Manager, Human Resources Division, Samsung Electronics, 25 January 2010.
#10 Managing Director, Rockwell Samsung Automation, 16 May 2006.
#11 Store Manager, Samsung Tesco, 6 July 2006.
#12 Branch Manager, Oriental Brewery, 23 December 2011.
#13 Team Leader, Corporate HR Management Team, Samsung Tesco, 17 May 2006.
#14 Executive Director, Homeplus Academy, Homeplus, 20 December 2011.

#15 Assistant Manager, Global Sales (North American Region), Hyundai Motors, 12 December 2011.
#16 Vice President, Corporate Strategic Planning & Coordination, LG Chemical, 6 December 2005.
#17 Senior Manager, Non-Memory Semiconductor Division, Samsung Electronics, 13 December 2011.
#18 Manager, Human Resources Division, Renault Samsung Motors, 28 November 2005.
#19 Manager, Internal Audit & Security, Homeplus, 21 December 2011.
#20 Workforce Manager, Human Resources Division, Renault Samsung Motors, 28 November 2005.
#21 Equity Research Analyst (Retail Sector), Hyundai Securities, 13 December 2011.
#22 General Manager, Power & LNG Business Development Team, SK Corporation, 7 December 2005.
#23 General Manager, Human Resources Team, Doosan Corporation, 25 November 2005.
#24 Executive Director, Finance Division, Renault Samsung Motors, 2 December, 23 December 2009.
#25 Equity Research Analyst (Retail Sector), Samsung Securities, 8 December 2011.
#26 Senior Manager, Marketing, GM Daewoo Motors, 2 December 2005.
#27 Branch Manager, Apgujeong-dong Branch, Standard Chartered First Bank Korea, 20 September 2006.
#28 Manager, HR Development Team, Samsung Tesco, 17 May 2006.
#29 Assistant Manager, Supply Chain Management Team, Samsung Electronics, 3 January 2012.
#30 Managing Director, LS Industrial System (Vietnam), 10 December 2011.
#31 Equity Research Analyst (Brewery Sector), Kiwoom Securities, 10 December 2011.
#32 Equity Research Analyst (Brewery Sector), Samsung Securities, 7 December 2011.
#33 General Manager, Human Resources Team, Oriental Brewery, 21 September 2006.
#34 Manager, Finance Division, Samsung Motors Incorporated, 12 May 2006.
#35 Equity Research Analyst (Automobile Sector), Samsung Securities, 7 December 2011.
#36 Analyst, Product Quality Information, Samsung Electronics, 10 December 2011.

Index

advisory roles 88–92, 98, 105–106
affiliated firms 8, 16, 29, 65–66, 70
agency theory 9, 89, 105
Asian Crisis 47, 111–112, 114, 116, 121

behavioural characteristics 88–92, 95, 97–98, 101, 103, 105–107
binary variable 46–48, 54
brand royalties 18, 23, 29
business functions 117–118
business groups 8, 10–11, 39, 45–48, 52, 54–55, 65–73, 75, 77, 79–81, 83, 122–123; families 46, 54–55

capability transfers 114, 120, 123–124
CEO succession 8, 68, 72, 74, 80–81, 83
chaebols 2, 4–7, 10–11, 16–23, 25–28, 30, 32–34, 45, 47, 66, 74–75, 111–116, 122, 124–125; affiliates 9, 112, 114–115, 117, 122, 125; families 6, 17–18, 20, 24, 28; owners 9, 17, 22–24, 27–30, 34, 113; reforms 4, 11–12, 56; subsidiaries 10, 111
Clement, M. 97
conformist monitoring 95, 97–98
Confucian culture 39, 42, 44–46, 48, 52, 55, 57
Confucianism 7, 11, 39–40, 42–44, 52, 54, 56–57
control variables 46, 75, 77, 96, 98
corporate governance 2, 4–7, 10–11, 18–21, 25–26, 32–34, 40, 56–57, 87, 93; reforms 4, 6–11, 16–17, 19, 24, 34, 55, 87–88, 97, 102, 105–107
corporate restructuring 38–48, 55–57, 113
cross-border capital 9–10
Crossland, C. 41
cultural value system 42

Daems, H. P. 21
data analysis 7–8, 26, 46, 48, 73, 94
databases 73–74, 94–95
data collection 73, 94
dependent variables 7, 26, 46, 48, 74, 77, 95, 97, 101

extortions 22, 33–34

Fairchild Korea 119, 121
family business 39–40, 42–44, 46, 55, 57; strategy 57
family capitalism 4, 6
family conglomerates 40, 56
family firms 2, 38–40, 42–43, 56–57
family ownership 20, 22, 34
family rents 22–23
family successions 17, 21, 26–27
financial revenues 26
Finkelstein, S. 68–69
firm insiders 66, 69, 72, 75, 77
firm-level rent seeking 21
first child 44, 46, 52
first son 7, 20, 43, 46, 48, 52, 54–55
foreign acquisitions 111, 114–115
foreign ownership 9–11, 93, 96–98, 103, 105–107, 114–116, 123, 125
foreign pressures 9, 11–12, 21, 24
foreign shareholders 93

gender 39–40, 43, 94–96
global financial crisis 55, 67, 72–73, 75, 79–80
governance 19, 33, 111–112, 114–116, 122–123, 125
Granovetter, M. 8, 68
group-affiliated firms 66–69, 71, 80, 83
group outsiders 66, 69, 71–72, 75, 77, 79–81

Hambrick, D. C. 41, 69
Hamilton, S. A. 48
HCS chaebols 22–30, 32
Hoetker, G. 52
holding companies 17, 21–26, 29–30, 32, 123
holding company system (HCS) 17–30, 32, 34
hypothesis development 67

independent variables 46, 74, 95–96, 98
indirect ownership leverage 24, 30, 32
in-group outsiders 8, 66, 69, 71–72, 75, 77, 79–81

institutional variation 52
intragroup trading (IGT) 5–7, 17–19, 22–24, 27–28, 30
inward investment 112, 124

joint ventures 115–116

Karaevli, A. 65
Korea Fair Trade Commission 18, 66, 73–75
Korea Listed Companies Association (KLCA) 95
Korean business groups 8, 39, 43, 45–46, 55, 57, 66, 69–70, 82–83
Korean chaebols 2, 8, 10–11, 18–19, 24–25, 34
Korean-controlled chaebol affiliates 9, 115, 123
Korean-controlled firms 111, 123
Korean corporate governance 5, 17–19, 34
Korean economy 4, 33, 55, 112
Korean firms 21, 87–89, 106, 114, 116, 119
Korean government 45, 47, 55–56, 73, 88, 114, 122–123

Lafarge 116, 119, 121
Li, S. 20
liberal market 48, 52, 57

management committees 117–119, 122–123
management practices 42, 106, 111
managerial decision-making 116
managerial discretion 39–42, 46, 55–56, 69, 72, 80; sources of 55–56, 69
managerial transformation 112
marginal effect 52, 54–55
market development 48, 52, 57
minority shareholders 16–17, 122
moderating variable 9, 75, 96
monitoring roles 9, 87–88, 90–93, 95, 105
Moon, President 57
multinational subsidiaries 10, 114, 123–125

national culture 7, 11–12, 39–42, 55–57
negative effect 8, 66, 71–72, 77, 79, 91
new corporate governance 6–7, 19
new institutional economics (NIE) 2, 19
non-dividend incomes 18, 22–24, 29, 32

Oriental Brewery 116, 119, 121, 124
Otis Korea 116, 119, 121, 124
outside directors: behaviour 87–88, 90–91, 95, 97, 105–107; expected roles 89
outsider succession 65–68, 71, 73, 79–80, 83
Ouyang, M. 20
ownership 4, 16–17, 23–24, 28–29, 34, 77, 89, 96–97, 111, 115, 122–125
ownership-control disparity 7, 18, 34

patriarchal ideology 43
practical implications 10, 33, 56, 82, 89, 105, 107, 124
proactive behaviour 9, 91–94, 98, 103
proactive monitoring 95, 97–98

Quigley, T. J. 69

relevant theory 67
Renault Samsung Motors (RSM) 116–117, 120–122
rent sharing 6–7, 11, 16, 19–20, 25, 32–34
rent sharing view (RSV) 6, 19–20, 33
resource 120
resource allocation dimensions 74

Samsung Tesco 118, 120–122, 124
social interaction 96–97
social networks 8, 67–68, 71, 96
South Korea 16, 25, 33, 38, 40, 42, 45, 54–55, 57, 123
Stern, I. 96–97
strategic changes 7–8, 10–11, 39–42, 47, 56–57, 65–74, 79–84, 92; degree of 65–66
strategic motivations 115
subsequent strategic change 70, 74–75, 77
subsidiaries 10, 22–24, 29–30, 114, 117–118, 120–125
succession 7, 11, 17, 24–25, 30, 32, 34, 38, 40–46, 52, 54–57, 69–71, 74
successor's discretion 38–41, 44, 48, 52, 55, 57, 70
supplementary analysis 79
supplementary test 45, 48, 54–55, 57

taken-for-grantedness 43
TCG chaebols 24, 26–30, 32
Therneau, T. M. 48
total group revenues 26–27, 30
transaction cost economics (TCE) 2, 19

upper echelons 67

valuable resources 91, 93–94, 105–106
values 39, 41, 44, 46, 54, 98, 118, 124
variables 45–48, 52, 54–55, 73, 75, 77, 79, 95, 97–98, 103

Westphal, J. 96–97
Wiersema, M. F. 74

Zajac, E. J. 65
Zhang, Y. A. N. 74